Guns
and
Garlic

Guns and Garlic

Myths and Realities of Organized Crime

by Frederic D. Homer

The author acknowledges the contribution of
David A. Caputo

Purdue University Press
West Lafayette, Indiana
1974

Eighth printing, May 1991

© 1974 by the Purdue Research Foundation
Library of Congress Catalog Number 73-88132
International Standard Book Numbers
clothbound edition 0-911198-37-7
paperbound edition 0-911198-38-5
Manufactured in the United States of America

*To the matrix that urged the book to its conclusion:
Carole Homer, Deena Weinstein, Ken Kofmehl, Bill
Shaffer, Cy Gerde, Jack Mortiarty, Steve Shoenholz,
Mildred Homer, and Charles Hyneman.*

Contents

Acknowledgments

I am mentioning my wife Carole's contribution first and not last, as is customary, for without her criticism, cajoling, and encouragement this book would not have been possible.

I owe profound thanks to my brother-in-law, Steven Shoenholz, for his incisive criticism of the earlier drafts of this manuscript. Two enforcement agents were particularly helpful and must be singled out for praise. Charles Siragusa, director of the Illinois Legislative Investigating Commission, patiently spoke to me about the myriad experiences he had investigating organized crime, and about his hypotheses concerning its operation. He prompted me to go back to the drawing board, so to speak, many a time, and to rethink my major propositions. Sergeant Nick Gulling of the Indiana State Police Organized Crime Unit gave me encouragement in my endeavors, and I am especially indebted for discussions with him which provided some ideas for the last chapters of the book.

My thanks also go to the many students at Purdue who challenged my hypotheses, helped me to refine them, and generally provided a congenial atmosphere for my efforts. I am especially obligated to Gerald P. O'Herren who patiently listened to my ideas and criticized drafts of the first four chapters. Robert Cory was unbending in his insistence on excellence in the first few chapters. I am grateful to Diane Dubiel of Purdue University Studies for the excellent editorial advice she rendered and to the others at Purdue University Studies who did so much to expedite publication of the book.

My thanks also go to many others who read the manuscript in its entirety and offered comments and encouragement, especially Kip Homer, Gerold Neudeck, and Henry Rufa. Also, I would like to thank Barbara Cummings who transcribed the original draft of the manuscript, and Ella Walker who did the bulk of typing on the manuscript.

This volume is the result of extensive interest and research dealing with organized crime. In 1971 Professor David A. Caputo and I discussed the research opportunities present and the need for political scientists to study organized crime. This common interest resulted in a jointly authored paper, "The Conceptual and Operational Problems of Studying Organized Crime: An Overview and Research Strategies," which was presented at the 1971 Southern Political Science Association Meeting. We had also planned to co-author this volume, but other commitments by Professor Caputo kept him from participating in that capacity. Despite his contributions and limited editorial assistance, I am responsible for what is contained herein. I would, however, like to acknowledge and thank him for his assistance.

Finally, I wish to thank those who cooperated with me in this study and must remain anonymous.

Frederic D. Homer
Murdock Park, summer 1973

Foreword

In the classical tradition of political science and sociology, represented by such writers as Marx, Weber, Durkheim, Lasswell, and Veblen, perhaps the highest achievement of scholarship is a definitive, comprehensive, and theoretically fruitful analysis of a significant human activity. In a period in which the social sciences are beset by the twin evils of narrow and fragmented empirical studies, and abstract and contentless theory, Frederic Homer's work on organized crime stands out as evidence that social phenomena can still be studied comprehensively and systematically with impressive results. His study encompasses a total social fact, rather than a fragment or a fiction, and infuses data with theory.

Homer's analysis of organized crime in the United States has several aims, each of which is fulfilled with rigor and imagination. First, and most important for the scholar, Homer puts the study of organized crime on a firm scientific basis. In the past this controversial and emotion-laden subject has been a field more for ideological polemics than for critical analysis. With the appearance of Homer's study, it is no longer possible to base any serious work about organized crime on the superficial debate over whether or not this set of activities is dominated by one or more particular ethnic groups. Homer removes the study of organized crime from the realm of sensationalism and ethnic chauvinism, and places it in the context of contemporary American social structure. He reviews the prevalent myths and hypotheses about organized crime and critically analyzes them in the framework of contemporary organization theory. In this context, organized crime is analyzed in its economic, political, ethnic, and social class dimensions.

A second goal of Homer's work is to make a theoretical contribution to the study of organized crime and to the analysis of human activity in general. Basing his theoretical construction on the perspectives which human actors have about organized crime, Homer finds that this phenomenon can be explained either as the result of the activities of a coherent social group (in his terminology, "a society") or as the consequence of complex activities and role systems aimed at specific ends ("matrices of activity"). Setting up a fruitful dialectic between "society" and "matrix," he shows that focusing on visible or mythical membership groups serves the ideological purposes of simplifying and emotionalizing law enforcement, while it distorts scientific analysis by narrowing the field of study in advance of observation. The notion of "matrices of activity" gives Homer's work a significance beyond its particular data base. For example, the Watergate affair can be adequately analyzed through the concept of "matrix." Those involved in the Watergate case and related campaign activities were evidently not members of a well-defined social group, but instead constituted a web of roles and functions which mediated between established groups and organizations to realize certain purposes. Thus, in Homer's analysis formal and visible collectivities become the instruments and containers for more fluid associations oriented towards the pursuit of particular aims. The dilemmas confronted by such associations in their activities (for example, the dialectic of secrecy and efficiency) form much of the substance of Homer's discussion. As a result of their theoretical power, Homer's distinctions can be applied to the study of any secretive, subversive, illegal, or rebellious activities which appear in contemporary societies, from office politics to affairs of state. His examples of gambling, loan-sharking, and other activities are not confining, but are illustrative of widespread patterns of social dynamics. It is this generality of application which places Homer's study squarely within the classical tradition of social science. Rather than borrowing abstract models and paradigms from past or present thinkers, or indulging in particularized ethnography, Homer allows his concepts to develop through critical observation of collective representations and interpretation of factual data. This method permits him to discover non-obvious dynamics in contemporary society. How much of current social life is disguised rather than illuminated by focusing on formal rule systems and visible organizations and groups? How much public policy is misdirected and vitiated by legalism and regulation of established structures? How much of our tendency to confine ourselves to the visible in social life is an exercise in self-deception and rationalization? By raising these questions, Homer's study falls into the tradition of systematic social criticism represented best by Veblen's *Theory of the Leisure Class.*

The third aim of Homer's work is to provide perspectives on law enforcement policy. Here he remains a scientist by disclosing a range of alternative possibilities instead of advocating a particular line of policy. He shows how treating organized crime as a well-defined "society" may be conducive to peace of mind by offering a visible enemy or scapegoat, and may allow law enforcement agencies the illusion of effectiveness. However, he also implies that in the long run this approach will tend to obscure the extent of organized crime and its close relations with other, more "legitimate," activities. In this phase of his analysis, Homer poses a dilemma for American citizens. Will we choose to ease our consciences by pretending that organized crime is an anomaly in American society to be eliminated by punitive action against particular groups, or will we recognize that criminal matrices functionally interlock with many other aspects of everyday life? Only the latter recognition will permit us to make a free decision about how we wish to act with respect to organized crime.

In the tradition of classical social science, Frederic Homer's work is an intensely personal and committed effort. Underlying his most obvious commitment to objective scientific inquiry is a more basic dedication to reason and freedom. The very choice of organized crime as his subject for investigation is an example of his belief that only by realistically confronting all of the aspects of their existence, however unpleasant, can human beings attain freedom and, perhaps even more important for Frederic Homer, honesty and decency. In this era of team projects and grant research, it is a hopeful sign that a single scholar can still combine humane values and scientific objectivity in a work of impressive proportions.

Michael A. Weinstein
Professor of Political Science
Purdue University

Chapter 1

Introduction

The Myth of Organized Crime

American folklore is replete with the legendary exploits of criminal societies such as the Black Hand, Murder Incorporated, and the latest group to catch the public imagination, La Cosa Nostra. The activities of these societies capture newspaper headlines only intermittently, but their words and deeds are constantly thrust upon the public through novels, short stories, TV, radio, and motion pictures. Each generation of Americans hears of a pervasive criminal organization and of new protagonists in the never-ending battle between organized crime and enforcement agencies.

In the twenties, an era tainted by organized crime, criminals belonged to the "Syndicate," and Al Capone, Johnny Torrio, and Arnold Rothstein fought Elliot Ness and other enforcement figures. These conflicts have been immortalized on the TV and motion picture screen by actors such as James Cagney, Edward G. Robinson, Robert Stack, and David Jansen. During the late thirties and early forties, attention centered on Abe Reles, a Brooklyn-born racketeer whose revelations led to the trial and convictions of several members of a gang (called Murder Incorporated by the press) which specialized in murder and other criminal activities. District Attorney Thomas E. Dewey's exploits in combating prominent organized criminals of the time (Lepke Buchalter, Charles "Lucky" Luciano, and Dutch Schultz, among others) catapulted him first into the governor's mansion in New York and then into presidential politics.

Monitoring organized criminal activity became the pastime of millions of Americans in the fifties when hearings of the Kefauver Committee were televised. Senator Estes Kefauver's name became a household word along with those of many organized criminals, most notably Frank Costello, a purported organized crime boss. Events of the late fifties and early sixties again put organized crime up for public scrutiny. In 1957 in the small town of Apalachin, New York, the police accidentally stumbled upon a meeting of individuals from many sections of the country, most with criminal records and many known by the police to be important figures in the underworld. Independently, the McClellan Committee ceaselessly hammered away at the role of criminal groups in organized labor. The work of this committee received considerable publicity when Joseph Valachi, a member of an organization identified as La Cosa Nostra, testified on his activities and associations with other participants in organized crime.

In the seventies, attention also has been riveted on organized crime. Meyer Lansky, a purported gangland leader, refused to return from Israel to face charges in the United States stemming from his involvement in Las Vegas gambling casinos.[1] Mayors of several New Jersey cities were suspected, indicted, or convicted for their association or involvement with organized criminals.[2] Joseph Colombo, reputedly the head of a Cosa Nostra family, was shot at a rally he helped organize to protest allegedly unwarranted discrimination against and harassment of Italian-Americans by the FBI and other enforcement agencies.[3] Publication and TV dramatization of *Honor Thy Father*, the story of gang warfare within the family of Joseph Bonanno, further alerted a new generation to the existence of organized crime.[4] Most notably, the publication of the best-selling novel, *The Godfather*, and its subsequent screen adaptation (both have been attended by remarkable critical acclaim and financial success) have aroused public interest in organized crime.[5]

In sum, from Capone and Torrio to Bonanno and *The Godfather*, organized crime has become part of popular lore and has stimulated the public imagination to an extent equaled by few other aspects of American life. Fact and fiction on the subject command public attention because organized criminals appear to live in another world and to share a set of experiences alien to everyday American life. Their lives are shrouded in secrecy which arouses the curiosity of at least some persons. For a segment of the public, books on organized crime can be an escape from the problems of everyday life, an indulgence in a world of fantasy.

For other readers and movie-goers, interest in organized crime is stimulated by the observation that behavior of organized criminals differs in degree but not in kind from that of everyday experience. During the post-depression years, many people could identify with criminals who fought the wealthy and the government in their quest to achieve wealth and status. The audience could also identify with the collapse of the criminal at the end of the film or novel. Today, the theme has changed somewhat (the "bad guys" don't always lose), but individuals still can identify with the experiences of organized criminals. In today's society asserting one's own individuality and authority has become more and more difficult. This theme dominates popular and scholarly literature and, one might suspect, some individuals' everyday lives. For instance, C. Wright Mills speaks of a power elite which dominates the country, making individual actions difficult; Herbert Marcuse notes the political and technological dominance of the system over individuals, and, more recently, Theodore Lowi in *The End of Liberalism* notes the dominance of selected groups over the decision process.[6] In contrast, the gangster film, such as *The Godfather*, portrays organized criminals as people with unlimited powers. The godfather solves personal problems of friends, bribes public officials, has senators in his pocket, and can help a family friend sign a movie contract with a famous producer against the latter's will. We can identify with the godfather, vicariously share in his exercise of power over men and circumstances, and long to have such powers for ourselves.

Beyond this, the modern gangster film or book stresses a value lost to American society, but one we can long for and identify with: the continuing primacy of the family and strength of interpersonal relationships. The criminal belongs to a society in which virtues of loyalty and reciprocity are admired and reinforced. The viewers or readers can admire this sense of community and belonging, which seems to be lacking in their society.

Finally, there don't seem to be many distractions or complications in the life of an organized criminal. Robert Lane describes man in contemporary society as beset by many tiny little messages.[7] Conflicting goals and the myriad human interactions occupy one's time and detract from any pattern, meaning, or purpose in an individual's life. In contrast, the celluloid gangster has a simple set of loyalties, receives few extraneous messages, and knows clearly who his friends and enemies are. The participants ensure, without hesitation, that justice is done, and they dispense it in accordance with factual considerations rather than moral ones. Life is much less complex; there are no Hamlets in organized crime. Thus, in the modern saga of the gangster, the lost virtues of power, community, and goal orientation which are missing in the lives of many Americans can be obtained vicariously.

Paralleling media portrayal of organized crime in American life, serious scholarship shows two similar interpretations of the criminal experience. The first treats organized crime as deviance, proposing a qualitative difference between organized crime and American experience, and claiming that non-criminals share *no* common experiences with the "grim reapers," the "merchants of death," the "murderers," the "brotherhood of evil."[8] This interpretation inhibits understanding of organized crime and lends to the reinforcement of stereotypes we already have. A second interpretation, one which has the author's sympathies, suggests that organized crime arises from some of the same conditions which shape many other aspects of American experience, and cannot be understood apart from that experience. Much of the behavior manifest in organized crime can be understood in light of propositions about human behavior which have been gathered in the social sciences.

This book is a reorientation of the study of organized crime away from the popular myths, away from the treatment of organized crime as deviant, aberrant behavior, and toward the study of organized crime as an aspect of the American experience, rather than something divorced from it. Organized crime will be studied from the standpoint of individual and organizational behavior in much the same way a social scientist would study any other organization.

From this orientation comes a definition which highlights organized crime as a system of power and interaction, not as an invincible organization with mystical powers. In the framework of this definition, the analysis of the organization itself points up syndicated crime's strengths and weaknesses from an organizational standpoint, and emphasizes organizational dilemmas faced by these criminals. As in every organization, to maximize one goal or value is often to do it to the detriment of some other value. The policy orientations in the study follow from the definition and the substantive conclusions as to the nature of organized crime. They are not policy recommendations, but behavior maxims, policy alternatives that stem from the perspective outlined in this book and which will serve to orient debate on public policy in the area of organized crime.

As well as being a personal orientation to the study of organized crime, this book will attempt to attune individuals to the substantive and methodological problems and issues involved in the study of organized crime. I will be developing, testing, keeping, or discarding concepts and hypotheses found in social science literature, popular fiction, newspapers, and writings by public officials throughout the book. This may be illustrated best by a short discussion of the contents of each chapter. In the remainder of this chapter a definition of organized crime will be set forth and problems of data gathering and analysis will be summarized.

In Chapter 2, enough historical background is provided to sensitize the reader to some of the points at issue in the study of organized crime while providing sufficient background information to follow the remaining analysis.

A profile of the participant in organized crime will be developed in Chapter 3 by examining facets of his personality and learning how social characteristics such as ethnicity, class, and age influence his behavior.

Chapter 4 deals with the economic and political organizational structure of organized crime. It will be suggested that organized crime is a social order and a system of power within a larger society and government. Knowledge gained from the study of economics and politics will guide understanding of how a "confederation" of crime operates.

A discussion of the various activities in which organized crime has been engaged—for instance, bootlegging, narcotics, loan-sharking, and the theft of securities—will follow in Chapter 5. Here the interaction between organized crime and the broader economic and political system will be discussed in detail, with emphasis on enforcement policy, corruption, and services organized criminals provide which have not been provided by the wider economic system. The concluding chapter spells out the policy orientations which follow from the earlier description of organized crime in the book.

One caveat must be mentioned with respect to this book. It will concentrate on groups for which data is available, and will not give equal time or emphasis to every major group or entity in organized crime. The amount of time spent in analysis of one group or series of groups is not a statement as to the power of that group or groups. In the course of this study it will become obvious which groups are powerful in organized crime, but the major emphasis here is not on "who governs" types of questions but on the discovery of how criminal groups function in the United States.

Definition of Organized Crime

Critique of *Task Force Report* Definition

The way organized crime is conceived and what policies are made to counteract it depend on the conceptualization of the problem. The definition of organized crime set forth here is similar to the one criticized, for it sees organized crime as a system of power relationships. But the similarity ends there, for the definition to be proposed here differs substantially in scope and emphasis from preexistent definitions and may substantially alter the way analysts will look at organized crime in the future.

Since definitions are but arbitrary stipulations, it is rare in social inquiry when a consensus of scholars exists on a definition of a central concept. It is particularly unusual in a substantive area such as organized crime where one would expect a variety of perspectives and profound disagreements on fundamental concepts. There is considerable consensus, however, on the following definition of organized crime which appears in the report of the President's Commission on Law Enforcement and Administration of Justice:

> Organized crime is a society that seeks to operate outside the control of the American people and their governments. It involves thousands of criminals, working within structures as complex as those of any large corporation, subject to laws more rigidly enforced than those of legitimate governments. Its actions are not impulsive but rather the result of intricate conspiracies, carried on over many years and aimed at gaining control over whole fields of activity in order to amass huge profits.[9]

A similar definition was formulated by participants at a conference on organized crime in 1967 at Oyster Bay, New York, and the *Task Force Report* definition is widely cited in other government reports and scholarly works.[10]

This definition has a great deal of merit and warrants considerable attention, but I feel that it is necessary to highlight my disagreements with it. Fundamentally, this definition could better be described as a set of conclusions as to the nature of organized crime rather than as a definition which opens the way to inquiry. It would be preferable if the definition merely designated organized criminal groups and allowed us to generate our own series of hypotheses. This would permit the testing of hypotheses and the drawing of inferences about these groups and their activities. Instead, the definition draws conclusions as to how organized, monolithic, and distinctive the behavior of organized criminal groups is. These are researchable questions and analysis of them should not be precluded by the definition of organized crime.

An analogous situation would be to define the concept of alienation and then do empirical research to see what characteristics are shown by those individuals defined as alienated. If those characteristics are included in the definition of alienation, the scope of the inquiry is limited. Thus in the study of organized crime, I do not want to assume that the organization is set inalterably in opposition to government, monolithic and totalitarian. These are several of the very relationships I want to explore in the study of organized crime. Not only do these conclusions by the commission block the way to inquiry, they are unacceptable in other ways as well.

For instance, the definition concludes that organized criminal groups are in total opposition to the rest of society when it says that "organized crime is a society that seeks to operate outside the control of the American people and their governments."[11] However, the aspirations and behavior of organized criminals may in fact be similar to those of many other individuals in society; the organized criminals may not always seek to act in a way that sets them off from or in opposition to others in society. There is, for example, some indication that organized criminals will pursue legitimate businesses in legitimate fashions as they get older.[12] Conversely, most Americans are not unalterably opposed to what organized criminals do; as Ramsey Clark, former attorney general, suggests, organized crime provides many services the public wants and condones.[13]

If we still want to assume that organized criminal groups are inalterably opposed to the rest of society, consider the difficulties in determining just who is an organized criminal and what constitutes a criminal society. For instance, a man might purchase two dozen television sets for his retail outlet from a seller at half the wholesale

7

price. He asks very few questions. Is the retailer an organized criminal? What about his willing customers? Are they part of the criminal syndicate? These questions are especially vexing when we speak of victimless crimes such as gambling. Do we consider as criminal those who swear to an oath of allegiance to the "organization," those who run a horse parlor and pay a commission to the oath-takers, or those who place bets of five, ten, or a hundred dollars at the horse parlor?

The actions under discussion are those traditionally identified with organized criminals that seem to set them apart from the rest of society. There is also behavior by the rest of society that resembles that of organized criminals in many ways, but which is not identified as criminal. When we step out of a taxi and pay the fare registered on the meter, we are informed that we owe the driver a tip. If we refuse to pay, we will perhaps be the target of an abusive verbal assault. Most of us end up paying. Similarly, truck drivers pay for preferential treatment on the docks, building contractors pay extra for building permits, and we slip the *maitre d'* some cash if we want a table near the stage and good service. A doctor refuses to treat a patient before charging him an initial examination fee, an allergist refuses to continue to treat a patient until he consults with the patient (for $10 the patient tells him everything is okay), or the garbageman throws refuse on your lawn if you forget or don't want to give him a Christmas present. We ordinarily accept these as aggravating business practices, but they are all forms of extortion. Organized crime's methods are not always qualitatively different from those employed in the wider society.

A second conclusion in the commission's definition which raises questions is that organized criminals are "subject to laws more rigidly enforced than those of legitimate governments"; indeed, the word "totalitarian" is used in the report to describe the internal structure of the organization.[14] It is misleading to speak of laws, for there is no written codification of laws. More important, obedience in organized criminal groups is far from total, organization is not strictly hierarchical, and leaders do not have a monopoly of information.[15] The impression the commission conveys about the internal organization of criminal groups ignores the complexity of social organization.

Even if we were to concede that the unwritten laws of organized criminal groups are more strictly enforced than the written ones of legitimate governments, it would be wrong to imply that control is not a problem in these groups. The conflict between political and economic goals, disputes and disagreements over organizational and societal norms, and a "generation gap" weaken internal discipline. Major gang wars are good examples of the breakdown of cooperation between criminal groups as well as manifestations of conflicts within groups. The inter-gang Castellamarese War in the early 1930s involved tensions between old and young, Sicilians and non-Sicilians.[16] The Gallo-Profaci war, an intra-family dispute, saw two factions fighting over the distribution of income and status within a single family.[17] The usual rationale for suggesting the totalitarian nature of organized criminal groups is the use of murder as the sole means of social control. But investigations have found that murder is costly in terms of resources and is used sparingly by criminal groups.[18] As we know from the study of international politics, the threat of ultimate force does not necessarily deter all transgressions by parties threatened. Some may wish annihilation; others, realizing it may be costly for the aggressor to utilize his ultimate weapon, feel they can risk defiance. We must distinguish between the ultimate sanctions a group or state may have at its disposal and the limitations of such sanctions in maintaining discipline. One may say that criminal groups utilize killing to maintain discipline, but the very use of this resource may indicate weakness in the organizational mechanisms of control.

As noted previously, another complaint with the definition, aside from the conclusions it draws, is that it limits the scope of inquiry into organized crime. It is perfectly acceptable to define organized crime as La Cosa Nostra, the Mafia, or the Syndicate, and to keep your investigations centered on these organizational entities. The commission talks of organized crime as "a society" and uses the word *it* several times in referring to organized criminal groups.[19] It thus seems to be speaking of organized crime as if it were one monolithic group,[20] a view that coincides nicely with that held by most people. A preferable definition, however, would allow broadening the scope of inquiry to consider and do research on other organized criminal groups. Paradoxically, this suggestion is implicit in the report's definition—the very definition which seeks to limit inquiry to the study of one group. In the first part of the definition, the emphasis is on organized crime as a single group, and in the last part the suggestion is made that "its actions are not impulsive, but rather the

9

result of intricate conspiracies, carried on over many years and aimed at gaining control over whole fields of activity in order to amass huge profits."[21] If one utilizes this latter part of the definition, carefully defines key words such as conspiracies, changes the word *its* to *their*, and sets a reasonable limit to profits, one can broaden this inquiry to include many other groups. By altering this definition, a wide variety of groups could be examined, such as moonshiners, car theft rings, NCO service club operations, and groups of students involved with the transport and distribution of marijuana. Altering the definition would permit escape from a tautological possibility. If the analyst defines organized crime as a single society or a single activity, he usually ends up by concluding that La Cosa Nostra is the only organized crime group or that gambling is the major activity of organized crime. In other words, if the analyst suggests in the beginning of his study that organized crime is defined by characteristic X, he usually ends up concluding as a matter of empirical observation that characteristic X is the only one exhibited by organized criminal groups.

It is incumbent upon me to ask why the Task Force on Organized Crime reporting to the President's Commission on Law Enforcement and the Administration of Justice came up with its particular definition. Much of this will be pure speculation on my part; nevertheless I feel it is worth a try. The president's commission was formed without a charge to deal separately with the question of organized crime. In May 1966, almost nine months after the commission had begun working, a task force of experts to deal with organized crime was added. As well as being pressed for time, the separate task force was short on funding. Since no new funds were appropriated for it, the money had to be culled from the existing budget.[22]

More important perhaps than the restraints of time and money were the public policy benefits that accrued from the point of view that the commission espoused. First, it wanted to suggest that there was some danger in this country from organized crime, a fact not even acknowledged in the original make-up of the commission itself. To mobilize public concern, it is often easier to simplify a problem and personify it by citing a singular enemy, either a specified individual or an identifiable group. Hank Messick, an organized crime reporter, openly suggests this was the government's reasoning during Robert Kennedy's tenure as attorney general. "Somewhat cynically," writes Messick, "despite the best motives, Kennedy and his advisors decided to limit their attack [on organized crime]. They recognized that the National Crime Syndicate was too vast, too sophisticated, to be understood by the average citizen. On the other hand, the Mafia was compact enough, crude enough, exotic enough to capture the imagination of people who thought of organized crime in terms of Al Capone and *The Untouchables.*"[23] Thus for mobilizing opinion, and as Messick suggests, for bringing government investigative agencies such as the FBI into the battle, the designation of a monolithic, totalitarian, purposive enemy may have served a useful bureaucratic function.[24]

The tactic of singling out a publicly identifiable group or individual is not a new one devised by the Task Force on Organized Crime. For example, prior to 1776 the Revolutionaries, in attempting to mobilize the colonists for war against Great Britain, chose George III as the subject for scorn and hatred though they knew very well that Parliament (which lacked the king's public identification) was the real power in England. This reflected the realization that people can more easily focus their attention and vent their animosities on one man or on one monolithic group than on less recognizable targets. The same seems to hold whenever there are real or imagined threats to the internal security of the United States.

The logical extension of this view for enforcement purposes is to make it illegal to be a member of the subversive group. Defining La Cosa Nostra as a subversive group was suggested by Senator John McClellan to Attorney General Kennedy at a hearing before the McClellan Committee. "I am thinking in terms of making it a crime, making it illegal to belong to a secret society or organization or association, whatever term we want to give it, where allegiance is taken that assumes disloyalty, and individuals pledge disloyalty to the Constitution and laws of the United States."[25] Of course, Senator McClellan recognized some of the problems that would come with acceptance of his proposal. "I know it will have some problems, constitutional problems maybe," he said, "but to me it seems that we have established the fact, and I think we all know it, that such an organization exists, that we might be able to enact some laws striking directly at the source."[26] If Senator McClellan's suggestion was enacted through laws, then one might strike directly at organized crime, but protecting civil liberties, as he indicates, would become a severe problem.

If public opinion could be mobilized and laws passed which would deal directly with suspected groups, then, one would think, the goals of the task force would have been achieved. However, to combat organized crime successfully, an accurate picture of its structure and functioning must be rendered. A monolithic group with a charismatic leader would best be fought with different strategies and focus than would a confederation of groups. Perhaps eradication of the leader might be the best policy to pursue in combating a monolithic organization, while a confederation might not be so dependent upon leadership. Agencies might feel that one image of organized crime provokes public opinion, but if they act upon this belief, their policies may turn out to be ineffective.

A New Definition

Dissatisfaction with the commission's definition prompts me to suggest possibilities for a viable alternative. My definition will propose as hypotheses some of the statements which the commission treats as conclusions, and these hypotheses will form an integral part of a new analysis of organized crime.

The first component of the definition states that organized crime consists of a set of interactions that takes place over a continuous period of time, such as a gambling operation running for five years, rather than an isolated event, such as a bank robbery. One must distinguish, however, between the individuals who share in either a permanent organization or in recurring patterns of behavior. Organized criminals may continuously work together in a structured organization engaged in a variety of activities, or may not belong to any nominal organization but be bound together with others in a recurring activity. The former is exemplified by groups such as La Cosa Nostra, the Purple Gang, or Murder Incorporated. The latter is exemplified by a man who steals continually over a period of years, uses a "fence" to dispose of his goods, uses the same bail bondsman, and continuously supplies himself with weapons from the same source. A further example of the latter is in narcotics traffic, in which members of three or more national groups continually do business with each other; the growers may be Turks, Corsicans may do the refining, Italians the importation, and blacks the street sales. To differentiate between permanent organization and recurring patterns of behavior, I will call La Cosa Nostra and the Purple Gang *criminal societies*, and networks of individuals involved in turnover of stolen property and traffic in narcotics *matrices of crime.* This distinction allows one to see how many ethnic groups may be involved in organized crime, rather than necessarily assuming that Italians predominate. For instance, there may be a society of Italian criminals, but they may find themselves part of a matrix stealing securities with Protestants, smuggling heroin with Turks and Corsicans, or selling lottery tickets with blacks. Non-Italians may even outnumber Italians in the activities by their participation in specific matrices of crime.

In sum, an organized criminal "society" may be engaged in a wide variety of economic enterprises and be held together by influence relationships on the basis of profit, loyalty, ethnicity, or friendship. "Matrices" of crime describe the pattern of influence relationships that usually evolve around one or only a few economic activities that bind them together. The activities might be gambling, selling narcotics, theft, stealing of securities, or a variety of others. This distinction between societies and matrices allows us to look at the complexity of organization in crime and the complex interrelationships between individuals and groups. A person may owe loyalty to the head of a society and live in fear of him, and also owe allegiance to a matrix of crime in which very few or none of the members belong to the society. The distinction between societies and matrices allows the study of organized crime over a period of time by avoiding the identification of organized crime with a specific group. If there is no more Purple Gang, Cosa Nostra, or Mafia, we can keep track of criminal matrices which involve complex, organized activities and may be just as detrimental to the public weal as criminal societies designated by name. It would be foolish to assume that when there is no more Cosa Nostra, there is no more organized crime, or that Italians invented or perfected what we know as organized crime. This component of the definition is necessary if only to allow us to explain the past and anticipate the future.

The distinction between societies and matrices not only describes actual behavior and institutions in the real world but represents differential perceptions that commentators may have about the real world. For instance, one reporter may look at all of organized crime as a matrix or he may look at all of organized crime as a society, regardless of the structure of actual behavior and institutions. As we shall see, these perceptions tailor much of what is discovered and done about organized crime.

The second component of the definition of organized crime classi-fies activities of these societies or matrices. I will not restrict myself to gambling, narcotics, and loan-sharking, even though they are traditionally considered activities of organized crime. Rather, I will also include as possibilities such activities as stock frauds, labor ex-tortion, car theft, personal blackmail, poaching and sale of the pelts of spotted cats (leopards, etc.), and collusion with public officials on the sale of land. To define activities of organized crime as the traditional three, gambling, narcotics, and loan-sharking, is not useful or workable; they are usually chosen because groups identified as organized criminals make much of their money from these three activities, not because these are the only illegal activities organized criminals engage in. What is needed is a means of classifying the whole range of criminal activities so that societies or matrices that participate in them may be designated as organized criminal groups. Pre-existent definitions do not tell us if societies or matrices that steal copper tubing or a farmer's trees or break other laws are orga-nized criminal groups.

An activity is designated as *legal* or *illegal* by law. For instance, it is legal to sell cigarettes and illegal to sell heroin in the United States. Often the definition of what is legal varies from one political jurisdiction to another. Prostitution is illegal in most jurisdictions, but in Nevada, counties have a local option to make it legal. In the study of organized crime, the designations *legitimate* and *illegitimate* are also used to differentiate between activities in organized crime; for example, operating a bar and grille is a legitimate business and selling narcotics is an illegitimate one.

Although the words *legitimate* and *illegitimate* are used in common parlance to differentiate between legal and illegal businesses, I will redefine them here to distinguish between those activities which are normatively acceptable to the public and those which are not. An activity, like gambling with the neighborhood bookie, may be *illegal* (against the law), but *legitimate* (a practice accepted by the people who live in the neighborhood). Activities are viewed as legal and illegal from the perspective of the law, and viewed as legitimate and illegitimate in the eyes of the public.

Another factor will aid in distinguishing between types of activi-ties. A business such as a supermarket may be legal, but the way it is run, illegal. For example, the supermarket manager may buy products he knows are hijacked or purchase merchandise that does not meet federal standards. Conversely, businesses such as gambling that are illegal in many places may be conducted according to business standards acceptable where the activity happens to be legal. For example, gambling in a state where it is illegal may be run so that the customers are always paid off in the correct amounts and employees get fair and regular compensation; the "illegal business" would be run by "legal means." In sum, we now have three important distinctions which allow us to classify activities: legal vs. illegal business, legitimate vs. illegitimate business, and legal vs. illegal means of running the business.

This classification allows, first of all, a differentiation between criminal and non-criminal activity. Any activity that is not a legal business run by legal means—one that is illegal either in itself or in its means of operation, or both—could fulfill part of our definition of organized crime. It could be argued that legal businesses run by legal means that are condemned by the public, such as the manufacture of the cheap handguns known as "Saturday Night Specials," are "criminal." However, one might narrow the definition and call these by another name, perhaps "conscienceless businesses," to avoid the possibility of referring to all businesses one feels are not in the public interest as criminal. One can also see the large role governments have in defining activities as legal or illegal; gambling is the best example. In other words, much of the definition of crime is dependent upon local laws. Finally, activities legal or illegal that are condoned by the public are extraordinarily difficult to combat. Public support is lacking and enforcement agencies are most liable to be lax.

One can now decide which activities are criminal. If groups or matrices meet the other conditions of the definition and are engaged in criminal activities, it can be concluded that they are participants in organized crime. Thus, groups or matrices whose activities are illegal in themselves, in their means of operation, or both, whether legitimate or not in the eyes of the public, would qualify as participants in organized crime.

This scheme, of course, could benefit from further refinements. For instance, legitimate and illegitimate activities might be classified according to various publics. The voting public of a municipality may condemn an activity like prostitution, but a large segment of the population may condone it.

In the third component of the definition, we must specify the number of people that must be part of a matrix or society before it is considered to be organized crime. The Organized Crime Control Act of 1970 was partially designed to control gambling operations taking place on a large scale. Part of the lawmakers' definition of an "illegal gambling business" was an operation which "involves five or more persons who conduct, finance, manage, supervise, direct, or own all or part of such business."[27] In practice, then, the number of individuals that must be involved in an operation before it is labeled a criminal business or conspiracy has been set. Perhaps the minimum number of participants necessary to make up a matrix or society could be set at ten, twenty, or even one thousand in our definition of organized crime.

An alternative to counting the number of participants is to call crime organized if gross or net profits surpass a given dollar amount. This is implied in the *Task Force Report* when it speaks of organized crime "gaining control over whole fields of activity in order to amass huge profits."[28] This definition will make reference to numbers of individuals which are often difficult to discern, but infinitely easier than trying to estimate the profits of groups or matrices. If activities which have over two thousand participants are defined as organized crime, there may be only one criminal society or matrix in the country, and significant activity ordinarily thought of as organized may not fall under scrutiny. If only two people are needed for crime to be organized, then all criminal activity comes close to being lumped under the organized crime rubric. Arbitrarily, I would suggest that five or more individuals (consistent with the Organized Crime Control Act) must participate in the society or matrix before it is called organized crime.

Finally, the fourth component is a measure of the degree of involvement of individuals in illegitimate activity necessary before speaking of them as criminals, or of their organizations as criminal matrices or societies. For instance, is a corporation criminal if it does most of its business according to law, but if all of its salesmen pay kickbacks to customers when the law requires competitive bidding? Is the ex-bootlegger, whose only connection with organized crime today is in the settlement of labor problems, part of a criminal society? In determining the degree of involvement one could take into account several variables: time spent in illegal activities, the participant's knowledge that these activities are illegal, and percentage of income from illegal activities.

The *Task Force Report* is not systematic about measuring the degree of involvement of individuals and groups in criminal societies. Instead, it speaks of twenty-four "core" groups which are allied with "other racket enterprises." This is a way of suggesting that organized criminals are those belonging to a national organization and that the others, regardless of their involvement in illegal activities or the number involved in their group or matrix, are only on the periphery of organized crime. My classification designates individuals or groups as part of organized crime in terms of their degree of involvement in organized crime activities.

In determining involvement, a distinction can be made between producers and consumers in organized crime; the former, who run the activities and provide the labor, include numbers runners, narcotics pushers, loan sharks, and lay-off bettors. Among the latter are those who gamble, go to prostitutes, borrow money from loan sharks, and buy stolen merchandise. Those who are engaged full time as producers I will call "professionals." They are "persons whose income is gained primarily from the full-time pursuit of criminal activity."[29] Although the report this definition is drawn from suggests that professionals work alone, my usage suggests they may either be working alone or as part of matrices or societies. There are also several types of part-time producers. They may be "apprentices," people who are learning the trade but have to hustle work on their own; "retirees," individuals who used to be full-timers or professionals and now deal in organized crime only on occasion; or those persons who have chosen to work on a part-time basis or haven't been allowed full membership in matrices or societies. Members of this last group frequent the bars and restaurants the others favor and pick up different jobs as they come along. I will call them "free-lancers."

Consumers also perform their functions on either a part-time or a full-time basis. Some persons habitually gamble, take out loans from sharks the day before payday, and support some kind of addictive habit. People who range towards this kind of involvement we will call "steady customers," while those who unwittingly buy products stocked by organized criminals, pay more money in taxes to pay for police protection, and have costs of stolen merchandise passed on by department stores, I will call "innocents." Those who knowingly buy stolen goods, borrow from a loan shark, and gamble, but only occasionally, I will call "opportunists."

TABLE 1

	Producers	Consumers
Full-Time	Professionals	Steady Customers
Part-Time	Apprentices Free-lancers Retirees	Innocents Opportunists

It is evident that judging the extent of organized crime depends on which groups are included as organized criminals. Using the *Task Force Report* definition, Ralph Salerno suggests that "Italian gangs—Cosa Nostra—do make up the center of organized crime: a group of 5000 to 7500 formal members to which an equal number of non-Italian groups are linked by alliances and for which independent groups and individuals work. The total number of Cosa Nostra and their associate gangs and employees and underlings may be 100,000 to 250,000."[30] I would suggest that professionals may be in La Cosa Nostra or other gangs, for my designation cuts across given societies and matrices. Apprentices and retirees also may be associated with La Cosa Nostra, as Salerno calls it. My designation is more relevant because enforcement agencies should be more interested in catching active full-time participants than those who merely belong to a society. Also, designation of consumers allows us to account for a wider group that wittingly or unwittingly contributes to the maintenance of organized crime by purchasing its services.

This revised definition of organized crime has many virtues. It takes account of criminal matrices and societies often overlooked in the analysis of organized crime, and avoids defining such crime as a single society. The analyst can look at the history of organized crime not as the rise, decline, and fall of a particular group, but as the complex interplay between criminal societies and matrices. Utilizing this definition, one can account for activities such as car theft, moonshining, management of certain NCO clubs, and poaching of spotted leopard pelts as organized crime. It is easier, for instance, to understand narcotics traffic as a matrix of crime than as the work of a criminal society.

A few questions arise with the acceptance of this definition; for one, it is necessary to distinguish between economic and political organized crime. In reality, gambling, loan-sharking, and other organized criminal activities which are often dependent upon corruption of government may bring economic gain in addition to weakening the structure of government. Similarly, the threat to burn down public buildings may be avowedly political in nature, but the group may also commit robberies to support its militant political goals. The distinction between economic and political organized crime is necessarily difficult to draw, but a case can be made by differentiating organizations whose goals are avowedly political from those whose goals are avowedly economic. Problems, of course, arise when rhetoric no longer matches reality and a radical political group coheres only for the economic benefits of its members while masking its behavior in an elaborate political ideology.

Thus, the distinction between economic and political crime is not an esoteric one, for it could be suggested that the wording of the Organized Crime Control Act could lead to the arrest of public officials as well as organized criminals. Senator Carl T. Curtis, for instance, has lamented that the immunity statutes in the Organized Crime Control Act were meant to get at the top echelons of organized crime and not to be used against the president of the United States in the prosecution and Senate hearings involving the Watergate break-in.[31] In the last chapter, it will be argued that no such double standard should exist and laws should not designate special targets.

It also seems odd that violence or threat of violence is not mentioned in the definition. Often it is the blood and gore of the films the public associates with organized crime. The problem arises in classifying violence with organized crime and including all of those individuals and groups the public associates with organized crime in this classification. The amount of violence in organized crime has been decreasing, making it impractical to define as organized criminal societies or matrices those groups that commit a specific amount of violence in a given year. Many groups or matrices may utilize low levels of violence or threats of violence in their activities, yet we might want to label them as participants in organized crime.

Another method of classification would investigate the levels of violence that groups perpetrated at their inception and in their formative years, when violence was more widespread. However, this would be defining a group not by what it is, but by its origins. Two societies may be solely involved in skimming the profits off the top in a Las Vegas casino; one could be designated as involved in organized crime because its members used force to achieve their goals during Prohibition, while the other group, even though it is engaged in selling narcotics and stealing securities, would not be so designated because its origin is recent and its methods peaceful. For these reasons, violence was excluded from my definition of organized crime.

Data Sources

Primary Data

One source of primary data is from defectors, those individuals who were once a part of organized crime, or who were associates of organized criminal groups. The most famous of the defectors is Joseph Valachi, who appeared on the televised hearings of John McClellan's Permanent Subcommittee on Investigations in 1963. Valachi told the committee and hence the public of the formative years of organized crime, and chiefly of the Castellamarese War in which present gangland configurations were established. He recounted much of his personal participation in organized crime, including those events which led up to his incarceration and his decision to divulge all of this information to federal officials.[32] Valachi's revelations provided the public and enforcement agents with a wealth of information, but one must be aware of certain limitations. Most of his experiences dealt with organized crime in New York City. His modest standing within the organization precluded a more comprehensive picture of organized crime from a perspective of leadership. Nevertheless, his revelations focused attention on organized crime and allowed officials to test their hypotheses and assumptions against Valachi's words.

Gay Talese's *Honor Thy Father* promised to reveal a good deal about the workings of organized crime. To quote the book jacket, "the 'inside' book [on organized crime] that has so far eluded other writers has now been written."[33] The key to this book is access to Bill Bonanno, a member and officer in a Cosa Nostra family, but, more importantly, the son of family head Joseph Bonanno. There is hesitation in using the word *defector* to describe Bill Bonanno's role in the writing of the book. He "defects" when it comes time to tell about his personal life, which does not involve his day-to-day activities in business, and when he selectively describes events which lead up to and follow the disappearance of his father.[34] He withholds a good deal of information. We learn little about family enterprises and how they work; we never find out where the elder Bonanno was taken or what he did when he disappeared. Much of the information for the book comes from the same sources that are available to other interested journalists and social scientists; nevertheless, there are some interesting insights in this book, and Talese does an excellent job of reporting.

Other defectors have come forward, but none with the overall perspective of a Valachi or a Bonanno. Paul Siciliano, son of a Prohibition bootlegger; Vincent Teresa, purported grandson of a Cosa Nostra don; Sidney Slater, an associate of members of a Brooklyn crime family, and a host of others provide some insights into the workings of organized crime and are worth reading.[35]

The shortcomings and advantages of using information from the defector should be obvious. First, when we speak of defectors as primary sources, we are not using the term *primary* as a synonym for *reliable* or *valid*, for all men see only a selective picture of reality. The defector is especially prone to see one side of particular issues. In the cases of Valachi and Siciliano, it was their hate and fear of organization members that drove them to speak in the first place. Take, for instance, Siciliano's description of the man who has continually tried, according to Siciliano, to kill him: "I will tell you about the biggest mistake I ever made and about the biggest louse I ever met. The mistake and the louse are one and same, Robert Cervone."[36] We must take into account the defector's biases and his ambivalence towards the organization he has deserted when analyzing the data.

Data from a defector may be subject to filters other than his own eyes, ears, and biases. As in the case of Peter Maas with the *Valachi Papers* and Gay Talese with the words of Bill Bonanno,[37] the data may be interpreted by an editor. When Valachi spoke before a congressional committee, his responses were structured by the congressman's questions, which may have distracted Valachi from the context within which he thought and acted, and caused him to ignore other issues he might have thought were important. In many cases, the congressmen might be motivated by their own concerns, constituent demands, and public opinion, and not by the goal of finding out all they can about organized crime.

Nevertheless, defectors can tell us a good deal about the workings of organized crime. Their own perspective may be a source of bias, but at the same time, these biases are a source of information. How do organized criminals perceive their own role in society? How do they justify committing murder and selling narcotics? Answers to these and other questions can best be gained from the defectors' perspectives.

Another source of primary data comes from electronic informants, bugs or wiretaps placed in the home or office of an organized criminal. Three sources of information are extraordinarily interesting and are relied upon quite heavily in this study. One is the transcript from a microphone placed in the office of the plumbing business of Samuel Rizzo de Cavalcante, a purported head of a small crime family in New Jersey. His business dealings, as well as aspects of his private life, are detailed in the transcripts.[38] Another good source is a set of airtels (FBI summaries of eavesdropping) gathered on Raymond Patriarca, purported boss of a New England organized crime family.[39] Both the de Cavalcante and Patriarca transcripts became available when they were turned over to the courts upon request of the defendant's attorney. Previously, government officials had dropped charges when asked to place such transcripts on record to see if evidence had been obtained illegally by aid of the transcript. Much to the surprise of the defendants' attorneys in these two cases, the transcripts were turned over to the courts and became a matter of public record.

Another excellent electronic informant is a tape recording of eight conversations of organized criminals prepared by John Hughes' New York State Joint Legislative Committee on Crime. Selections chosen by the committee illustrate interesting aspects of the organization and activities of organized crime; for instance, the tapes mentioned a securities theft, a loan-shark collection, reminiscences about a murder, and mention of La Cosa Nostra.[40]

Data from electronic informants, like data from defectors, has its limitations. The individuals subject to eavesdropping might suspect they are being listened to and thus guard their conversation. They might transmit important or confidential information in a pre-arranged manner. What we find with the de Cavalcante tapes is a curious phenomenon: at times the principals are guarded in what they say, and de Cavalcante, in a fashion we have been accustomed to in TV gangster shows, turns up the radio to drown out conversations. But most of the time he forgets about caution and, as we shall see, talks about a variety of sensitive issues.[41] One can only speculate as to why he does not take such precautions, although one reason might be that to do so would almost preclude doing business. It is difficult to work under and acknowledge conditions that justify paranoiac behavior, and certainly preferable to believe that we are not under constant surveillance.

It is certain that after the release and publication of these tapes, and subsequent publicity about the federal government's enthusiasm about utilizing the wiretap as a weapon against organized crime, there has been more caution by organized criminals concerning their private conversations. In fact, there has been an interesting "war" between the government and organized crime with respect to electronic surveillance. There have been successive stages of government initiatives and organized criminal responses. The pattern is not strictly a chronological progression, for more primitive relationships may still exist between organized criminals and enforcement officials in some localities.

In the first stages of the relationship, organized criminals are listened to, and, as is described with de Cavalcante, suspect the government of electronic eavesdropping.[42] Next, organized criminals use pay phones for important business calls. Enforcement agents take advantage of the fact that in low income neighborhoods and in other sections of the cities, pay phones are often out of order. They break all but one of the pay phones near the office or home of an organized criminal and tap the line of the one left in good repair. At this stage the Bonanno family replied in two ways: first, by developing a telephone answering service, and second, by working out an elaborate code with pay phones.[43] The answering service was placed in the home of a relative of one of the members and registered in a fictitious name. Members could call in to indicate, by a pre-established code, who they were and where they were presently located. The pay telephone system went into effect when two members conversed on a home phone and slipped two digits into the conversation. The first digit would represent the locale of the phone booth and the second digit indicated the time at which the call would be placed. Under this system, as Bill Bonanno suggests, it was imperative that the telephones be in good repair. "The condition of the coinbox was of vital importance to him [Bill Bonanno] and the other men, and he knew how infuriated they had all been at one time or another by malfunctioning phones and how they swore vengeance on the petty thieves who tamper with outdoor phones."[44] Organized criminals may be the phone companies' most constant critics because they continually call in repairs and check to see that phone numbers have not been changed. What we see here is the increasing suspicion by organized criminals of federal, state, and local wiretap procedures, and perhaps increasing difficulty for the researcher to obtain good electronic eavesdropping data.

Another problem with data from electronic devices is that researchers cannot ask the crucial and probing questions they want, for the agenda is set by the participants themselves. This may mean hours of sifting through irrelevant materials, and fragmentary answers to questions which researchers want to probe in more depth.

Finally, some of the information is not "primary," since someone else has edited the materials. The choice of tapes in the recording made by the New York State Joint Legislative Committee may have been made with a different set of criteria than the political or social scientist might use.[45] Of more significance is the procedure the FBI follows when its agents summarize incoming information. Here we clearly have second-hand information, and not the words directly from the mouths of the criminals. Nevertheless, the virtue of electronic eavesdropping as a source of primary data is obvious. You are intruding into the day-to-day activities of organized criminals and getting a feel for and ideas about how they run their lives.

Government information in the form of committee hearings, commission reports, and agency releases also serves as primary data on organized crime. A variety of congressional committees have reported on the activities of organized crime: hearings of the Kefauver Committee, 1950-1951, received a lot of publicity and gathered a good deal of hitherto disparate materials on organized crime. More recently, as suggested earlier, the Senate Permanent Subcommittee of Investigations has taken over the major burden of intelligence and research on organized crime. In the late 1950s, it did extensive investigative work into labor racketeering with Robert Kennedy as chief counsel; in the early 1960s, it heard Joe Valachi's testimony; and recently it has held hearings on stock fraud and securities theft by organized criminals.

Many of the problems faced with this data parallel the problems with data from defectors and electronic informants, for we cannot control the questions to be asked. For example, Senator Javits once seemed on his way toward checking up the relationship between Italians and non-Italians when Valachi was being questioned about the relationship between Genovese, an Italian, and Lansky, a non-Italian.

> SENATOR JAVITS: Are they associated, Lansky and Vito Genovese?
> MR. VALACHI: Yes, they do everything together.
> SENATOR JAVITS: And it persists to this day?
> MR. VALACHI: Yes.[46]

At this point, the researcher may want to interject the whole question of Italian-non-Italian relationships, but to his chagrin, the committee is disposed to talking about gambling in Las Vegas.[47] A problem which faces us with all of the primary material is how to reconstruct the workings of a social system from slices of information which are not totally representative of the activities of organized criminal groups and might not reflect a representative sample of individuals in organized crime. These drawbacks present the researcher with both problems and challenges.

Three government reports—the Wickersham Report published in 1931, the Kefauver Report, and the section on organized crime in *The Challenge of Crime in a Free Society*—provide the most comprehensive thinking by government on the problems of organized crime.[48] These documents are subject to all the weaknesses of government reporting—the tendency to compromise and to attempt to mobilize public opinion, and the sometimes-inadequate time and resources for preparation. Agency releases are subject to the purposes of the initiating agencies, and may not be subject to verification by competing sources of information. They may release information to publicize their enforcement efforts and may play up or play down the problems of crime in the society.

In summary, the so-called primary sources of data may not actually be primary if the organized criminals are guarded in their comments, if the questions asked are structured by a second party, or if the material is edited before we read or listen to it. Little field research goes on; we are dependent on others for information, and this information comes in spurts and concerns a variety of groups and individuals. To dwell on the shortcomings of this data is necessary to sensitize the critic to the problems of analysis. Yet there is considerable information to be gained from these sources, and in comparison with past years, researchers are sitting on a gold mine of information.

Secondary Sources

Some interesting interpretations of the primary source data by newspaper journalists, magazine writers, and biographers of organized crime and criminals have been made; one has only to sample the work of Nicholas Gage, Gay Talese, Sandy Smith, and Hank Messick.[49] However, most writing by journalists lacks comprehensiveness in dealing with organized crime; journalists often rely upon discrete bits of information and don't worry about the overall picture. When they do reflect on organized crime as a whole, distinctive styles or biases may be reflected.

The first tendency of the journalists is to gather materials on a day-to-day basis without any attempt to include them in a larger corpus of events or explanations. This is an occupational hazard for reporters writing stories on any given event and is not necessarily unwarranted. People who read the papers affix their own interpretation to events, or read the afternoon papers which attempt a bit more analysis. To show that reporting of organized crime involves discrete reportage of events, one has only to clip articles from a newspaper for a month or two and look for concepts or ideas that tie the events together. This form of reporting tends to be more endemic to crime coverage than to many other areas of journalism. Nicholas B. Katzenbach, the former attorney general, asks, "On the average newspaper today, who covers the police beat? I do not know and can find no studies to say. But I would strongly suspect that in a number of cases it is the greenest rookie on the staff, lacking training in his own profession, let alone that of the policemen, lawyers and judges he covers."[50] He is unlikely to have the methodological skills to understand events and fit them within a broader perspective or world view.

Nicholas Gage appears to recognize the lack of sophisticated crime reporters or investigative reporters who are assigned full-time to stories and issues and are not cursed by having to follow day-to-day business. He recognizes as accomplished investigative reporters "William Lambert of *Life* magazine, who discovered that [Abe] Fortas had accepted a $25,000 check from Louis Wolfson when Wolfson was under indictment for stock manipulations,"[51] and

"Stanley Penn of *The Wall Street Journal* [who] reported that a number of the ruling party's leaders had accepted consultants' fees from land developers and casino operators," revelations which led to the fall of the Bahamian government in 1966.[52] Yet he understands the difficulties of getting competent people to do the job, and more important, of getting newspapers and magazines to hire and retain these individuals. There are difficulties in convincing publishers to retain investigative reporters, for their work requires considerable time and expense, and often the payoff is not a story of any importance. Legal fees may mount and the investigative reporter with a good deal of independence may unearth information that is damaging to the publisher or those who advertise in the publication. These factors make it difficult for newspapers, magazines, or wire services to hire many investigative reporters.[53]

Even if attempts are made at comprehensive analytical reporting, certain modes of explanation recur in the writings of reporters. In an article, "Is Television Biased?," Paul Weaver suggests that all political reporting is biased, but that the perception of political candidates as liberal, conservative, Republican, or Democrat is not what is important. More significant is the reporters' theme of elections as a struggle between two or more individuals for victory, with their actions moving towards or detracting from that goal. Thus, in the 1968 campaign, Humphrey is seen by the media as the underdog, Nixon as the frontrunner, and Wallace as the precursor of violence; they are not viewed as liberal, moderate, or conservative candidates.[54] The same kind of anthropocentricity is seen in crime reporting in what I call the "crime reporter's theme." What reporters perceive are continuous struggles for power between various charismatic leaders in organized crime. All their reporting concerns these struggles, or the never-ending battle between the forces of good embodied by the district attorney and the forces of evil manifest in the gangland boss.

Interest invariably centers on the identity of the current "Mr. Big" and various names are always suggested: Al Capone, Vito Genovese, Meyer Lansky, Frank Costello, Lucky Luciano, Lepke Buchalter, Carlo Gambino.[55] We are concerned here not with whether the newspapers are right or wrong about Mr. Big, but with the reasons why this is the question continually asked. One senses a touch of nostalgia in reporters who suggest that charismatic leaders in organized crime are dying or being displaced by a newer, less colorful band. For these reporters, it is almost as if organized crime would die with these individuals.

Reporters cannot be entirely faulted, for their readers want to hear when key gangsters are arrested, are involved in gangland intrigue, or die. Investigative agencies count success against organized crime in terms of personalities captured and number of arrests made. In view of the public's desire to learn and conceptualize about organized crime through personalities, the information that qualifies as "news" involves conflict between individuals. Gang wars, as well as confrontations between criminals and investigative committees, are excellent data sources and in contradistinction to the day-to-day activities in crime, these events highlight personalities. Thus, where reporting goes beyond discrete facts or events, it begins to resemble a military history with focus on personality as opposed to social organizations or social structure. This leads to the possibility that much needs to be investigated by the social scientist that is not covered by the reporter.

Can the social scientist do any better than the journalist? It is better to ask if the social scientist can supplement what the journalist has to say, for the latter has an excellent grasp of primary information and does provide us with a running history or chronicle of organized crime.

It is my belief that the social scientist does have something to say, but the arguments of those who might say social scientists have little or no first-hand information on organized crime and don't know as much as public officials must be overcome. Much of what either the journalist or the social scientist would want to know about organized crime is classified or confidential and only those in enforcement or in the organization itself really can "know" it. Much of what Jimmy Breslin calls "Italian geography" is not available to many others, journalists or social scientists. "Italian geography," writes Breslin, "is the keeping of huge amounts of information on gangsters: the prices they pay for clothes, the restaurants in which they eat, the names of all relatives out to the fifth cousins, their home addresses, and their visible daily movements."[56] However, a public official may only have first-hand knowledge of a small segment of organized crime, just as the social scientist does. He may be less likely to avail himself of other knowledge available on the subject than the social scientist who may pursue the subject at his leisure. Also, in talking to public officials and crime reporters, it is evident that little which would shed greater light on the structure or functioning of organized crime is withheld from the public. Information is withheld for legal, rather than intellectual, reasons. Public officials with a first-hand knowledge of organized crime have been very open, short of specific references to names and places (when legal restrictions are involved), and are rarely reluctant to give their opinions on organized crime.

Finally, the man with first-hand knowledge of organized crime sees his events from his own perspective and not from that of his adversary. This does not free the social scientist from this difficulty; he, too, is a participant-observer and carries with him his own beliefs as a citizen. More important, the social scientist is prone to a position perhaps more insidious than that of one who does not recognize and acknowledge his own biases. In looking at the events from every perspective and hunting for social and psychological explanations of behavior, he may take a deterministic view toward all of the events. He thus may sacrifice commitment to his subject, assume no sense of responsibility for what occurs, or develop no perspective on what public policy on organized crime should be. I shall try to maintain that delicate balance between participant and observer and to recognize a commitment to describe organized crime and develop consistent, intelligent policy alternatives to deal with it.

Chapter 2

The History of Organized Crime

The societies and matrices described in the definition of organized crime are not merely contemporary American phenomena. In France in the early 1300s, the Church encouraged the enfranchisement of the serfs, and by the standards of the time, there was general prosperity. With the onset of the English Wars in 1336 this prosperity disappeared and "these wars gave rise to a dangerous class of criminal (known as Gueux or Beggars) who got the length of forming themselves into an order with their own government, hierarchy, and laws, to say nothing of a separate language."[1] A similar group of wandering beggars existed in Elizabethan England. "There was no single head of *the* beggars but there were petty chiefs who ruled their particular districts and they were known as Upright Men. Any thief, beggar, horse-stealer, trull, sham-madman, or any other member of the various degrees of crime who frequented the countryside where one of the Upright Men held sway was obliged to become a loyal subject, and submit to the taxation."[2]

Organized criminal groups and matrices existed in other parts of the world as well. In the last century, the Phansegars or Thugs of India lived off the earnings of others by murdering travelers to relieve them of their possessions. Like the organized criminals we are more familiar with, the Thugs often had some menial job that would serve as an alibi for their more nefarious activities.[3] A society known as the Assassins emerged in the Near East around 1863 and they thought of themselves as the "true" interpreters of the Koran.[4] The Assassins often operated in ways similar to those of contemporary criminal matrices and societies for "rather like the Mafia of later times, [they] operated from their strongholds a protection racket under the threat of death."[5] In the city of Singapore, Malaya, the offshoot of a Chinese revolutionary society called the Triad ran illicit activities. "The gambling industry, opium trade, prostitution and other activities of the society, as well as the struggle against the British authorities and Christian missionaries, had little to do with the fight for the imperial throne."[6] Their ideology might have been revolutionary, but their structure of rewards, incentives, in fact their whole *raison d'être*, centered around their criminal businesses.

In the United States, organized criminal groups are not strictly a twentieth century phenomenon. Many of the eighteenth and nineteenth century groups (especially the ones which have captured the public imagination) operated in rural, frontier settings. After the Civil War, there were many train and bank robberies, such as those perpetrated by the Reno brothers of Indiana and the Jesse James-Cole Younger group from Missouri.[7] At the same time, and even prior to the Civil War, societies and matrices of criminals existed in the large urban areas, but were subject to much less public attention. These groups were usually restricted to urban slum neighborhoods. Typical of these groups were those located in the Five Points and the Bowery in New York City.[8] Many of these early gangs operated around the wharfs of the city, often with little interference from the police.[9]

One of the urban matrices to receive substantial publicity was formed by the two Matranga brothers in New Orleans in the 1890s. They set up a protection racket on the docks which governed all loading and unloading of cargo. The brothers ran into competition from a matrix run by the Provenzano brothers and the dispute resulted in numerous killings. The local chief of police, a man named Hennessey, investigated the murders and he was shot just a few days before the opening of the grand jury. Indictments were brought against nineteen and a now-familiar pattern emerged. At least half of the jury was intimidated or bribed, excellent lawyers were hired for the defense, and acquittal was won for all but three.[10] A mob of several thousand gathered and dragged eleven out of jail, hung them by the neck and riddled them with bullets. In the aftermath, nobody was prosecuted for the lynching.

These early gangs primarily preyed on their own countrymen and were neighborhood-based. Jurisdiction, as is the case between the Provenzano and the Matranga brothers, often was fought on a block-by-block basis. There was no trace or hint of a national organization and these early societies and matrices were not the special province of Italians, but were made up of many ethnic groups, each having its own criminal societies and matrices. At the end of the nineteenth century, organized crime was more in the hands of Irish, Jewish, and "native American" societies and matrices than Italian groups.[11] The first two decades of this century saw the growth of the cities and the continuation of the pluralistic pattern of societies and matrices in organized crime. Certain individuals became well known for their exploits, but the specter of a national organization was not yet with us. Ciro Terranova gained widespread notoriety. Arnold Rothstein gained fame as a prominent gambler in New York City and caused quite a stir when his name was associated with the fixing of the 1919 World Series.[12] Big Jim Colisimo was his counterpart in Chicago. With the advent of Prohibition, organized crime was still in the hands of local, parochial, ethnic societies and matrices, but many were beginning to operate on a moderate scale. Joe Valachi does a good job in capturing the atmosphere of the times when he describes night life at the Venezia Restaurant on 116th Street.

> Guys were coming there from all over the city. Besides us Italians, there were the Diamond Brothers, Legs and his brother Eddie, there were other Jew boys, and Irish guys from down around Yorkville. Sometimes you saw Lepke and Gurrah and also Little Augie from the East Side downtown. But the big man on 116th Street was Ciro Terranova, the Artichoke King. He got the name because he tied up the artichokes in the city. The way I understand it he would buy all the artichokes that came into New York. I didn't know where they all came from, but I know he was buying them all out. Being artichokes, they hold; they can keep. Then Ciro would make his own price, and as you know, Italians got to have artichokes to eat.[13]

His description predates any overarching organization, but we begin to see potential for association and communication.

It is part of the conventional folk wisdom that the growth of organized crime coincided with the Volstead Act that took effect at 12:01 A.M. on January 7, 1920, ushering in the era known as Prohibition. In reality, Prohibition profoundly affected organized crime by changing the public's attitudes towards organized criminals and altering the structure of criminal societies and matrices.

With the advent of Prohibition, a very wide spectrum of the public demanded the services of organized criminals. In accepting these services the public was acknowledging that those who performed the services were not moral freaks or degenerates. Organized criminals distinguished between those who provided a good quality alcoholic beverage and those who dealt in contraband that was of inferior quality and might cause blindness and death. The public also made this distinction. Enforcement was difficult because of the complicity of customers and the public in general with bootleggers, but also because of problems in getting enforcement agents to enforce unpopular laws. In this society there is little impetus for enforcement when an illegal activity has the complicity of the upper and middle classes. The marijuana laws remained on the books unchallenged until the children of middle and upper class families began using it and were affected by enforcement policy. The moral onus is now upon agencies of enforcement rather than the users or distributors. The marijuana distributors are not seen as dope peddlers or pushers, but as college kids. The whole thrust, then, of Prohibition on the public was toward acceptance of the individuals involved in the manufacture, distribution, and sale of alcoholic beverages, and disrespect for enforcement agents and their respective agencies. Meanwhile, little attention was paid to other illegal activities criminals pursued while publicity centered on bootlegging.

Prohibition also wrought extensive changes in the internal structures of organized criminal groups and matrices. The most significant change from the point of view espoused here is what I call the "nationalization" of the distribution of illegal commodities. Before Prohibition, most societies and matrices were local in the scope and extent of their activities; often they were confined to single ethnic neighborhoods. The onset of Prohibition encouraged attempts to control criminal activities of more extensive territories, such as cities or even regions.

Much of the pre-Prohibition business centered around certain well-defined districts in the cities. In Chicago, for instance, it was an area known as the Levee. "Bounded north and south by Twenty-second and Eighteenth streets and east and west by Clark and Wabash, the Levee had one of the world's heaviest concentrations of crime and vice."[14] Some of the vices, such as prostitution, drew a heavy contingent of upper and middle class customers; but it was still to most people an evil, the other side of the tracks. Prohibition changed all that and liquor became accessible to almost anyone anywhere. "In Chicago alone, in 1930, Federal officials estimated that ten thousand speakeasies were operating, each buying weekly six barrels of beer at $55 each, thus giving the gangs a weekly $3,500,000 revenue."[15] Thus, "nationalization" occurred when illegal use of alcohol and hence distribution became widespread. Illegal services were no longer confined to certain districts in cities.

More universal demand led to the process of nationalization of organized crime, but this process was also furthered by the distribution procedures. Sales were often made from one city to another and alcohol and alcoholic beverages were often smuggled in from other countries. Cooperation between criminal groups in various localities was necessary to keep the public supplied. In the pre-Prohibition days such cooperation was unnecessary because the illicit activity was very often a service such as gambling or prostitution, or protection rackets which often don't necessitate larger distribution systems. The only exception was the occasional transfer of labor from one region to another. For example, the importing of hired killers or muscle prevented easy identification and arrest, and the importing of prostitutes (the white slave trade) sometimes was necessary to keep the houses of prostitution going.

At the same time the nationalization of distribution systems took place, there was a proliferation of competing groups involved in the illegal alcohol industry. There were high profits to be made, low risk, and widespread public acceptance of bootlegging activities, which encouraged many individuals to become involved in the "criminal" process. As in the distribution of marijuana today, the sources of supply could not be monopolized easily by larger criminal groups, so individual entrepreneurs were encouraged. Every tenement was a potential source of supply. In Chicago, for example, one matrix headed up by the Genna brothers persuaded hundreds of individuals to install copper stills in their homes. To earn fifteen dollars a day, all the tenant had to do was keep the fire burning and skim the distillate.[16] All of the people formerly engaged in legal enterprises involving the alcoholic beverage industry and even those engaged in making industrial alcohol became potential participants in the now-illegal trade.

The two trends which came with Prohibition, the nationalization of distribution and the proliferation of groups involved in the distribution process, explain both the violent character of the era and the growth of criminal organizations beyond the confines of the community. What existed was a wildly competitive market situation with few established businesses, very similar to the conditions that exist in any infant industry.[17] Unlike legitimate businesses, there were no legitimate or effective organs in existence to regulate the markets for alcoholic beverages. Violence and defensive alliances naturally spring up in an unregulated market situation. This explanation of violence during Prohibition seems more plausible than ones which tend to pass off violence of the period as a symptom of the bawdy, gusty, carefree atmosphere of the times.

Other forces were also at work during Prohibition that contributed to the trends just described. Increasing transportation and communication allowed the public to travel to reap organized crime's services as well as enabling criminal societies and matrices to organize on a more national level. We now find a continuation of this trend today when people can afford to travel to Las Vegas, the Bahamas, or even England to gamble. Also, one can not ignore the Americanization of various ethnic groups which facilitated communication and cooperation between them. Various ethnic matrices did business together during Prohibition, whereas in the past this was often impossible.

It must be recognized that although Prohibition formally began and ended with passage and repeal of the Volstead Act, organized criminals anticipated its coming and planned what to do upon repeal. By the time it went into effect nationally, twenty-four states had already accepted it by local option, the first acceptance being by Georgia in 1907. Many in organized crime made a smooth transition into the bootlegging business by either prior practice or sufficient foresight. Once in effect, it became a dominant economic enterprise for many organized criminals, but many retained and developed other legal and illegal activities along with it. Diversification is not a totally new concept for industry. With the end of Prohibition, groups had to find other sources of income, and those who had stuck to the principle of diversity or had the foresight to create new business lasted in organized crime.

As Prohibition drew to a close, more and more Italian names were mentioned in discussions of organized crime. The question was naturally raised again as it had been earlier in the century when the term "the Black Hand" was used, as to whether organized crime in the United States was an offshoot of the Mafia in Italy. It is an argument that continues to recur.

One argument which suggests importation of Mafia members to

the United States referred to the widespread use of notes picturing a black hand which were used in extortionate transactions around the turn of the century. The Black Hand was the symbol of an idea, not of an organization. Just as the visitor to the United States might think that the peace sticker affixed to cars signifies some organizational solidarity, so might the observer surmise that the Black Hand referred to some organizational entity. On the contrary, this fear of organizational conspiracy was used by individual criminals working in small groups to extort money from others. Any individual using the note making reference to the Black Hand found it struck fear into the recipient. "The genuine Black Hander (the real terrorist of 'Mafiuoso') works alone or with two or three of his fellow countrymen."[18]

It has been suggested that the American Mafia might have been imported directly from Italy because organizationally American and Italian criminal groups have many similarities. Donald Cressey, while suggesting that American organized crime and the Sicilian Mafia are not the same, is still troubled by the similarities. "While we are confident that American organized crime is not merely the Sicilian Mafia transplanted, the similarities between the two organizations are direct and too great to be ignored."[19] He has trouble accounting for these similarities, but others have devised a set of concepts to explain them. A distinction between organizational structures and culture was made by Arthur Train, at one time an assistant district attorney in New York City. In 1925 he suggested that "by far the greater portion of these criminals [in New York City], whether ex-convicts or novices, are the products or by-products of the influence of the two great secret societies of Southern Italy. These societies and the unorganized criminal propensity and atmosphere which they generate, are known as the 'Mala Vita'."[20] The same distinction between culture and organization is recognized by other analysts, such as Gaetano Mosca, Giovanni Schiavo, and Francis A. J. Ianni.[21] Ianni suggests that "Mafia is a word which has at least two distinct meanings to Sicilians. When used as an adjective, it describes a state of mind and a style of behavior that Sicilians recognize immediately. It is bravura but not braggadocio."[22] "Such a man (mafioso) may or may not be a member of a formal organization in which he has a clearly defined role. Yet even in Sicily, the word Mafia also clearly denotes just such an organization when it is used as a noun."[23] Thus, the culture of the Mafia may be transplanted, but it does not necessarily follow that the American organization has to be an offshoot of the Italian organization. The sharing of a common culture would suggest that organizational entities would end up being similar.

Words which may stand for a culture and organizational entities (such as Mafia, Black Hand, and more recently, La Cosa Nostra) have bedeviled law enforcement officials and analysts in their quest to understand the workings of organized crime. One of the biggest follies is to attempt to track down whether or not officials in various cities had heard gang members use the phrase *Cosa Nostra* to refer to organized crime.[24] Some took Valachi's use of the term to signify the existence of a nationwide conspiracy, and others noted its use exclusively in New York, and thought it signified a local organization. The data shows that in different cities organized criminals call themselves the outfit, the syndicate, the organization, the mob, or Cosa Nostra. They may be using it in the sense of a noun or adjective, and their use of the word does not prove existence or non-existence of an extensive network of organized criminal groups. Even if every group used the same word, we still could not deduce a single organizational entity. A word like *Mafia* or *Cosa Nostra* should not get in the way of understanding organized crime.

The numbers of years it took for Italians to gain a foothold in organized crime is another argument which suggests that the culture but not the organization of the Mafia was transplanted to this country. The massive immigration of Italians to the United States took place from 1900 to 1910 when 2,045,877 entered the country, and about half as many came from 1910 to 1920. After this period immigration slowed and only about 330,000 Italians have entered this country since 1930.[25] Their success or impact in organized crime was by no means immediate, which suggests that either they started on a small scale, or had to become Americanized Italians, adapted to American ways, before they could be successful in criminal activities.

Spread of the organizational Mafia to the United States would be plausible if we saw the Mafia of Italy exhibiting similar imperialist tendencies towards other countries or provinces of Italy. On the contrary, the Mafia did not spread to Northern Italy, nor even to the eastern end of the island of Sicily. There always has been a suspicion of outsiders and a tendency to keep within the confines of the extended family in their business activities.

If the organization of the Mafia were transplanted from Italy to the United States, there would have to be a single organizational entity called the Mafia. Commentators and historians talk of Mafia organizations in the plural. For instance, Gaetano Mosca suggests that the Mafia as an organization "signifies a number of small criminal bands."[26] Luigi Barzini, an Italian legislator, captures the structure of the Mafia in Italy.

> It is not a strictly organized association, with hierarchies, written statutes, headquarters, a ruling elite and an undisputed chief. It is a spontaneous formation like an ant-colony or a bee-hive, a loose and haphazard collection of single men and hetero-geneous groups, each man obeying his entomological rules, each group uppermost in its tiny domain, independent, submitted to the will of its own leader, each group locally imposing its own rigid form of primitive justice. Only in rare times of emergency does the Mafia mobilize and become a loose confederation.[27]

It is, therefore, difficult to see how the Mafia as organization can be a transplant from Sicily.

Finally, not all of the Italian criminals in the United States or their ancestors were from Mafia strongholds in Sicily. Two important organized crime figures of the past, Vito Genovese and Frank Costello, were from Naples and Calabria, respectively.[28] The ranks of Italians in organized crime in this country were filled with individuals who came from at least three different regions, each supporting separate criminal cultures: the Camorra from Naples, the Mafia from Sicily, and the Onorata Societa from the province of Calabria. These cultures and the groups they spawned had no affiliations with one another in Italy and indications are that Italian organized criminals in this country held steadfast to their regional loyalties.

The Castellamarese War, the next important event in the history of organized crime, serves to illustrate this point as well as suggesting other trends in organized crime. Until recent revelations by Joseph Valachi, little was known about the events in the war. Dixie Davis, Dutch Schultz's lawyer, found out from one of Schultz's lieutenants that a man named Salvatore Maranzano was killed on September 10, 1931, and throughout the rest of the year, "there was a terrific number of Sicilian murders all through the country."[29] Valachi filled in the details. In 1930 Joe "The Boss" Masseria and Salvatore Maranzano were struggling for power in the Italian underworld. Joe the Boss decided to eliminate Maranzano as well as other gang leaders who came from the vicinity of the town of Castellamarese del Golfo in Sicily. Masseria had many Neapolitans allied with him and the dispute had a distinct ethnic flavor with individuals loyal to people of the same towns or provinces allied against others from different towns or provinces.

The war had an added significance, for it took place between Italian groups that thrived during Prohibition and set the tone for criminal organization in the future. According to Peter Mass, Valachi's biographer, two of Masseria's trusted sidekicks, Charley Luciano and Vito Genovese, turned against him. "In return for their promise to have Masseria killed, Maranzano agreed to halt the war."[30] Maranzano proceeded to organize Italian families under his command and he attempted to rule the families by forming his own palace guard. Valachi joined this guard even though he formerly worked for Tom Gagliano. Maranzano tried to rule as dictator over the organization and perhaps the last straw was a banquet held to honor Maranzano as a sign of obedience of all the family bosses throughout the United States. According to Valachi, $115,000 was collected.[31]

Maranzano was killed by several criminals who got access to his office by pretending to be policemen. In the aftermath of his death at least forty men were killed throughout the country. According to Peter Maas, "The murder of Maranzano was part of an intricate, painstakingly executed mass extermination engineered by the same dapper, soft-spoken, cold-eyed Charley 'Lucky' Luciano who had so neatly arranged the removal of Masseria just months before."[32] After these events, violence between organizations subsided for quite a while.

It appears that Maranzano's big mistake was his erroneous assessment of the structure of power in organized crime. Clearly, power lay with individual family heads, many of whom formed their crime families from scratch. By giving up his power base in an individual family and trying to establish a palace guard more powerful than the combined organizations, he fundamentally misunderstood the limitations any overall leader of the organization would have. From this time on, no one asserted himself as the top man in the manner of Maranzano. The family structure survives him as does communication between the groups, but the title, boss of all bosses, was abolished.

Also significant is that much of the particularism of Italian groups was no longer of overriding importance. Italian groups began doing business with other ethnic groups as well as forgetting differences among themselves. A symbol of this cooperation was the murder of Maranzano, which was performed mostly by non-Italians. According to Maas, the war was based upon generational conflict as well as based upon regional loyalties. Younger members, for instance, Luciano and Genovese, were in favor of forgetting regional and ethnic differences and doing business with other ethnics, while the older members with old country ways (the "Mustache Petes") were much more particularistic in their outlook.[33] This is presumably why Luciano and Genovese turned against Masseria and Maranzano. In Chicago, criminal matrices were ahead of their time, for business had already taken precedence over nationality in criminal organizations.

Information available on the period from the early 1930s to 1950 describes individual activities and selected groups, but we have little information on the organizational structure of crime during that period. In 1936 Charles Luciano was sent to jail to serve a thirty- to fifty-year sentence. The same man who put him in jail, Thomas E. Dewey, commuted his sentence in 1945 in his capacity as governor of New York. It has never become clear, but apparently Luciano helped to safeguard the port of New York from sabotage during World War II.[34]

In 1940 the district attorney and his staff uncovered evidence of a criminal matrix in Brooklyn that specialized in murder and participated in other activities such as bookmaking, running dice games, and a variety of other illegal activities. Unfortunately, the history of this period was distorted when the members of this matrix became known to the public primarily as assassins, and were given the name Murder Incorporated. On the contrary, as Burton Turkus, assistant district attorney in Brooklyn (the man who helped uncover their activities), said, "murder, I must emphasize, was not the *big* business. The rackets were. The assassinations were ordered, contracted and performed solely to sustain those rackets."[35] This matrix of crime was composed of men of several ethnic groups who contracted work out to other groups. At times they worked for Lepke Buchalter, a gangster in Manhattan who specialized in industrial and labor extortion, and at times for Albert Anastasia, boss of a Brooklyn-based crime family.[36] One may conclude from reading about them that organized criminal societies and matrices of this period did have

connections and acquaintances that extended beyond the neighborhood they operated in; there were many ethnic groups involved, and
Italians were not adverse to doing business with other ethnics.

In 1950 Senator Estes Kefauver became chairman of a special
committee to look into organized crime in interstate commerce,
popularly known as the Kefauver Committee. When the hearings
moved into New York on March 12, 1951, the events were televised
and "for the first time brought tens of millions of people into
simultaneous contact with senators, lawyers, hoodlums, and assorted
other characters."[37] Not only did the hearings publicize the activities
of organized crime, but they helped gather together significant
materials heretofore in the hands of investigative agencies and
citizens' crime commissions, but not available in any one place. It
was the first important effort since Dewey's push in New York to
concentrate attention on organized crime. Television interest centered on Frank Costello, purported head of the organized crime
family formerly headed by Vito Genovese and Charles Luciano.
The hearings dealt primarily with the structure of economic activity
and concentrated on personality rather than organization. As a result, their conclusions about organization differ from ones made by
commissions today.

> There is no doubt in the minds of members of the committee
> that there do exist at least two major crime syndicates. There is one
> with an axis between Miami and the Capone Syndicate now headed
> by Tony Accardo, the Fischetti brothers, and Jake Guzik. There is
> another with an axis between New York and Miami headed by
> Frank Costello and Joe Adonis. These axes have branch lines that
> extend into many cities and areas and there is apparently a gentle-
> men's agreement, if the operators of these mobs can truthfully be
> called gentlemen, not to infringe on the activities of each other.[38]

They found men of several ethnic groups at the heads of these
syndicates and vast contacts between groups. This was an accurate
assessment of the network of economic activities which cut across
ethnic designations and is similar to the conclusions of Turkus and
Feder as to the structure of organized crime in the later thirties and
early forties. It was only in reporting of subsequent events and in
concentration on nuclear Italian families that people began to identify, totally, Italians with organized crime. In other words, the
Kefauver Committee tended to perceive of organized crime as a
matrix of activity rather than as a society or societies. They mistook

for formal societies the networks of interactions between various criminals.

In 1955 when the Democrats took control of the Senate, John McClellan became chairman of the Senate Permanent Subcommittee on Investigations and Robert F. Kennedy became chief counsel. Their investigations began by looking into improprieties in the clothing procurement program of the armed forces. They found some "East Coast gangsters, Albert Anastasia, Johnny Dio and his brother Tommy, and others were involved directly or indirectly in the manufacturing or trucking of uniforms."[39] This led to knowledge that organized criminals had muscled into the labor movement, and subsequent investigations were made into the relationship of organized crime to labor, especially with the Teamsters union. Investigators were still interested in matrices, the web of labor crime, and if they tended to look at the operations of any societies of crime, they concentrated on the structure and functions of labor unions.

In 1957 the perception of organized crime as a society became dominant and has lasted until today. On November 14 of that year, in the small town of Apalachin, New York, a group of men gathered at the house of Joseph Barbara, who controlled part of the distribution of beer and soft drinks in the Binghamton area. The police surrounded the grounds and the guests fled in panic. Those picked up were known by the police in various cities as leaders of various crime families.

> Dynamic, chunky little Vito Genovese, who is the American underworld's greatest financier, with interests ranging from narcotics through gambling to labor extortion, was there with his two oldest friends and partners, Joe Profaci and Mike Miranda—only slightly less prominent than he. Big John Ormento, head of New York City's powerful 107th Street gang, Joe Bonanno, Carlo Gambino and a dozen other equally important top executives of organized crime were present, accompanied by their assistants and subsidiaries.[40]

The specific ties these men had with one another and the nature of the organized crime society they belonged to remained a mystery until the revelations of Valachi. Nevertheless, the government decided to prosecute these men for conspiracy, a charge finally thrown out by the courts upon appeal. It was at this juncture that a society became the dominant perception of organized crime.

Valachi's revelations in 1963 before the McClellan Committee continued to fix attention upon the existence of a criminal society, one which he called the Cosa Nostra. According to Valachi, the meeting was called by Vito Genovese to deal with the charge that he attempted to kill the man who became boss of his family in his absence, Frank Costello. He also wanted the blessings of the council for the murder of Albert Anastasia, a family boss who died in a barber's chair three weeks earlier. Anastasia was accused of selling memberships in the organization.[41] The view of the public and of enforcement agents was now concentrated on organized crime as a society and not as a matrix. Kefauver thought he was describing a formal society but he was in reality describing a matrix of activity. The change in the perception can be noted by reading the testimony of police chiefs before the McClellan Committee in an effort to verify Valachi's testimony.[42] Their emphasis is on the network of local activities; they had had no knowledge of any overall structure. Neither perception is correct; both describe two aspects of the same process.

After Apalachin, the next event which occurred in organized crime and became public knowledge was the inter-family dispute known as the Gallo-Profaci war. Joe Profaci was a family boss whose leadership dates back to the Castellamarese War. Ralph Salerno, who was with the Criminal Investigation Bureau of the New York City Police Department, suggests that the dispute erupted between the younger members of the family who objected to old-fashioned business methods as well as their own subordinate status.[43] In the opposition faction were the Gallo brothers, Larry, Joe, and Albert. In June of 1962, Joe Profaci died of natural causes and his brother-in-law Joseph Magliocco took over, but the war continued. Magliocco tried to enlist the help of the other bosses and got the cooperation of another family head, Joe Bonanno. He never gained internal control of his family and died of natural causes in 1963. Much of what we hear about organized crime currently comes from this family. Joseph Colombo, a much younger man than Profaci or Magliocco, took over the reins of the family after the latter's death. No more was heard publicly about the family and its disputes until the spring of 1970 when Colombo began picketing the FBI, which had accused his son of melting down silver coins into ingots.[44] At this juncture, the Italian American Civil Rights league was formed, and at the end of the year membership was said to number 45,000.[45] They held two rallies in New York City, one in 1970 and the second on June 28,

1971. The first was well supported and attended, but there were indications that family bosses had tired of all the publicity. The *New York Times* reports that "Federal Bureau of Investigation sources have said that Gambino [purported successor to Albert Anastasia] was upset because of the publicity Colombo had been getting after founding of the Italian American Civil Rights League."[46] On the date of the second rally, Joseph Colombo was shot by Jerome Johnson, a black who was immediately killed by an unknown assailant. Both Gambino and Joe Gallo, who had recently gotten out of jail, were questioned by the police.[47] The assault has gone unsolved, and Colombo, though released from the hospital, suffered extensive wounds. In 1972 Joey Gallo, celebrating his birthday with some friends in Umberto's Clam House, was shot and killed.[48] This shooting took place the week of the premier of the movie version of *The Godfather*, which features a scene in which a gangland leader is shot to death in an Italian restaurant. This coincidence tended to fuse myth and reality in the public's consciousness.

Another purported organized crime family, that of Joe Bonanno, also suffered from internal difficulties in recent years. In October 1964, Bonanno was reported kidnapped shortly before he was supposed to appear before a New York grand jury. On May 17, 1966, he showed up in court, accompanied by his attorney, to the surprise of even his son Bill.[49] Prior to his disappearance, Bonanno had been feuding with other family chiefs as well as with members of his own family. One basis for this dispute seems to have been Joe's insistence that his son Bill become *consiglieri* (counselor) of the family.[50] According to Ralph Salerno, Bonanno's ambitions had threatened some of the other bosses. "Bonanno was accused of trying to overreach and usurp some of the business interests of Carlo Gambino and Thomas Luchese, two of the other New York bosses."[51] During Bonanno's absence the family was split into two factions, one apparently led by Bill Bonanno and the other by Gaspar Di Gregorio, a member of the Bonanno family for thirty years.[52] There has been relative quiet in the family since Bonanno's return.

If a careful look is taken at the recent revelations about organized crime, including the 1967 *Task Force Report*, the emphasis on a society, La Cosa Nostra, and its intrigue is unmistakable. This replaces the prior emphasis on the matrix of activities and associations criminals are engaged in. It does not suggest a change in the structure of organized crime from a heterogeneous collection of organized criminal groups to dominance by La Cosa Nostra—just an entirely different perspective of the same phenomenon. Today instead of seeing more blacks in narcotics and gambling along with other ethnic groups, people who see things from a societal perspective describe these groups as encroaching upon La Cosa Nostra. Everything today is viewed from the societal perspective that grew from speculation about the Apalachin meeting and followed from the revelations of Joseph Valachi.

This short history of organized crime is highly selective and woefully incomplete. It is meant to provide a backdrop for the ensuing analysis, and also make a few cogent points about the nature of organized crime. It is centered on the main societies and matrices of crime that have received continuing attention, and does not cover other matrices and societies that are also of interest to enforcement agents and students of organized crime. More, however, is known about the major groups, and knowledge about them will help us to understand the other groups.

The history of organized crime is difficult to record because it is as much a local as a national history. Analysts have concentrated on events of Chicago or New York which grab the national headlines, but ignore those of many other municipalities. One can get the erroneous impression that societies and matrices do not appear elsewhere.

In the endeavor to cover history some significant occurrences have been left out, such as Meyer Lansky's battle against extradition to the United States, the basketball scandals of the 1950s and the 1960s, the probe on sports betting in 1972, and corruption in New Jersey.[53] Omission is due more to a lack of space and the feeling that the events covered serve to illustrate the major points made while serving as sufficient background information.

Chapter 3

Social and Psychological Characteristics of Organized Criminals

Criminal Personality

At the core of an individual's beliefs about the political, economic, or social system is an implicit or explicit conception of man. We can call upon an infinite set of concepts with which to describe man. Is he evil? Is he rational? Is he kind? Is he self-serving? The specialist in human affairs develops concepts to describe man. The economist asks: Does he seek to maximize profit in his dealings with other men? The political scientist asks: Does man seek to maximize his influence in all situations? Whether we study the behavior of the American Indian, the congressman, or the organized criminal, implicit or explicit in our thinking is a set of hypotheses or assumptions about the constitutional makeup or acquired characteristics of man. The dimensions developed to describe the nature of man are usually dictated by the behavior to be explained. In studying the voting patterns of senators, height would not be as important in explaining their votes as finding out whether or not they are open-minded individuals. Our conceptions of man may be held to describe all mankind, or simply classes of people; all people may be dogmatic, only senators may be dogmatic, or only certain senators may be dogmatic.

In the literature concerning organized crime and in the popular press, two dimensions (each embodying polar types) are used to describe the nature of the man who participates in organized crime.

One dimension discerns whether the individual who participates in organized crime is good or bad; a normative dimension with which to look at man. A second dimension looks at the organized criminal to see if he carries out the activities of organized crime with efficiency or inefficiency. Is he a superman, a James Bond, or a buffoon, a bungler, or a clown?[1]

'Good' Guys and 'Bad' Guys

Categories borrowed from the prominent sociologist Edwin Schur will help to determine if organized criminals are "good" guys or "bad" guys. We can see, according to Schur, what his constitutional makeup is, whether he is mentally ill, or whether he is a religious sinner.[2] All three avenues of investigation, depending upon the outcome, tend to place an individual in one of two categories: he is either "good" by some standard or "bad" by some standard. If it is found that organized criminals have damaged x chromosomes and other individuals in society do not, they can be categorized as an unwanted or bad influence on society. Or if a definition of mental illness is formulated, by use of that definition it can be determined whether the organized criminal is mentally ill, and a decision can be rendered as to whether his actions are good or bad. Finally, there is perhaps the oldest avenue of investigation: If it is decided that the individual is a sinner by religious laws or norms, or that he violates some of the consensually agreed-upon norms of society, then he can be labeled either good or bad.

Constitutional makeup refers to the traits which man inherits from his ancestors, and immediately this brings up the difficult methodological question of determining whether those characteristics believed to be inherited are not, in fact, caused by factors in the physical and social environment. The heredity-environment dispute will be bypassed by asking what traits characterize organized criminals and not by inquiring into origins of the traits.

First it might be suggested that organized criminals are less intelligent than other individuals in society, and that this lack of intelligence causes them to participate in organized criminal activities. The intelligence of organized criminals seems to vary greatly among members, and may vary depending on the degree of intelligence or skills demanded by particular organizational roles. On one end of the spectrum there are men like Arnold "The Brain" Rothstein, who manifested a variety of skills in laying the foundation for the profits of Prohibition, and Lucky Luciano, an individual engaged in a multiplicity of sophisticated enterprises. On the other end of the spectrum there is a man named Ali Waffa.[3] Ali Waffa lacked some of the sophisticated skills of a Luciano or Rothstein; his primary function in organized crime was a bodyguard to Joey Gallo, a principle in the Gallo-Profaci war. As Sidney Slater, an associate of Joey Gallo, once described, Ali Waffa would walk into a bar with Joey Gallo and they would place a bet on one of Ali Waffa's skills. Joey Gallo would bet that Ali Waffa could break a board with his head. "Someone would dig up a plank of wood and damned if Ali Waffa wouldn't run at it and with his head split it right down the middle every time."[4] There is a great range of skills and intelligence that characterizes organized criminals, and it is by no means correct or useful to depict them as less intelligent than the general population.

Second, it might be suggested, as it has in the study of criminology, that criminal tendencies run in families. It seems plausible, for organized criminals sometimes have many family members in organized crime. However, as Francis Ianni points out in his interesting article on the Mafia, many members of the biological family do not pursue interests in organized crime, and as time passes there is a tendency for many organized criminals and especially their offspring to enter legitimate pursuits free of ties or dependence on organized criminal structures.[5] This hypothesis suggests that organized criminals are not necessarily products of a bad family tree, or "bad seed," but that cultural and environmental influences are also important in determining their destinies. Thus, this particular attempt to establish a constitutional makeup peculiar to organized criminals has failed.

If it can be determined that organized criminals are mentally ill, perhaps they can be categorized in terms of being "good" or "bad," sick or well being loose synonyms. The key is being able to decide when somebody is or is not mentally ill, and it superficially seems correct to suggest they are ill. For instance, they commit murder; it seems likely that there is something wrong with those who commit murder. Not only do they commit murders, but they seem to do so in the most malicious and sadistic ways. Burton Turkus, in *Murder Inc.*, talks about a juke box business operator who is executed for withholding and concealing profits from his superiors. "The corpse was loaded into Pretty's (a member of Murder Incorporated) automobile and driven to the shore of one of the popular lakes dotting the mountains. There, a pinball machine was lashed securely to Sage's chest, and the entire package was dropped into the lake."[6] There are countless other instances of murder and brutality. Robert F. Kennedy described the plight of a man who angered a group of organized criminals.

> There was the union organizer from Los Angeles who had traveled to San Diego to organize juke box operators. He was told to stay out of San Diego or he would be killed. But he returned to San Diego. He was knocked unconscious. When he regained consciousness the next morning he was covered with blood and had terrible pains in his stomach. The pains were so intense that he was unable to drive back to his home in Los Angeles and stopped at a hospital. There was an emergency operation. The doctors removed from his backside a large cucumber. Later he was told that if he ever returned to San Diego it would be a watermelon. He never went back.[7]

Seemingly, there appears to be no alternative than to talk of individuals who commit some crimes as mentally ill, bad, or savage.

However, the question of who is mentally ill is not that simple, at least not in today's society. Violence is institutionalized in many contexts. The killing of men in wartime and brutality in boxing matches and in other sports where there is significant chance of physical injury are sanctioned by society. The astute reader asks the question: If organized crime fits into the same category of institutionalized violence, then why the sadism? Violence and brutality often are utilized as a rational strategy to get members or clients to comply with organizational imperatives. For example, Sam De Cavalcante, in conversation with one of his lieutenants, Lou Larasso, indicated that "he was having some trouble with the government and that he expected that someone was talking to the authorities."[8] Lou replied, "Sam, find out who this guy is and we'll cut him up in bits to make an example of him."[9] In the murder in which the individual was dropped into the lake with the pinball machine tied to him, the coroner noted that a great number of slashes were made in the body. "Now, a body immersed in water will rise to the surface because of the buoyancy of gases which fill the intestinal tract. These killers kept themselves informed on such matters. Imagine their surprise then, when the cadaver suddenly popped to the surface in just ten days, despite the perforation and the weight."[10] Jabbing the individual with an ice pick many times is going to serve the function of getting the air out of his colon and out of his intestines so that he won't float to the surface. Also weight is needed to keep him in the water and the pinball machine, if it ever did float to the surface, would certainly suggest to other people that one didn't fool around with this group of individuals. As for the cucumber, this horrible form of torture also served the organization's purpose very well. As Robert Kennedy said, "he never went back."

Certainly, these methods seem a bit sadistic; the killers go a bit further than warranted in terms of organizational imperatives. There are sadists in organized crime, and they may be retained by the organization because they will perform such functions. But it is unwise to ascribe this sadism to all the members of the organization. For most of the organization's members, violence is only a byproduct of other goals, and there are many indications that members in leadership positions wish to minimize the amount of violence in organized crime. For instance, Sam De Cavalcante warned the members of his organization to lay off rough behavior. Larry Wolfson, Sam's partner in the plumbing business, said, "Well, I won't go to extremes unless it's necessary."[11] In sum, one can not easily designate organized criminals who commit violence as mentally ill, for society sanctions violence in many other contexts not dissimilar to the circumstances the organized criminal finds himself in. Terms such as *deterrence* and *massive retaliation* were not invented by organized criminals. If the violence in organized crime seems inordinately sadistic, it appears this sadism is often functional, both in disposal of physical evidence and as a warning to their rivals, clients, or enemies. Some persons with a proclivity for killing are undoubtedly recruited and retained, but violence is not the *raison d'être* of the organization and often it is minimized by the leaders.

Another ground for suggesting someone is mentally ill is compulsive activity. Words like *kleptomania* or the cruder one that has been used on television, *homicidal maniac*, are used to describe compulsive activities. But few of the activities of organized criminals are compulsive. Most of them are very well planned and executed, and the ability to maintain self-control is valued highly in the appraisal of prospective new members. Violence and sadism may be functional for the organization, but self-control is also a trait respected by members and leadership of organized criminal groups. Calculating individuals commit murders to further organizational goals, but definitions of mental illness which refer to compulsive acts do not let us condemn these men, as a rule, to mentally-ill status. Organized criminals, as well as committing acts of violence, can and do perform functions similar to those performed by law-abiding members of society, and feel many of the same emotions. Their capacity for violence is not compulsive nor all-consuming, for if it were, they would not be able to perform some of the other chores and duties that they must carry out in life. Popular fiction often misleads us by concentrating on the violent acts rather then the humdrum day-to-day activities these men spend the bulk of their time pursuing.

Perhaps one can use a set of moral standards either gained from religion or some other set of norms to classify organized criminals as either "good" or "bad." The problem is to define and apply a standard which would differentiate the organized criminal from other members of society. In the abstract, there may be a set of principles which separate the "good guys" from the "bad," but in actual practice, religious groups often condone the actions of criminal groups and matrices. One could perhaps set up criteria to distinguish one group from another even if the Church could be sinful, but I will concentrate here on the relationship of the Church and organized criminal groups.

Historically, Italians in Sicily distrusted the actions of the secular Church, for far from being neutral politically and economically, the Church played an active partisan role. When the Church uses the expedient in politics, actively intervenes in secular affairs, and owes allegiance to organized criminals, the average citizen does not consider Church officials as morally superior to organized criminals. The words of the Church but not the deeds of the Church could be used to distinguish between the saint and the sinner. In the United States, many Cosa Nostra members and other organized criminals are seemingly involved in religious activities but do not allow their actions to be inhibited by the moral strictures of the Church. "Most Cosa Nostra men were raised in the Roman Catholic Church, and some still practice their religion, after a fashion. Unlike membership in the Knights of Columbus, this is not often a PR trick, though Joseph Profaci's face does appear in the corner of a mosaic on the ceiling of a New York church."[12] Important here is not just that organized criminals may be involved in a double standard, obeying ritualistic but not the ethical principles, but that religious organizations whether they be Protestant, Catholic, or Jewish, may be involved in the same kind of double standard. "The charitable, religious, and fraternal organizations who benefit from underworld largess are not always innocent dupes. Those familiar with organized crime in cities across the country report a general pattern of such groups knowingly inviting people of questionable reputation to be honored at fund-raising dinners because of their known ability to dispose of large blocks of expensive tickets."[13] "Sam (De Cavalcante) is active in raising money for the St. Joseph's Orphanage in Italy. The orphanage is a legitimate charity, but Sam naturally solicits contributions from those who owe him favors or who regularly do business with him. Thus, there is a slight odor of pressure about the way he gets funds, but probably no more so than from many other charities."[14] It is unclear from the actions of groups which group is following the norms of society and which group isn't. Often the groups which are supposed to set the example give knowing or un-knowing acceptance to groups of organized criminals. Thus, in theory, we can speak of organized criminals as bad and the rest of us as good, but in reality, these distinctions blur.

So far we have talked about society's attempt to label the organized criminal as good or bad. We might also ask if the organized criminal considers his own behavior bad or reprehensible. The film stereotype is of the gangster's mother wringing her hands at her son's funeral and asking where she and her boy went wrong. But in reality, there is a subculture of crime and the people involved in criminal activities do not think of themselves as morally reprehensible. It is not one individual who has gone bad, but whole families or even whole neighborhoods. Often we find relatives—for example, the three Shapiro brothers, Meyer and Jake Lansky, Joe Bonanno and Joe Colombo and their sons—purportedly involved in organized crime. Coming from a subculture where crime may be acceptable, these men would take issue with being called criminals or gangsters. For instance, Sam De Cavalcante treated his brother rather roughly when he asked for a favor, and did so ostensibly because of the following insult paid to him by his brother's wife: "Sam turned them down flat, and the meeting ended with Sam ordering them out of his office, reminding Marie (Sam's brother's wife) that her family had called him a racketeer and a gangster."[15] Joseph Valachi, in his testimony before Congress, indicated that perhaps in the beginning one thinks of his activities as crimes but after a while he doesn't think of them in this light. "Well, after you get used to burglarizing or committing crimes," Valachi said, "you don't feel these other things are crimes.

For instance, I had been in some machines. I don't think that was a crime; everyone else had them. I don't know how to explain them. I had dress shops. I had horses. Everyone was selling stamps. How am I going to explain it to you, senator?"[16]

Not only are organized criminals supported by the subculture within which they exist and able to rationalize that what they're doing is not wrong, but they also receive much support from the rest of society. Many professional and lay analysts suggest that the organized criminal is just providing services that citizens demand but by the quirk of law have been categorized as illicit. An interesting example appeared in Chicago politics when a former power in the Chicago Machine, William Dawson, suggested that the numbers game is an important service to blacks in Chicago. "Dawson visited him [Kennelly, the incumbent mayor] and explained that the nickel or dime a day a black person bet on policy was a needed diversion, much like the bingo in Catholic Churches, the bets made by society people at the race track, and the gin games in the private clubs to which Kennelly belonged. Our people can't afford the race tracks and private clubs so they get a little pleasure out of policy."[17] Neither the subculture the individual belongs to, nor the larger society of which he is a member, may view all the activities of organized crime as wrong or criminal.

In conclusion, it is not as simple as it first appears to label organized criminals as bad guys and the rest of us as good guys. This appears to be the least promising way to pursue the study of organized crime, yet the most practiced. From the standpoint of understanding the way organized crime operates, it is more useful to describe organizational patterns and requisites, often similar to the ones of "legitimate society," and not begin by setting organized criminals apart from the rest of the public in terms of personality and organizational structure. Even in the making of public policy, it is not useful to begin by differentiating organized criminals in terms of virtues. More often than not this differentiation may lead to a distorted picture of organized crime and hence an inability to deal with actual situations.

The analyst, however, must be careful not to adopt a strictly environmentalist view of organized crime, viewing organized criminals as merely products of society; one could not single them out for punishment without punishing us all. We as a society must make judgments as to what we think right and wrong, and then punish the offenders. Sidney Hook gives an interesting example of the trap that the pure environmentalist might fall into when he tells us of an individual in the Weimar Republic giving the environmentalist's position to exonerate himself from punishment from crime. The individual said, "If you, gentlemen, had a heredity similar to mine and had been sub;ected to the same influence as I, you would also have committed the burglary in this particular situation. With this theory I am in good company. I refer you to Spinoza and Leibnetz."[18] Hook notes the absurdity of accepting this argument in a court of law and relates the very interesting response given by the court. "We have followed the prisoner's reasoning with attention. Whatever happens is the necessary and immutable sequel of preceding causes, which, once given, could not be other than it is. Consequently the prisoner, by reason of his character and his experience was destined to commit the burglary On the other hand, destiny so decrees that the court, as a result of the submitted testimony, must judge the prisoner guilty of burglary."[19] Thus, moral judgments must be made, but they should not stem from a simplistic view of organized criminals as "good" guys and "bad" guys, nor should they overwhelm the analyst's description of organized crime.

Efficiency of Organized Criminals

Two works of popular fiction typify two very different perceptions of organized criminals; one pictures them as supermen, and a second pictures them as buffoons. These are two ends of a continuum which describes how efficient organized criminals are in fulfilling their goals. The first image is that of organized criminals as supermen, and the book that best manifests this image of organized criminals is Mario Puzo's *The Godfather*.[20] There are many passages in *The Godfather* where Puzo idealizes Don Vito Corleone, head of a Cosa Nostra family.

> Don Vito Corleone was a man to whom everybody came for help, and never were they disappointed. He made no empty promises, nor the craven excuse that his hands were tied by more powerful forces in the world than himself. It was not necessary that he be your friend, it was not even important that you had no means with which to repay him. Only one thing was required. That you, yourself, proclaim his friendship. And then no matter how poor or powerless the supplicant, Don Corleone would take that man's troubles to his heart. And he would let nothing stand in the way to a solution of that man's woe.[21]

Puzo often describes Corleone as a bit larger than life. "Nobody made the mistake of assuming that Don Corleone could be held cheaply because of his past misfortunes. He was a man who had made only a few mistakes in his career and had learned from every one of them."[22] The novel glorifies the life of a don in organized crime, an image that builds the mystique of Cosa Nostra. Organized criminals are similarly characterized on many of the TV dramas. Though slightly less brilliant than a Perry Mason, Elliot Ness, or Ironside, characters portrayed as infallible, they would defeat any lesser enemy.[23] Few fiction writers other than Mario Puzo have had sufficient candor to admit publicly to building efficiency and mystique into their characterizations. Puzo suggested in an interview that "I can't write about people without glorifying them a bit. If I'd met as many Mafia types before I wrote the book as I know now, it would have been harder to romanticize them."[24]

Such romanticism can lead to a situation of utmost irony. Organized criminals will in real life imitate vivid portrayals of gangsters they have seen in the movies, in novels, or on television. For instance, Joey Gallo, even in tough spots, acted as though he were Richard Widmark in an old movie, and prided himself very much in his resemblance to Widmark. When Sidney Slater, a restaurant operator drawn by loan sharks into illegitimate dealings, first met Joey Gallo, Gallo asked Slater if he had seen the movie, *A Kiss of Death*, and thought Gallo looked like the star. Slater assented. Gallo smiled with satisfaction, adjusting his tie, "You're smart, Sidney. A lot of people think I look like Richard Widmark."[25] It did not end with Joey Gallo merely thinking of himself as Richard Widmark, but he even acted the part. "I don't think that Joey was ever crazy. Some of the police disagree with me on this—but he had quite a sense of dramatic. Maybe what I mean is that he was a ham."[26] In Gary, Indiana, there is purportedly an organization trying to imitate the Corleone family as portrayed in *The Godfather*. They have met with a marked lack of success. Joey Gallo's attempt to act as suave and sophisticated as the celluloid image of Richard Widmark, the Gary group's crude imitation of the Corleone family, and Puzo's suggestion that there is too much romance in his novel upon meeting regular Cosa Nostra members are all indications that the supermen images of organized criminals are a bit too exaggerated.

The opposing view is that organized criminals are not supermen but buffoons, and the book that best captures organized criminals as

buffoons is Jimmy Breslin's *The Gang That Couldn't Shoot Straight.*
This is a light and amusing book, in which even the don of the
family, Baccala, fails to escape Breslin's comic touch.

> At eight A.M. Baccala got out of bed and ready to leave for the
> day. He was standing just inside the kitchen door while his wife,
> Mrs. Baccala, went out into the driveway in her housecoat. Mrs.
> Baccala slid between the wheel of a black Cadillac. Baccala sat
> down on the kitchen floor and closed his eyes and folded his arms
> over his face. Mrs. Baccala started the car. When the car did not
> blow up from the bomb, Baccala got up from the kitchen floor and
> walked out into the driveway, and patted Mrs. Baccala on the head
> as she came out of the car, got in, and backed down the driveway
> and went off to start another day.[27]

The rest of the organization is not spared either. "The Mafia relies
heavily on Jews. Boss gangsters are usually able to count only when
they take off their shoes and use their toes."[28] Finally, Breslin
describes a desperate chase, a matter of life and death, which takes
place in a puddle-filled alley.

> "The Water Buffalo [a syndicate criminal] who had his adrena-
> lin pumping because it was life and death, had taken the puddle in
> a big leap and hadn't gotten his $110 Bostonians wet. He was
> beating down the alley way. But Joe Miranda pulled up short of
> the puddle in his $120 Footjoys, and Julie DiBiasi stopped dead in
> his $115 Johnson Murphys. They tiptoed around the puddle. Then
> they started running down the alley in a fury."[29]

Most of us would agree that Breslin's book is a caricature of organized criminals, but as with the superman myth, somewhere in
organized crime there are situations which resemble the ones he
describes.

In fact as well as in fiction, there are conflicting images of organized criminals as supermen and as buffoons. Former Senator Estes
Kefauver gives an interesting example of the efficiency and skill of
organized criminals. "When California feared air attack by the
Japanese, a vital telegraph circuit which served an Air Force field
was knocked out by a plane crash. Continental Press managed to get
its wire service for the gamblers resumed in something like fifteen
minutes. It took the Fourth Army, responsible for the safety of the
entire West Coast, something like three hours."[30] Contrasting examples of humor and buffoonery on the part of organized criminals
abound in the literature. Cosa Nostra Don Sam de Cavalcante received an application for jury duty. He and Larry (his partner in the

plumbing business) amused themselves by reading off the questions and inventing interesting answers. "Larry told Sam to put down that he was a convicted felon and they wouldn't bother him any further. But Sam said he really couldn't serve on a jury because he felt sorry for all the defendants."[31] The following conversation is excerpted from a tape of the actual voices of organized criminals which was prepared by the New York State Joint Legislative Committee on Crime, and concerns a man named Mike who is telling another man how his gun jammed in a gangland execution:

> MIKE: It (the gun) was this far from his back. I got out of the fucking car and I ran. We had two cars and ran after him like a fucking madman. I tackled him. I fell into him. I was out of my fucking mind. I ran after him. The fucking hat went. I ran into him and I tumbled all over.
> WILLY: I'm surprised you wear a hat, Mike.
> MIKE: Huh?[32]

This does not sound like the smooth job efficiently carried out night after night on television.

What also adds to the comic touch are the nicknames given to some of the organized criminals—Charlie The Bug, Dutch, Kid Twist, Lepke, Pretty, and Blue Jaw Magoon.[33] The ways in which the names have been acquired often add comedy to the legends attached to organized criminals. "About 1925, a guest at Allie's father's place was one Jake Shapiro, a lumbering gorilla who growled orders in snarling bursts of sound. His stock command when annoyed was, 'Get out of here,' only it came out, 'Gurradahere.' So, his friends took to calling him Gurrah."[34]

It is most useful to explain the efficiency or inefficiency of organized criminals as a function of organizational characteristics and situations they find themselves in, not as a manifestation of a personality trait or traits. Peter Blau and W. Richard Scott in *Formal Organizations* emphasize the notion that every organization has built-in "structural dilemmas" which result from fulfillment of certain basic aims of the organization.[35] For instance, a democratic organization faces the dilemma of maintaining basic freedoms while remaining strong enough to survive. Groups which promote one goal may be inefficient in the pursuance of a conflicting goal. The structural dilemmas of organizations have been neglected by analysts but rarely as often as in the study of organized crime.[36]

In trying to decide what makes organized criminals efficient or inefficient we will first begin to uncover some structural dilemmas in the organizational configuration of organized crime. Second, the structural dilemmas which often prevent the police from being a viable opposition will be discussed and third, the activities of the organized criminals which hamper their efficiency will be examined.

In the recruitment of organized criminals the best man does not always get the job. As in other organizations, nepotism, scarcity of good labor, and loyalty to the organizational chiefs may be more important than merit. For instance, Sam de Cavalcante's nephew Bobby Basile achieved a high status with Sam even though many of Sam's subordinates were disappointed with Bobby's behavior.[37] Joe Valachi talks about Albert Anastasia, a Cosa Nostra boss, and his practice of hiring recruits based on their ability to pay a prescribed fee for membership, not on other characteristics thought as important or more important to the organization.[38] Loyalty, nepotism, and scarcity of good labor are all reasons for admitting to membership people who might not perform efficiently on the job. As in any organization, these factors, while promoting desirable traits of organization such as loyalty and cohesion, may preclude maximal effectiveness in other areas.[39]

Another feature of organization that takes away from maximal efficiency, yet is inevitable and even desirable, is that those at the bottom of the organizational hierarchy are not as efficient as those at the top. For example, consider the crudeness and lack of sophistication of the organized criminal whose mere function is to collect on a loan. In the dialogue which follows, Jack is the individual who is in debt, and Dom is the individual who has presumably been sent by his superiors to collect the money.

> JACK: There's no money. I don't have it with me. I got it down in my car. I got the money in my car.
> DOM: Well, go downstairs and get the money.
> JACK: I'm not going down with you, Domenic, I'm not leaving.
> DOM: I'll carry you out.
> JACK: You're going to have to then. You're going to have to carry me out.
> Then Dom, confused, has to make a phone call and then the conversation continues.
> DOM: I don't give a fuck if you go and fuck yourself.
> JACK: Nobody cares. I don't care either. . . .[40]

At the top of the pecking order criminals are more sophisticated, more sure of themselves, and better trained. It is unrealistic to expect to find well-qualified people at lower ends of the hierarchy because of the difficulties in finding talent, and the problem of inducing the skilled to perform such tasks in the first place. If highly talented people are doing menial tasks, the stability of the organization is often threatened.

A look at training procedures may further enrich our picture of efficiency and inefficiency in organized crime. The training itself is empirical, on-the-job training. With a new member, or a new routine, mistakes are made and those who survive become more proficient. Organized criminals have always been looked upon as especially proficient in murder but even with members of Murder Incorporated, known as executioners *par excellence*, training was empirical, on-the-job style, and they were very ineffective in the beginning. "All told, the rebels had eighteen shooting opportunities at Meyer [a rival gang leader named Meyer Shapiro] between June, 1930, and July, 1931, and eighteen times they missed. It was a most humiliating record for the gunmen who were later to win fame as the most able assassins in gangland."[41] What we see in recruitment, chain of command, and training of organized criminals are some of the same problems that every organization striving to maintain efficiency has. How do you recruit the best men? Can you build a staff from top to bottom with top-notch people? How do you train these people to be expert at their task? To some extent, organized crime families meet these organizational needs but they suffer from the same structural dilemmas that cause legitimate organizations to succumb.

What also leads to the exaggerated image of the organized criminal's efficiency is the set of characteristics attributed to his traditional enemy, the policeman. The image is of the brilliant policeman relentlessly pursuing the organized criminal and prevailing after a protracted, stimulating conflict. This is an idealized picture and there are very good reasons why this does not hold in reality. First, there is a good deal of corruption in police forces. This means that policemen are not always out to get organized criminals; they may be looking the other way or may even be aiding criminals in the performance of criminal activities. Second, they have other duties to perform and can not constantly be at war with organized criminals. For instance, former Attorney General Ramsey Clark suggests that we may expend far too many resources fighting organized crime than sound public policy dictates. "The greatest harm we could suffer from organized crime would be to permit it to distract us from the major problems we face if we are to control crime in America."[42] Clark is suggesting that fighting organized crime is not the full-time pursuit of police departments around the country, nor for that matter, should it be. Third, Hank Messick, a student of organized crime, says that top law enforcement officials, even at the level of governor, look the other way when organized crime is thriving and only respond to pressure in bringing enforcement agency resources to bear on organized criminal groups. "Governors such as Dewey in New York and Fuller Warren in Florida [according to Messick] were no problem [to organized gambling activities] except when the heat built up on the federal level."[43]

Finally, the police are not necessarily as brilliant and well trained as television's Ironside or Elliot Ness. When we think of the salaries policemen earn and the training they get, it would be foolish to expect the greatest skill and expertise. John Gardiner, in his study of the crime-wracked city he calls Wincanton, suggests how low these salaries are, on the levels of both the patrolman and the commissioner. "Wincanton police salaries have been quite low—the top pay for patrolman was $4856—the lowest quartile of the middle cities in the nation. Since 1964 the commissioner earned $10,200 and patrolmen $5,400 each year."[44] Ramsey Clark suggests that even if police departments are well trained, they are still not properly trained to deal with problems concerning organized crime. "Consequently, police departments have not been staffed, trained, or professionalized to cope with organized crime."[45]

A look at the nature of the activities of organized criminals also will suggest to us the limits of their efficiency. Behavior by organized criminals could be roughly divided into those matters that are routine and those that are non-routine. The routine or bureaucratic actions seem to give organized crime an aura of efficiency and rationality. Murder, for example, involves a division of labor, and rarely is the plan drawn each time from start to finish. Organized criminals utilize persons in prescribed roles—the gunsmith, the procurer of the gun, the look-out men, and the trigger men, individuals who already know what they would do during any given murder. The whole process is routine and seems very efficient even though the individuals involved may not be the most brilliant and not able to handle the intricate planning if they had to organize everything from start to finish.

At other times, the vicissitudes of business and violence, non-routine events, make for certain inefficiency and humorous, unpredictable events. In Hank Messick's book *Lansky* where the author tries to stress Lansky's extraordinary business acumen, he must also talk of Lansky's failures. When Castro completed his revolution in Cuba he showed unbending hostility to gambling interests. Messick describes Lansky's plight. "Yet the end came more abruptly than anyone had anticipated, and Lansky flew out of Cuba on Batista's heels."[46] Lower ranking members also fell prey to the vicissitudes of business. Joe Valachi describes his partnership in numbers and some of the problems he encounters.

> Bobby and me are only operating for maybe three weeks, trying to build things up little by little, hoping we won't get hit too bad. Well, this number pops that's got $12 or $14 on it, I think $14, and after we pay off our controllers and runners, we only had about $1,700 net that day and only a couple of thousand more in the bank. Now you can see how much we got banged for. We got hit for $8400. That was a pretty good hit in those days. I don't know what I'm going to do.[47]

The vicissitudes of violence also make problems for organized criminals; for instance, in the example given previously in which a gangster tries to commit a murder—his gun jams, his hat flies off. It's very difficult to prevent all the contingencies that are going to happen when you plan a murder.[48] Many things can go wrong and many of them may be quite pathetic or humorous in a macabre way. The murderer prepares for all contingencies but there is always some unanticipated event, and the way that people may deal with it may turn out to be amusing. The same kind of humor is found in events that take place in war. These are beautifully illustrated in the Joseph Heller's popular novel *Catch-22* and in many other comic portrayals of wartime situations.[49]

I think that we can safely conclude that the structural dilemmas of criminal organizations, the nature and limitations of the enemy, and the vicissitudes of business and violence make organized criminals less efficient in achieving their goals than the media would lead us to believe, but somewhat more effective than the clowns of Jimmy Breslin. Like many myths, the superman and the buffoon images are infused with grains of truth, but fail under intense scrutiny. Simplistic approaches to enforcement follow the acceptance of one or the other image; the lawman ignores the buffoons, and stays awake nights worrying about the supermen. Thus it has been necessary to challenge these images of the criminal so that more serious attempts may be made to explain the nature of organized criminals and their organizations. In the process, as in the study of men in other groups, organized crime can best be understood in light of organizational structure and behavior, and not in stereotyped descriptions of individual behavior. Knowing this has spoiled many a television mystery for me.

Social Characteristics of Organized Criminals

Ethnicity

Social scientists have always been interested in explaining the behavior of individuals by utilizing the social characteristics of ethnicity, class, and age. Here I will ask two fundamental questions: What are the social characteristics of organized criminals and do these characteristics explain their behavior and the structure of criminal organizations?

There is considerable debate as to the impact and degree of involvement of the various ethnic groups in organized criminal activity. Unfortunately, pressure from citizen groups and public officials prevent open, honest debate on these issues. There has been significant group pressure, such as that by the Italian-American Defense League, on government and the media to delete references to ethnic groups when making statements on organized crime. This league, originally formed by Joseph Colombo, a purported leader of an organized crime family,

> started casually, in one year it grew into a genuine vehicle of expression for thousands of Americans of Italian descent who had nothing to do with organized crime. Harnessing their honest sentiments, Colombo felt the Italian-Americans could achieve new pride as well as influencing government and industry to ease up on references to Italian-Americans and organized crime. For instance, they embarrassed the Justice Department and *The Godfather* film makers into dropping the words Mafia and Cosa Nostra from their vocabulary.[50]

In response to such pressure, or perhaps in the face of new evidence, Attorney General John Mitchell suggested publicly that the names

Mafia and Cosa Nostra should ,be stricken from use by federal agencies.[51]

There is a conflict between individuals (both scholars and public officials) trying to ascertain the ethnic composition of criminal groups, and other public officials trying to suppress or distort information as to the ethnic composition of these groups. This conflict is best exemplified by a senate subcommittee meeting in an exchange between Senator Jacob Javits of New York and Michael A. Amico, assistant chief of detectives in charge of the Criminal Intelligence Bureau, Buffalo Police Department.

> SENATOR JAVITS: Now, I know—I notice that you referred to a man named Weinstein and others to the chart under the heading "Jewish ties," and I would like to point out that the staff here has gone to great pains to eliminate a national or ethnic reference to the whole organization, and I think that is a splendid thing.
> Wouldn't you recommend, Mr. Witness, that the same be done as to "Jewish ties?"
> MR. AMICO: I certainly would. I should have better titled them perhaps "other associates" or nonmember associates.
> SENATOR JAVITS: . . . In no way should we give any feeling that criminal activities are the sole property of any religious, ethnic, national, or other group in our country. It is tragic and sad enough without loading them with that.[52]

Knowing the biases that exist with respect to the question of ethnic ties, an attempt will be made honestly and without prejudgment to assess the relationship between ethnicity and organized crime.

Garlic and Guns

There are two opposing views found in the popular press and the literature relating to the importance of ethnicity in explanations of organized criminal behaviors. The "garlic and guns" position not only argues that ethnicity explains everything in organized crime, but one ethnic group, Italian-Americans, is the embodiment of organized crime.[53] If members of other ethnic groups are involved in organized crime they are always playing subordinate roles. There is just not the supposition that all organized criminals are Italian, but if there were no Italians there would be no organized crime. Ethnicity explains the character and even the very existence of organized crime. This view is popular because it is inclusive and conspiratorial. The ethnic explanation is manifest often when commentators try to explain away a society's ills by making ethnic or religious groups the scapegoat. It offers a comprehensive and economical explanation of a confusing and often threatening situation.[54] As is the case with most stereotyped explanations, there is a grain of truth in the garlic and guns position. There are large numbers of Italians in organized crime.

Of course, there are problems with the garlic and guns position. The definition in Chapter 1 does not single out Italian ancestry as a necessary condition for criminal societies or matrices. Naturally, we would find only Italians in organized crime, if we had decided by definition that organized crime is Italian crime.

It is also clear that all manifestations of Italian culture are not amenable to organized crime, nor do they necessarily resemble its structural and organizational characteristics. Not everything that Italians do lends itself well to the purposes and functions of the organized criminals' organization, and this poses structural dilemmas for the organization.

The Melted Pot

The view at the opposite pole from the garlic and guns position is the "melted pot" position, which is that other variables, such as class or age, rather than ethnicity alone, may explain the nature of organized crime. Herbert Gans in *The Urban Villagers* suggest that in Italian-American families "peer group society" is better explained as a phenomenon of working class people than as characteristic of Italian-Americans. Gans argues "the class hypothesis offers a better explanation than the ethnic one."[55] Throughout his study, he marshalls evidence to show that non-Italian working class groups manifest the same characteristics which are dominant in the Italian community.

Edward Banfield in *The Unheavenly City* suggests another resolution of the question of class versus ethnicity.[56] Banfield certainly is not making a universal hypothesis that class is always more influential than ethnicity, but suggests that each may be important in a specific context. In his study, he posits what he calls "the statistical Negro—i.e., the Negro when all non-racial factors have been controlled for—is a very different fellow from what would be called the census Negro."[57] Even after correcting for everything possible, something is left that must be explained on racial grounds, especially job discrimination. Banfield suggests that ethnicity may explain certain attitudes or actions by ethnic groups, but other factors must be considered for before we will fully understand an action or situation. It is difficult to assess the strengths of one variable against the other. What is normally done in social science is to begin with one variable and to see how completely it explains a given set of circumstances. The process is repeated with other variables, and then a comparison is made. This procedure will be followed here, first with the variable of ethnicity, and then with social class and age.

There are several reasons why the melted pot position is interesting. First of all, it is a reaction against the garlic and guns position. It breaks down the Italian stereotype that many people have of organized crime. Secondly, it is normatively neat; if we wish to place blame or effect a cure, we point to discrepancies in social class in society and not to a particular ethnic group. In some countries where social class distinctions are held very strongly, it would be very bad to stigmatize organized crime as the phenomena of one or the other class. In this country, however, it is more acceptable to suggest that class, not ethnicity, is a prime cause of organized crime. But the melted pot view can not gain acceptance solely because it is normatively comfortable. Just because it is difficult to judge the strength of one variable as opposed to the other, the analyst should not downgrade the importance of one by fiat.

Both class and ethnicity are of use in explanations of organized criminal activity. For instance, Daniel Bell suggests that there is a "queer ladder" of social mobility in organized crime; that is, social class explains much about the nature of various groups active in organized crime.[58] However, the variable of ethnicity is needed to explain why some groups are in organized crime for a longer period of time than others. Everything cannot be explained under the rubric of social class. Certainly if all were known about the variables which constitute social class, the geographical circumstances, the climate, the natural disasters, it could be explained why those people labeled Italian, for example, speak the Italian language. However, it may be much more convenient to use the category of ethnicity in an explanation even though any variable, for instance, class or ethnicity, may be subdivided to explain the concept as a manifold of other characteristics.

Methodological Difficulties

To settle with more finality the dispute between those who adhere to the garlic and guns position and those who adhere to the melted pot position, the answers to two questions must be explored. First, it must be determined what ethnic groups are part of organized criminal societies or matrices. By my definition, it appears that many other ethnic groups are a part of the societies and matrices of organized crime, and not just in subordinate roles. Secondly, it must be asked why particular ethnic groups are involved in organized crime. To do this, the skills and organizational characteristics needed to sustain organized criminal activities need to be assessed. Do some ethnic groups manifest these skills or organizational abilities more than other ethnic groups?

For example, it might be that more Phoenicians are pirates than one might expect by chance alone; that is, as an ethnic or national group they are over-represented in a given activity. Phoenicians may be engaged in other types of activities and manifest the skills needed in piracy. Phoenicians might not only be sailors, but the best of all sailors; therefore, Phoenicians may have become pirates because they possess experiences, proclivities, or aptitudes which would lend themselves to piracy. Although this is the method to be followed here, it is best to present some possible drawbacks to this method. First, if the analyst tries hard enough, he can find reasons which explain why any ethnic group is found in a given activity. *Post hoc* explanations are not difficult to conjure up, and one must be sensitive to this possibility. Second, finding reasons why ethnic groups are involved in particular activities may blind us to the fact that the group may manifest some characteristics not ideally suited to that activity. For instance, pirates operate better if their members have a proclivity for violence, a characteristic which the Phoenicians may not manifest. Thus, even though they have seafaring skills, they may not be ideally suited to piracy. The characteristics of ethnic groups in organized crime will be scrutinized to see what characteristics they manifest which are not ideally suited for and thus pose structural dilemmas for organized criminal groups.

Third, the analyst must be aware that all organized criminal societies and matrices manifest similar characteristics. There are certain norms, such as secrecy and reciprocity, which play an important role in any criminal organization. If the analyst begins with a static picture of how organized crime is structured and operates he tends to think of all ethnic groups, past, present, and future, as conforming to that mold, instead of perceiving of a dynamic process whereby ethnic groups entering organized crime create new modes of organization and activity. Ethnic groups can create new patterns of organization and activity and do not find themselves out of organized crime simply because they do not conform to presently conceived norms. This is likely to be overlooked by the analyst, and he might not be able to see future patterns of organized crime emerging.

Fourth, ethnicity may only be a partial explanation of why particular groups participate in organized crime. For example, Martians may make very good Mediterranean pirates. However, if they are not on Earth, they are not going to be involved in this kind of activity. Closer to home, a particular minority group might make good organized criminals because they have the requisite skills to participate in gambling and lottery, but live in a country where the rest of the people are not given to gambling in any form.

Finally, what is thought of as an ethnic explanation of criminal behavior may be best explained by other social characteristics such as age or social class. The problem is not uncommon to social commentators. For instance, if one is trying to explain why some people do well on I.Q. tests, how does he decide whether quality of schooling, age, or some other variable explains high test scores? The best method of judgment is choosing the social characteristic which seems to do the best job at prediction. Since this study of ethnicity and organized crime does not involve a highly controlled experiment, only speculative conclusions can be drawn.

Ethnic Proclivities for Organized Crime

There are some proclivities of ethnic groups that make them more likely to participate in organized crime: hostility toward government, social norms of secrecy, loyalty, and reciprocity, and a penchant for systematic violence and entrepreneurial activities.

We know by the very nature of their activities that organized criminal groups or matrices will not be kindly disposed toward government. These groups may openly ignore or defy the laws of the society or cynically pay public officials to ignore the law. A multitude of factors may influence individuals to ignore or disobey the government: high profits, a poverty-ridden environment, or unpleasant encounters with authorities. The negative dispositions an immigrant group has about the legitimacy of government may also be a contributing factor to the development of organized crime. A survey will be made of ethnic groups that have participated in organized crime and it will be seen to what extent they manifest distrust of government, what forms this hostility has taken, and how much carry-over of negative feelings about government there has been to the New World.

The usual cliché about members of an immigrant group is that they resettled to escape governmental oppression or harsh physical conditions, and fondly embraced the laws and customs of the United States. On the contrary, the attitudes they held toward their former oppressors are usually carried over (sometimes for generations) to their feelings about the new institutions they encounter. Sicilians manifest a tradition of protest and organization against legitimate governments. The Sicilians continually had to protect themselves against foreign conquest and developed their own organizations to govern their everyday lives. Luigi Barzini in *The Italians* in references to Sicilians says: "The art of living, of defending oneself with one's own power, . . . supplementing the effectiveness of the state with one's own private virtues, corrupts, in the end, all forms of sound government. . . ."[59] There is a plethora of material on the Sicilians in particular and Southern Italians in general describing their mistrust of government.

Somewhat less is known and written about attitudes of other ethnics towards legitimate government. The philosophy of Diaspora states that Jews are to accept the mother country in which they live and the norms and mores of the country. It is doubtful in light of the many experiences of the Jews that the philosophy of Diaspora would prevail and Jews would feel kindly toward government. For example, it is widely known that the Jews in European countries felt they were exploited, and as a measure of discontent they did not pay as much in taxes as they should have. Under the pressures of Hitler's Germany and in Europe in the past, Jews were forced to live in and govern their own ghettos apart and at times in opposition to the larger community or state. There is no reason to believe that when Jews came to this country their suspicions about government would be lessened, or their reliance would immediately be placed on government.

The Irish suspicion of the political system took on a slightly different cast. Daniel Moynihan in *Beyond The Melting Pot* suggests that "the Irish brought to America a settled tradition of regarding the formal government as illegitimate and the informal as the true impress of popular sovereignty."[60] The Irish participation in the Catholic emancipation movement and other activities gave them some instruction in ruling and also a good deal of suspicion of government.[61] One of the implications of hostility toward government is the necessity for organizing and running one's own affairs. A penchant for organization and leadership developed within these three groups as a response to their European experiences. These organizational abilities allow a group to establish its interests in politics, in interest group activity, or in organized crime.

Puerto Ricans and blacks are in varying degrees alienated from existing government but suffer from the lack of leadership and organizational experiences. Puerto Ricans, like the other ethnic groups, are primarily law-abiding citizens. However, their feeling of obligation toward the American system is weakened because they view themselves as transients or visitors to the United States and participate little in the formal and informal institutions of government. Another factor is that in Puerto Rico gambling is legalized, and when they find gambling is illegal in the United States they feel no strong compulsion to obey these laws. Puerto Ricans, like most ethnic groups, manifest some suspicion toward government, but it is not as overwhelmingly as with other ethnic groups.

Blacks have always manifested some mistrust of American government and today, of course, it is expressed more openly. The movement for black consciousness not only expresses a feeling of mistrust of government, but a feeling that blacks ought to create their own social and economic organizations; it is a movement resembling the other ethnic groups' mistrust of government and reliance on their own organizational entities. In the same manner, they are beginning to reject organized criminal activities imposed and directed from outside their community and creating their own organization. For example, in a telephone conversation Sam de Cavalcante notes the reluctance on the part of members of his own organization to take revenge on a black who had beaten one of Sam's men. "Since Matthew Shumate who had administered the beating was Black Muslim, they were afraid of further retaliation."[62] Sam's organization could not retaliate swiftly and openly against Shumate for the feelings of the black community have intensified against non-black criminals. Within the black community we find a hostility towards government, a stress on group pride, and a desire for internal leadership, all of which may lead to the development of a variety of ethnic-based groups and configurations, from black power groups to coalition politics to organized crime.

A counter-argument can be offered that mistrust of government is not a manifestation of ethnicity but a manifestation of class behavior; for instance, poor whites also exhibit distrust of the government. There is no doubt, however, that some of the experiences of ethnic groups here or in other countries have made them more suspicious of legitimate government than one might ordinarily suspect on the basis of class status alone. Some ethnic groups are not only mistrustful of legitimate government but have, as suggested, organized to handle their own business and personal affairs while ignoring legitimate government.

Hostile feelings of a group toward government are not the only characteristics that make them amenable to organized crime. Organized criminal groups exemplify some of the following behavioral norms: loyalty, or putting other members of the organization before oneself; secrecy, or keeping affairs of the organization exclusive of outsiders; and reciprocity, or willingness to return favors.

Many of these norms are imperative to the operation of any illegitimate organization. For instance, loyalty and secrecy are necessary to prevent disclosure of the clandestine activities. These norms are in effect in Marseilles, for example, where Corsicans process morphine into heroin. An effective way for the Bureau of Narcotics and Dangerous Drugs to capture people in the narcotics trade is by paid informants. Because of the tight secrecy that surrounds their operations, the Corsicans have been immune to this form of law enforcement. Also the milieu in which Corsicans work is suspicious of strangers and supportive of the heroin processors and makes surveillance of their activities most difficult.[63]

Force and fear play a role in insuring organizational cohesion, but loyalty and reciprocity also insure cohesion. As in any organization where all activities cannot be governed by binding legal restrictions (for example, the United States Senate) informal norms of reciprocity are important. These norms plus others which are necessary to bring cohesion *vis-à-vis* other groups must be based upon some commonalities, which may be the necessity for profit, common hate of authority, or the factor under investigation here, strong ethnic ties. Norms of reciprocity, loyalty, and secrecy are often identified with immigrant political cultures, particularly the Jews, Italians, and, to a lesser extent, the Irish. The norms of loyalty and reciprocity between members of the group are very strong and the family structure shows great cohesion, even in times of stress. On the other hand, blacks decry the lack of ability to organize themselves, the inability to keep things secret. With Puerto Ricans this is to some degree less so, but one still finds in these organizations some mistrust between individuals.

Certain ethnic groups may be more amenable to organized crime than others because of their entrepreneurial skills or proclivity for violence. Violence may be endemic to Italian political culture and blacks manifest a good deal of violence, although in both these cases there is evidence that violence is as much a function of class as it is of ethnicity. Violence in black and Italian cultures also seems to reflect different historical and cultural traditions. Blacks, until recently, rarely used violence to achieve collective goals. Although murder rates are high in black ghettos and in· southern counties which are primarily black, much of the violence involved is a function of household disputes and fights with friends. Today, however, groups like the Panthers espouse the use of violence to achieve collective ends. In Southern Italian political culture, murder is often committed on behalf of collective as opposed to purely personal ends. For instance, Barzini describes "a feud which cost hundreds of lives almost a century ago between the Stoppoglieri of Montrioli and the Ratuzzi of Bragheria, (and) is still remembered."[64] Within organized crime it is the proclivity for systematic as opposed to random violence or crimes of passion that helps the organization to function.

A different set of proclivities is necessary for participation in the entrepreneurial activities so central to organized crime. Jews, Puerto Ricans, and Italians have demonstrated skill in developing small business where entrepreneurial skills are necessary, while neither the Irish nor the blacks have shown quite the same aptitude or interest. Of course, for many, the way to get started in organized crime is to participate in what are essentially small business ventures. The differential skills of ethnic groups suggest a pattern of activity that might be characteristic of organized criminal societies and matrices. Ralph Salerno in the *Confederation of Crime* recognizes a fairly interesting phenomenon. He says, "There are signs that organized Negro and Puerto Rican gangs have been making similar alliances (to the Jews and the Italians). They are joining together against the power structure as the Jews and Italians did in the early 1930s. In a curious reprise of the confederation, the Puerto Ricans seem to be assuming the Jewish role of money managers and businessmen for the ghetto alliances while the Negroes represent the Italian muscle."[65] As the analysis of business activity and violence suggests, this may often be correct, but it would be unwise to conclude that this is an invariant pattern. For instance, in a reading of *Murder, Inc.* one discovers a good number of Jewish enforcers or "muscle" and certainly a number of Italians who have assumed the entrepreneurial role.[66]

There is much that can be discovered about the relationship of ethnicity to organized crime by examining the economic activities organized criminals pursue. Certain activities attract organized criminals—gambling, bootlegging, narcotics, numbers, unions, bars, restaurants, and often other businesses that have a low cash flow. Both by historical accident and also because they may possess some requisite skill, certain ethnic groups are found in activities while other groups are not. For instance, Italians and Irish developed requisite skills for the manufacture of alcoholic beverages. These unique skills, coupled with historical circumstances, led to the development of bootleg outfits during Prohibition. Certainly, other ethnic groups were involved with the breaking of Prohibition and in every facet of activity, from the growing of the grains to the distribution of the finished product. Thus, the ethnic explanation gives us only a partial insight into the workings of organized criminal groups during the Prohibition era.

Jews populated the garment industry in New York. Labor unions lend themselves to a whole new set of activities attractive to organized crime, such as extortion and sweetheart contracts. Puerto Ricans who came from a country where gambling was legal found illicit gambling activities attractive business opportunities. Another interesting example of an ethnic group's involvement in an activity by a blending of historical circumstances and requisite skills was the Chinese involvement in the transportation and processing of opiates at the turn of the century. Harry Anslinger, former head of the Bureau of Narcotics, states that in 1930, "The Chinese still had a virtual monopoly on the opium trade in the country: opium dens could be found in almost any American city. The Chinese underworld of dope—combined with gambling and prostitution—had its own special Oriental ruthlessness which filled the aura of violence and brutality and killing that has always been the hallmark of the narcotics underground."[67] Today there are indications that other groups such as the Mexicans, Turks, Italians, Corsicans, Latin Americans, and Southeast Asians are involved in manufacture, sale, transportation, or distribution of drugs, basically because of their geographical location and because of the organizational proclivities they possess. Finally, on the docks there has been a succession of ethnic groups, first Irish, then Italian, and now Puerto Rican, following each other in both legitimate and illegitimate activities.

It appears then that certain activities are amenable to organized crime and any ethnic group that is engaged in these activities will pursue criminal activities. The nature of the enterprise and not the ethnic affiliations of the employer or employees may be the critical variable in determining whether organized crime pervades an activity.

A final example may illustrate the interrelationship of ethnicity with historical, geographical, and social characteristics in determining the nature of organized criminal activity. It appears that Corsicans have requisite skills for organized criminal activity they can utilize when they are not out at sea. "A popular legend maintains that Corsicans become gangsters, cops, or priests once they reach the mainland."[68] Besides having requisite skills, Corsicans also find themselves in circumstances that foster organized crime. First, they settled in Marseilles, a seaport whose location is a natural for the Turkey to United States drug traffic. Second, the city affords "30,000 villas suitable for hiding a lab (for conversion of morphine to heroin)."[69] Third, the French until recently did little to discourage the trade. Until late 1969, the city's anti-drug squad was composed of eight men. Thus, we can not depend on ethnicity alone to explain the participation of particular ethnic groups in organized criminal activity.

Structural Dilemmas in Italian Organizations

It has been assumed that certain groups have the propensity for organized crime and when matched with particular historical, geographical, and social circumstances, they find their way into it. But this does not imply that the ethnic groups with the requisite skills for organized crime are perfectly suited for organized criminal activity. These ethnic groups in pursuit of criminal activities may be laced with structural dilemmas that make them less than ideal participants. In particular, many characteristics of Italians are not fully amenable to crime in this country, or work to their disadvantage if they do become involved in organized crime. This is of great interest because it is often suggested that Italians as a group are "ideally" suited to organized crime.

The strong family structure and the distrust of outsiders in the Italian-American family structure make for close-knit, secret organizations, but they are less functional in criminal organizations in the United States than they were in Italy. Hostility and suspicion of outsiders limits the kinds of opportunities organized criminals in the United States may pursue. For instance, one of the basic causes of the Castellamarese War was that the "Mustache Petes," Italian criminals with Old World ideas, did not want to let other powerful ethnic groups in on their criminal activities. The Mustache Petes wanted to organize crime specifically on an ethnic basis which turned out to be impracticable in this country. Those who most strongly held to the exclusiveness of the Italian family and hostility towards outsiders did not survive in organized crime.

Another characteristic attributed to Italian-Americans is the deference and honor they show for one another in social relations. Italians in Southern Italy have always treated deference and honor as much more important than money. This characteristic may still be important in Southern Italy, but in the long run, other factors became more important than prestige to organized criminals in America. "The old basis of friendly relations among gangsters and politicians was being superseded by considerations of cash."[70] This statement was written in the 1920s by the head of the Chicago Crime Commission and increasingly holds sway today. Even in Italy, inter-family feuding and other internecine warfare between families prevented Italians in crime from taking advantage of all business opportunities, and in the United States criminal groups seem to put business ahead of honor.

As Hank Messick suggests in *Lansky*, Italian-American ideas about pageantry are also dysfunctional for Italians in organized crime and often jeopardize other norms such as secrecy and anonymity. The Apalachian meeting was a terribly risky pageant and its discovery allowed police to piece together a hitherto complex organizational puzzle.[71] The large-scale weddings and funerals also allow police intelligence to draw a bead on criminal matrices and societies. Police can learn much about the leadership structure by the deference shown to those in attendance and by who is conspicuously absent. Although it was not infiltrated by the police, the wedding of Bill Bonanno and Rosalie Profaci in 1956 was typical of celebrations in which the curtain of secrecy is or can be raised to interested outsiders. Since publicity about organized crime has heightened since that time, however, few celebrations today are of such magnitude.[72]

Finally, one would expect that strong moral strictures against gambling, prostitution, and drugs would restrain ethnic groups from participation in organized crime. It is particularly surprising to find Jews in organized crime, for their participation in violent crimes and their rates of alcoholism and drug addiction are very low. The same moral strictures against certain activities of organized criminals can be noted in Italian families. Luigi Barzini suggests Italians feel a need to participate in worthy business. The norm of the Mafia is against participation in such things as narcotics or prostitution—these are looked down upon. Certainly this is an attitude that Italians had to overcome to participate in all facets of organized crime.[73]

The sale of narcotics became an issue when some organized crime families banned participation in the manufacture, sale, and distribution of narcotics, while other families continued to participate. Frank Costello had originally suggested the ban and the Chicago Cosa Nostra, then led by Tony Accardo, went a step farther; it is Valachi's recollection that each one who left the dope trade received $200 a week out of family funds to help make up for the loss of income.[74] Nevertheless, families and individual members began trading in narcotics. There were some pragmatic reasons for staying out of the trade; penalties were high, and law enforcement was more stringent in this area. Moral strictures might have played some part in the decision, but in the end, the profit motive prevailed. Thus it is easy to see how a moral stricture or a norm is disfunctional for certain ethnic groups even though others may see that group as ideally suited for organized crime. In much the same way one can see other groups fall prey to the same kinds of temptations when involved in organized crime; opportunity structure may turn out to be more important than the norms of a particular ethnic group.

In sum, several factors seem to override moral strictures to allow individuals to participate in organized crime. It may be a function of social class or considerations of profit superseding moral strictures. Moral qualms can subside if the following rationalization is given: if we don't deal in the product or service, someone else will.

Conclusion

In conclusion, it appears that Italians are not "ideally" suited for organized crime in this country. Many of the characteristics attributable to Italians make it difficult for them to participate in organized crime and make their involvement less effective than it might be. Most important, ethnicity may explain a group's aptitude for criminal activities, but may also point up certain structural dilemmas. Many of the proclivities of an ethnic group may be contradictory or dysfunctional for an organization's goals. Also, ethnicity is not the sole determinant of the role an ethnic group will play in organized crime. In many of the geographical areas of the country, Italians are not found and yet the activities that are suited for organized crime are so organized. There is a great deal of interchangeability of roles in organized crime. Jews are not solely money movers, Italians enforcers, but a variety of ethnic groups play a variety of roles.

Finally, although there are factors heretofore attributed to ethnicity that can be explained by reference to class, age, opportunity structure, or some other variable, some phenomena can be explicated more easily by reference to ethnic groups. One hypothesis in which ethnicity seems to be a prime variable, and class, age, or urbanism lend little to the explanation of events, is that when a local government is composed of one ethnic group and other ethnic groups in the community are involved in organized crime, there is *less* organized crime than if the government and organized criminal groups are from the same group. For instance, Daniel Moynihan has suggested that the Irish politicians kept the lid on Italian-dominated organized crime.[75] In this situation, organized crime is merely one of the many interest groups involved in government activity, and certainly not part and parcel of government activity or the dominant force.

Organized crime is much more pervasive when local government and organized crime recruit from the same ethnic group. In this case, it may be very difficult to distinguish between government and organized crime. For example, when Italians are in power and Italians are in organized crime, there is a greater level of cooperation and exchange between the two. If care is not taken in defining organized crime, a good deal of activity might be overlooked and legitimized that might not ordinarily be sanctioned. If organized crime is defined as Italian crime, then one might say that when criminal activities are Irish and Irish are in power, there is no organized crime—there is only "corruption," or "machine politics." Of course, there are many activities of a political machine which may be considered as organized crime. There may be an Irish mayor making deals with land developers in the community, regulating gambling in the community, and sanctioning prostitution, all under the umbrella of the government. But if in fact it's not Italian government and Italian crime, it ordinarily is not thought of nor treated as seriously as organized crime. Many other imaginative hypotheses about ethnicity in crime can be generated and although there are limits in the use of ethnicity in explaining organized crime, it still at times, has its utility.

Social Class: "The Queer Ladder"

Ordinarily the individual who works with the variable of social class becomes engaged in arduous discussions about whether he is going to use objective or subjective indicators of class. Methodological discussions revolve around whether or not one should consider class as the individual's perception of what class he is in, or whether measures of income, social position, or social attitudes should be used to indicate class. In this study, social class will not be measured with great precision, but objective measures such as income, position, and hierarchy will be used to give an indication of social class. It will be seen how the social class of criminals affects criminal organization, and reference will also be made to the victims of organized crime and how exploitation varies according to the social class of the victim.

The reigning hypothesis in the study of social class and its relationship to organized crime is Daniel Bell's "queer ladder of social mobility." Bell suggests that,

> . . . the desires satisfied in extra-legal fashion were more than a hunger for the 'forbidden fruits' of conventional morality. They also involve, in the complex and ever-shifting structure of group, class, and ethnic stratification, which is the warp and woof of America's 'open' society, such 'normal' goals as independence through business of one's own, and such 'moral' aspirations as the desire for social advancement and social prestige. For crime in the language of the sociologist has a 'functional' role in the society, and the urban rackets—the illicit activity organized for continuing profit, rather than individual illegal acts—is one of the queer ladders of social mobility in American life . . . (the specific role of various immigrant groups is they, one after another, become involved in marginal business and crime. . .).[76]

Bell's hypothesis has been applied in an abstract and general way to account for the passage of one group and then another in and out of organized criminal activity. To test this hypothesis was to show that the Irish, Jews, and now perhaps Italians are beginning to move out of organized criminal activity.[77] Under closer scrutiny we will see movement of groups in and out of organized crime is far more complex and uneven than Bell leads us to believe. The reasons adduced for the movement in and out of organized crime will also need to undergo intensive scrutiny. In Bell's thesis, illegitimate business is one avenue poor struggling groups have to help fulfill the American dream of social advancement and social prestige. The intimation is that if given an alternative, individuals will always chose the legitimate over the illegitimate avenue, and abandon the illegitimate after achieving success. To determine if the queer ladder does exist and if the explanations for its existence are correct, the recruitment of organized criminals and the possible movements toward legitimacy by organized criminals will be examined.

Recruitment

Sociologists differentiate among the various types of subcultures of crime. For instance, Richard Cloward and Lloyd Ohlin have found that there are three major types of delinquent subcultures, one which they call "criminal," a second called "retreatist," and a third called "conflict." The criminal subculture is one in which theft and racketeering predominate; the conflict subculture is dominated by gangs; and the retreatist harbors the drug culture.[78] Irving Spergel's book *Racketville, Slumtown, Haulberg* is an updated study of criminal subcultures. He finds the retreatist subculture overlaps with the others and does not exist as a separate subculture, and feels that the drug culture may be part and parcel of all the other subcultures, but does not form a distinctive one of its own.[79] Spergel suggests there is not just one unitary criminal subculture, but that it can be divided into a racket and a theft subculture. Thus, he deals with three basic subcultures: the conflict, the racket, and the theft subcultures. The racket subcultures provide the proving and training grounds for organized crime.

> Racketville represents the subculture of young delinquents in neighborhoods where the racket is the chief means of achieving success-goals, and it arises within a social context in which legitimate opportunities are limited, but illegitimate opportunities are available. Here, many youths with aspirations for success status find themselves under pressure, direct or indirect, to use the criminal learning opportunities accessible to them; their relatives are often engaged

in the numbers, policy, gambling, and loan shark rackets, as well as in other lucrative criminal activities.[80]

How, then, do these subcultures come into existence? For the conflict subculture, the answer appears simple:

> Slumtown represents the conflict subculture of delinquent youths in the most deteriorated slums; it is seen as a response to social conditions that provide people with extremely limited access to either legitimate or illegitimate opportunities for reaching conventional success goals. In such an area many youths with high aspirations create for themselves a special kind of opportunity—gang fighting.[81]

In Spergel's study the lowest class of individual does not participate in organized crime, nor is he recruited for organized crime, for both legitimate and illegitimate means of livelihood are blocked to him.

In trying to distinguish between the theft subculture and the racket subculture, it becomes somewhat less clear why one group does not participate in rackets and the other group does. Spergel suggests that

> for a number of reasons, a highly organized criminal system has not gained a dominant position in this neighborhood. It is possible that here, initially, access to legitimate opportunities was not as limited as in areas such as Racketville, where the development of an extensive alternate means or criminal system was required. Furthermore, a stronger and more fully accepted legitimate organization may have set up the barrier to the creation of a fully integrated criminal structure.[82]

Spergel thus concludes that organized criminals do not come from a destitute class, but from lower middle class neighborhoods where both legitimate and illegitimate opportunities are available. In terms of the queer ladder, ethnic groups must achieve some modicum of success before they move into organized criminal activities. Spergel also distinguishes between racket and theft subcultures and concludes that since income differentials between theft and racket subcultures are so small, ethnicity may be the key explanatory variable. This is in stark contrast to those who hold to the queer ladder of social mobility. Their assumption is that illegitimate activities abound and that each group takes advantage of these opportunities in the process of moving on to legitimate activities. However, the activities of organized crime are professions in much the same way that we speak of law, medicine, and accounting as professions. All take a good deal of skill and training as well as an aptitude for the profession. Henry Barrett Chamberlain, director of the Chicago Crime Commission in the early 1930s, agrees with this perspective. "It (organization of professions) differs from the old gangs in that it is not an outgrowth of neighborhood play groups. It is becoming a development of occupational skill and apprenticeship."[83]

It would be unwise to ignore the fact that certain groups, because of prior socialization, do better in and continue to be recruited for certain professions. For example, military officers come from the South in greater numbers than one would expect by chance alone. As mentioned earlier, Italian culture presented many characteristics that make Italians amenable to the kinds of organization and activities organized criminals are involved in. Francis A. J. Ianni, in *A Family Business*, a case study of an organized crime family in New York City, suggests support of Bell's notion. "An era of Italian crime seems to be passing in large measure because of the changing nature of the Italian community which resides in American culture and its inclusion in the society. To that extent, the pattern of Italian crime seems to be following that of previous ethnic groups."[84] Yet the whole argument of the book mitigates against any simple acceptance of a "queer ladder." Organized crime is a family business and the Italian family is well suited to it. Organized criminal activity was carried on and still is being carried on through several generations. Although organizational ties did not carry over from Italy to the United States, occupational patterns were well established, even in Italy. Just as for the Chinese, for whom laundries and restaurants were good business, and the Jews, for whom law and medicine were good professions, for the Italians, organized crime was good business.

At first glance this has a horrible ring to it, but only if we treat organized criminals as totally bad, and the rest of us as beyond reproach, or if I am interpreted as suggesting all Italians aspire to a life in organized crime. Very few go into this avenue of endeavor, but it did turn out to be comfortable and lucrative as a profession for them. In summary, Italians have remained in organized crime longer than other groups, suggesting that ethnicity as well as class tends to lend itself to explanations of participation in organized crime.

The notion that organized criminals are recruited from the lower middle class and never from the middle or upper classes is not correct. There is a built-in structural dilemma caused by the success of criminal organizations. In the earlier years, members are "generalists," individuals who can run a numbers game, operate as a loan shark, commit violence, and steal merchandise. The close family ties and abiding loyalty to the boss is characteristic of the generalist. Thus he is not recruited to organized crime as much for his skills as for his loyalty. The more sophisticated the organization gets, the more necessary it is to bring in the "specialist" (the staff as opposed to the line position) to help run the enterprises. These people may be accountants and lawyers, certainly not drawn straight from lower class status. The specialist is less likely than the generalist to owe an abiding loyalty to the boss so that cohesion may suffer at the expense of expertise. Recruitment from the ranks of middle and upper class professionals again goes against the queer ladder hypothesis, for some middle class individuals actually move into organized criminal societies and matrices.

Organized criminals tend to recruit subordinates from areas in which they do business. If organized criminals, be they Italian, Jewish, or Puerto Rican, are going to run a gambling operation in Harlem, then the lower echelons of the enterprise will be comprised of poor people strictly from the neighborhood. For instance, George C. Edwards, police commissioner of Detroit, described a raid on the Gotham Hotel on November 9, 1963. The estimate of the annual "take" was $21 million at the Gotham Hotel. When questioned about the composition of this criminal organization, Mr. Edwards suggested the following:

> This was a Negro numbers operation. There wasn't a single white person in the hotel, so far as I can recall, when our raiders hit it. We have done quite a lot of work in relation to this since then. We have tried to ascertain just what the relationship was between the thing we call organized crime in Detroit and this which was its largest obvious manifestation. And we found the following: that they took the numbers from the Mafia; that they took the dream books which they sold to their customers from the Mafia; that they took their pads, the numbers pads—they could only be purchased from one supplier and that was supplied by the Mafia. And we found in Johnny White's (the manager) private phone directory Pete Licavoli's private telephone number and Tony Giaclone's private telephone number. And then we began to find after the raid that there was consternation because subsequent to the raid we told the people of Detroit that not only had we found that this thing was illegal and big but in addition to that we found evidence that it was completely crooked.[85]

Recruitment from the ethnic or religious group provided with the goods and services is also characteristic of legitimate sales and service organizations. At the lower levels and where lesser skill are needed, you can recruit from the area within which you work. If a store sells food to an Italian neighborhood, it is better off working with Italian clerks even though the supervisors are of non-Italian lineage. Eventually the groups which man the lower echelon positions may demand their fair share of the pie. For instance, in the speculation as to who wounded Joseph Colombo, a purported family boss, there are references to blacks who are described as impatient with their current position in the organization.[86] The question, of course, is whether blacks or other groups will supplant Italians in organized criminal activity much the way Italians supposedly supplanted the Irish and the Jews.

Many observers seem to feel that blacks will be taking over a substantial share of organized criminal activity. For instance, Nicholas Gage, a perceptive observer of organized criminals, notes the stratification in organized criminal groups, and the breakdown occurring in this hierarchy. "Blacks never used to rise higher than controller in the numbers hierarchy partly because of race prejudice among white gangsters and partly because slum residents feared that their fellow blacks would not be able to pay off heavy winnings without the resources of established banks. But now, law enforcement officials say, some blacks are gaining a toehold in the slums. Thomas Greene, whose numbers network is in central Harlem, has a substantial bank in operation."[87]

Paul Maisano, a pseudonym for an organized criminal Francis Ianni talked to, feels some pressure from other ethnic groups. "There are a growing number of 'independent' lottery operations in East Harlem, particularly the *bolita* lottery that Puerto Ricans and Cubans patronize. In addition, there is increasing pressure from Blacks in the area who want to take over the numbers operation that is still controlled by the De Maio family."[88]

However, the queer ladder of social mobility does not quite hold. Blacks have provided lower echelon personnel for gambling establishments in their neighborhoods at least since the end of Prohibition. In fact, it was the end of Prohibition and the push by other groups to find lucrative enterprises that led to the takeover of the blacks' own lotteries by other ethnics. According to Dixie Davis, Dutch Schultz's attorney, the numbers banks in Harlem were independently run by blacks in the early 1930s. "The bankers were mostly West

Indian Negroes, and to show their prosperity they rode around in limousines as long as locomotives, flashing their diamonds. There was a big profit in the game so long as the law of averages held good, and if a series of popular numbers came up the bankers just went broke and others replaced them."[89] Davis also tells how Schultz organized them to protect them for himself and from the authorities. When Schultz died, the rackets were passed on to other whites.

A group may populate the lower echelons of organized crime for generations, perhaps forever, and not take over organized criminal activities. What happened to blacks at the end of Prohibition was almost a reversal of the queer ladder. Businesses started by blacks, "the newly emerging group," were taken over by the long-established ethnic groups.

The queer ladder hypothesis also assumes a finite set of activities organized criminals may engage in. If organized crime is defined only as gambling and loan-sharking, one group inevitably must push the other one out to succeed. In the language of game theory, they are playing a zero-sum game. In reality, organized crime is not a zero-sum game; a new group can enter, such as college students selling marijuana, Latin Americans pushing cocaine, or Hoosiers stealing automobiles, without pushing another group out of organized crime. Thus, if we read about a new group in organized crime, this does not imply that it is taking another group's place. They may be starting a new form of racket or opening up new markets for time-tested rackets.

In the early seventies, publicity has been given to the non-Italian groups that are playing a role in organized crime. This tends to give credence to those who see the queer ladder of social mobility as a reality. Most of these groups have been there, but the press has chosen to ignore them in favor of emphasis on Italian societies. Now focus on these groups leads to the conclusion that Italian groups are on the way out. As I have suggested, the relationship is far more complex than that. Many of these other groups have been there for some time without substantially increasing their power.

In sum, the recruitment of new groups to organized crime indicates that the queer ladder of social mobility is an oversimplification of reality. Organized criminals do not necessarily come from the lowest class, and specialists are often drawn from the middle and even upper classes. Also, it is not necessary for one group to replace another when it begins organized criminal activity. The group may create a new form of activity or open new markets for old activities without displacing other groups. Some ethnic groups may show a propensity for organized crime and remain in the business for generations while other groups may never take advantage of the opportunities. Finally, the queer ladder assumes that a single ethnic group dominates criminal activity, but it appears that several ethnic groups operate in every era.

Upward Mobility

If the queer ladder theory is correct, then as criminals move up the status ladder they or their offspring must abandon a career in organized crime. After several generations the percentage of organized criminals in a given generation involved in organized crime begins to decrease. According to Ianni, "In 1970, forty-two fourth-generation members of (pseudonyms) the Lupollo-Salemi-Alcamo-Tucci family could be identified. . . . Only four of the twenty-seven males we traced are involved in the family business."[90] There does seem to be a high attrition rate to other careers as generation succeeds generation.

However, as Ianni points out, there still is a large family business and it continues to deal in illegitimate enterprises, even though business has increasingly concentrated on legitimate sectors of the economy.[91] Although a gambling operation in Brooklyn is being phased out, loan-sharking, a major activity, seems to be on the increase.[92] The family business is still intact and involved in legitimate as well as illegitimate business. This represents no major alteration in the family because the founder of the family also held a variety of illegitimate as well as legitimate businesses.[93]

Thus relatives of original family members increasingly go into other businesses, yet the businesses have persisted for several generations. Ultimately this may mean a loss of cohesion based upon family loyalty, but as of now few of the early empires have crumbled, some remaining in existence for over forty years.

So far I have gathered information to suggest whether the queer ladder of social mobility was followed and it appears that recruitment to organized crime does not follow this straight and narrow path. Succeeding generations of Italians follow their parents less and less into organized crime, yet enough still do, combined with new recruits, to keep the families functioning. Now it remains to see whether Bell's explanation for the queer ladder intrinsically helps us to understand why groups move in and out of organized crime. Central to Bell's explanation is the notion that as people take on middle class values they will abandon illegitimate enterprises. By implication, the natural pressure is towards decency and honesty as one moves up the social ladder. Daniel Bell, interestingly enough, calls this the embourgeoisement of crime and notes that "many of the top 'crime' figures had long ago foresworn violence, and even their income, in large part, was derived from legitimate investments (real estate in the case of Costello, motor hauling and auto franchises in the case of Adonis) or from such quasi-legitimate but socially respectable sources as gambling casinos."[94] There are other evidences of the movement from less respectable to more respectable crimes, and there is an indication that organized criminals believe it is good to do so. Sam de Cavalcante suggests that one of his lieutenants, a man named Frank Cochiaro, should be brought into a new business. "He (Sam) described Frank as a 'professional thief', heading for disaster as he got older, but that now, since he was connected with a legitimate business, Frank could spend the rest of his life in dignity."[95] In fiction, we see an excellent portrayal of this phenomenon in *The Godfather* when the son of the don, Michael Corleone, goes to Las Vegas and presumably withdraws from the more violent and corruptive influences of organized crime.[96]

Similarly, Robert Merton suggests that in American society, criminals strive for the same goals as other Americans—wealth, status, and security. They differ from other Americans in that their means to achieve these goals are blocked by barriers of education and other obstacles.[97] Consequently, one would expect organized criminals to use legitimate means as soon as the barriers to legitimate enterprises are removed.

Explanations of Movements toward Legitimacy

Merton and Bell are suggesting that the changing attitudes of criminals when exposed to middle class values substantially moves them more and more into legitimate businesses, perhaps because of a desire to be like everyone else. I have serious reservations about this hypothesis which I will register, and I will attempt to provide an alternate explanation which does not rely upon the middle class's inexorable movement towards goodness.

Merton and Bell are perhaps correct in suggesting that Americans strive for material comfort, respectability, and well being. However, in American society business and personal lives are often separated. Respectability in the broader society is more a function of consumption patterns than the nature of one's occupation. A person can be in organized crime and still live in the suburbs, be a pillar of the community, and conspicuously consume.

More important, organized criminals do not perceive of their businesses as rougher or more crooked than many other enterprises. To them, politics is not only more dishonest, but public officials have to be hypocritical as well. In reality, it would be hard for them to conceive of severe ethical differences between the behavior of many businessmen they deal with and organized criminals. Data on this score backs them up. Edwin Southerland's study of 70 of the largest corporations indicates that "legitimate businessmen" commit many crimes. "Every one of the 70 corporations (over a 45 year period) had a decision against it and the average number was 140. . . . About 60 percent of the 70 corporations had been convicted by criminal courts."[98] It is foolish to suggest that middle class members will be more honest in business transactions than lower class individuals. The folly of this suggestion became apparent to me in my own business affairs. When I moved to Earpsville, a real estate agent told me that her agency was the best in town because the owner was a millionaire many times over and no longer needed to make money. Therefore, he would not have to be dishonest with me in his dealings. The transparency of the notion that the wealthier an individual gets, the more honest he is, should be apparent. Why then should we expect that organized criminals or their relations become more honest when they move into legitimate businesses or that legitimate businesses are completely distinguishable ethically from organized crime activities and are attractive to former criminals or their siblings?

To make more sense of Merton's and Bell's explanation, it might be said that organized criminal societies and matrices suffer from high risk and have more recourse to violence than legitimate business organizations. Perhaps these values are more consonant with lower as opposed to middle class culture. It is not moral qualms but risk that drives organized criminals into legitimate businesses.

Violence often draws the harshest legal sanctions and there is evidence that as criminals move up the status ladder they have less inclination, but also less need, to have recourse to violence. In organized crime, violence involves high risk and low pay; therefore, people at the bottom of the status hierarchy perform these acts. Ralph Salerno reports a conversation with Joey Gallo, a purported member of organized crime who was seeking a higher status position in the Profaci family. Gallo is complaining about the low status of strong-arm and murder: "Me, I can't even get to run a crap game. Why? Ya need a college education to run a crap game? When you want somebody hit (killed), we're good enough. But not good enough to come to the house."[99]

In business, two motives seem to have overriding importance, the maximization of profits and the minimizing of risks. Offhand, it seems that legitimate businesses are less risky than illegitimate ones, yet organized criminals spend few years in jail for their activities and often receive significant support for their activities from governmental officials and the public. The wealthy can often remain in organized crime at low risk because their employees insulate them from the law. Thus, legitimate businesses do not appear much safer or less risky to them. Even if a business is perceived of as risky by individuals, the profits or the hope for profits will keep them in the business.

In sum, as people do get wealthy and move up the status hierarchy in organized crime, there may be a push into legitimate businesses and a movement from activities of violence. It may not be due to any pangs of conscience on their part but to minimize violence and risk. Exclusive of ethnicity, many impediments may occur to deter organized criminals from completely coming into legitimate business. Some individuals or ethnic groups may spend several generations in organized crime while in others only one generation may be fully involved in organized crime. First, profits may keep people in organized crime; if an individual can make greater profits through illegitimate rather than legitimate business, he is motivated to continue in these businesses. As long as objective or perceived risks are not so great, organized criminals will sustain these activities for a long time. Violence and risk may encourage individuals to move into legitimate businesses but does not insure a steady progression of defection from organized crime as the queer ladder leads us to suspect. More importantly, movement to legitimate businesses is not necessarily a function of middle class conscience.

There is an alternative explanation for the movement of organized criminals into legitimate businesses, one which does not rest upon the coercive moral power of the middle class. When ethnic identification decreases over succeeding generations and opportunities open up in many fields, ethnic groups are found in a diversity of occupations. Today there are Jews in a large variety of occupations, whereas thirty years ago they were clustered in a few professions, small ghetto businesses, and trade unions. Blacks are increasingly found in many occupations where they were not before. No immigrant group continues to have successive generations ritually succeeding their fathers in those occupations closely identified with the immigrant group. Succeeding generations need not have gotten out of organized crime out of moral revulsion but merely to participate in opportunities presented by other businesses or occupations. David Finn in *The Corporate Oligarch* suggests that next to making money, the most important consideration of a businessman is whether or not to bring his son into the business. In the United States where the value of achievement takes primacy over the value of ascription, the sons of immigrants are likely to strike out on their own whether their business is medicine, petrochemicals, or loan-sharking. Finn also notes the difficult psychological problems sons have in trying to match their father's accomplishments.[100] In *Honor Thy Father* we can see Bill Bonanno suffer under the shadow of his father's manifold business successes.[101]

The values of achievement as opposed to ascription and the manifold job opportunities opened up to sons and daughters of immigrants are hallmarks of middle class society. In that respect, middle class values prevent an ethnic group from dominating an organized criminal activity forever. Yet, the same is true of any area of American life in which an ethnic group originally predominated; they no longer retain hegemony. Of course, some ethnic groups show amazing persistence in occupations depending on the strength of the family ties and ethnic identification, and this appears to explain the continuing participation of Italians in organized criminal activity.

The social class an outsider or victim belongs to will profoundly affect the nature of his contacts with organized crime. When ethnic groups such as Italians, Irish, or Jews get involved with organized crime, they exploit their own community first and then other ethnic groups, in the "inside-outside" pattern. Harry Anslinger, former head of the Bureau of Narcotics, tells an interesting story about Mafia violence in America around the turn of the century. Anslinger worked on a road gang made up primarily of Sicilian immigrants. One of their numbers lived primarily on protection money gained from the other workers, a pattern which was not uncommon early in the 1900s.[102] In New Orleans, as well as other cities, the Italian criminals exploited other Italians on the docks for protection. The Jews in the garment industry were early victims of extortion of other Jews in the garment industry. After a time, with Jews and Italians and all ethnic groups, exploitation moves from within their own community to outside the community. In the case of blacks, for example, today we find narcotics peddling in the black community and would suspect that after a while, the blacks will move out and exploit the wider community. The inside-outside pattern occurs because there is a need for larger markets, the demand for their services in their own neighborhood decreases as income levels rise, and language and cultural barriers that inhibited interaction between ethnic groups break down as "Americanization" takes place. One qualification is that organized criminals would tend to ban the harder vices such as narcotics from their own backyard faster than activities like lotteries and sports betting where demand still exists and a minimum of harm is perceived.

Social classes are also differentially affected by organized crime. Individuals who live in the ghetto are affected more overtly and can readily identify organized crime. They all know about it. They play either nickel and dime games or higher stake games, borrow money from loan sharks or know of someone who does. Some look upon it with favor and others with scorn or hatred. Middle and upper class persons have less direct and continuing relations with organized criminals and consequently "see" less crime. They feel the impact of organized crime when lower or higher prices for some merchandise are passed on to them indirectly, but they may be unaware of the store's relationship to organized crime. Isolated individuals from middle or upper classes, however, may be hit extremely hard by organized crime. For instance, in *Sam the Plumber*, individuals talk with Sam about an interesting way to exploit a wealthy individual. "Pat Brennan and Jack Delarusso called Sam about a man who has been bragging about losing $30,000 in Las Vegas under an assumed name. Since Las Vegas doesn't have his name, he won't have to pay— he thinks. Pat and Jack wanted to shake him down for $15,000 by bringing him to Sam. Sam agreed."[103]

Finally, the same kind of activity, e.g., gambling, narcotics, or prostitution, may be provided to all classes, but the different classes may receive different qualities of services. An interesting example of differential services is found in a very early description of prostitutes in Joseph Crapsey's *The Nether Side of New York*, written in 1872.

> When a woman offers to sell her body to a man she never saw before, for 50 cents, she has fallen low indeed, and this offer will be made at least a dozen times during the hour to any observer at the spot mentioned, whose appearance does not absolutely forbid appearances.
>
> Next stand for the same period at Amity and Green Streets. As many women will pass in about the same ratio as to reappearances. They are a shade better in appearance as to dress, and some of them have the faint remnants of former personal beauty. They are vulgar yet, but are a vast improvement on the set first seen.[104]

In gambling as well differential services are provided. Compare, for example, the slum dweller who plays craps in an alley or books a $2 bet with his bookie to the middle or upper class gentleman who may spend much money on an airplane junket to London, Las Vegas, or the Bahamas to gamble.

Thus social class affects the characteristics of the members of organized crime, and crime differentially affects the victimized classes in our society. Organized crime affects members of the ethnic group from which the criminals are drawn before it affects outsiders, and hits the lower class in a more obvious and pervasive manner than the middle class. Finally, the same services may be provided differentially for the rich and the poor.

Age

Researchers have tried to develop at least some crude notions about most of the approaches analyzed so far, yet there is virtually no discussion concerned with the variable of age. Age differentials affect the nature of organized crime in two ways. First, older people behave in a different manner than they did when younger. For instance, risk taking is less prevalent among older people, and older people manifest a tendency toward political conservatism. A second resultant of age differentials among people is that generational differences cause conflicts between young and old. This may reinforce or confound the effects of an individual's chronological age. Attitudinal differences may be a function either of maturation or the perceiving of differential environmental stimuli in their formative years; for instance, today's generation grew up on television and other technological wonders and previous generations did not. Obviously it is hard to tell whether the differences between generations described are due to age or the changing values between different generations, but this distinction should be kept in mind during the discussion of age and organized crime.

One of the major structural dilemmas in criminal organizations and matrices has been to keep both old and young at peace with each other. The differences between young and old has contributed to several major disputes in organized crime. In the Castellamarese War, the issue was the maintenance of ethnic homogeneity of organized crime. There were some who felt that no one but Sicilians should be in the organization, and others who thought membership should be broadened to include at least Neapolitans as well as Sicilians and other ethnic groups. Some emphasized the virtues of power and deference, while others, caught up in the "Americanization" of organized crime, stressed profits. The difference seems to be between the older immigrants and the younger members (either born here or brought to this country at an early age). Major generational disputes occurred in the Gallo-Profaci war and in fights over control in the Bonanno family. Both involved impatient young men who wanted to rise to leadership positions in the organization, but whose claims were contested by the older individuals.

Today the conflicts between old and young have not abated. Anthony Downs' *Inside Bureaucracy* describes the "age lump" phenomenon in organizations. During the early years of an organization, growth is very rapid, and those who originally joined stay with the organization for a long time. "This means that a high proportion of its total membership consists of persons who joined it during the fast-growth period (unless it has a very high turnover). This group constitutes a "lump" of personnel, all about the same age."[105] Ralph Salerno, in describing recruitment practices in organized crime families, gives us an idea of how the "age lump" formed in organized crime. "The sizes of families were originally set after the Castellamarese War in 1931, and except to fill openings no new members were taken in until World War II when 'the books were opened.' They were closed again shortly after the war and reopened between 1954 and 1958."[106]

Downs notes, "As they (the members) grow older, the average age of the bureau's members rises too, since they form such a large fraction of its total membership."[107] Leaders of organized crime families today are very often old men. Sam de Cavalcante gives an indication that the age of members of his group is advanced in his use of the word *kid*. "Kid," according to Henry Ziegler, the editor of *Sam the Plumber*, is a term often employed by Sam to mean a person ranging in age from about 20 to 45, usually not a Cosa Nostra member, but often an experienced felon.[108]

The age lump in organized crime causes a great deal of internal dissention. The different age groupings reflect different attitudes, and conflict sets in along these lines. Always at issue is the increasing impatience of the younger people for advancement in the organization. In other organizations conflict may be avoided by younger members seeking opportunities elsewhere. That safety valve is not open to criminal organizations for they discourage defection, and they control all of the significant opportunities in a given area for young people. The young stay and fight within the organization. In the Profaci family it was demands by the younger faction for more of a share in the activities as well as their complaints about anacronistic practices that led to conflict. Conflict within the Bonanno family was partially caused by the elevation of Bill Bonanno, the don's son, to a high position in the family.

Attitudinal and behavioral differences between generations as well as vaulted ambitions exacerbate the conflicts. First, as in most organizations, innovation is often opposed by the elders, and in organized crime the elders show less of a propensity towards violence. For instance, Bobby Basile, Sam The Plumber's nephew, is discussing Frank Cochiarro, an individual in Sam's family.

> "Sammy, Frank ain't got no brains. He never had any and he never will. He's like a kid. He hasn't grown up yet. He thinks he's playing games yet. He thinks this is fun. He wants to go around hitting (killing) guys . . . this is all kids' stuff, Sam. The only thing is that if we get him out of this, then he has been told."[109]

Second, the elders believe that the younger generation is not as loyal as the elders and have not been as carefully chosen for membership. Mike, in the tapes made by the New York State Joint Committee on Crime, expresses worry that his ranks are being filled with informants.

> MIKE: Underground. Underground and reorganize and come up. And leave a couple of fucking bodies on every fucking corner. And every fucking stool pigeon we got a line on. There hasn't been any of that. I don't want to be vicious. I don't want to be bloodthirsty,

but, Pete, you talk to people and they're not afraid no more. They're looking to defy you.[110]

Later in the conversation he indicates that old-fashioned recruitment methods were better. It may be that the elders are no more loyal than the young, but conflict is generated by such beliefs. The younger generation in organized crime seems to lack the charisma, organizational skills, and commitment of the older generation. This may be a statement which is always made about a younger generation. The observations, however, are probably correct and the changes occurring in organized crime parallel what occurs in other organizations, such as unions, when the founding fathers begin to die out. For instance, when unions were founded, their leaders were charismatic types who drew membership and loyalty on the basis of personality. Second-generation leadership is composed of bureaucrats, less colorful figures wanting in certain charismatic qualities and having certain managerial skills. These leaders are often from the first age lump, cronies of the original founders, who lack inspiration but continue to speak for their age cohorts. When the younger generation steps in, they often have managerial skills but lack the sense of tradition or commitment that their elders had. In organized crime now, few of the younger generation such as Colombo and Bill Bonanno have moved or tried to move to positions of influence in their families. With power still lying for the most part with the cronies of the founders, there promises to be future turmoil with the transition of power to some of the younger members.

Chapter 4

Organized Crime as an Economic and Political System

Organized Crime as an Economic System

There are many ways to conceptualize organized crime; one may view it as an economic system, a social system, a political system, or a distinct subculture. Within each of these frameworks, there are many concepts that could be used to describe organized crime. The starting point here is necessarily arbitrary and based upon the author's predispositions and biases as much as upon any other considerations. Donald R. Cressey in *Theft of a Nation* has done a very comprehensive job of analyzing organized crime as a social system and I can not improve upon his analysis here.[1] Francis A. J. Ianni has given us some interesting concepts to deal with when he speaks of the difference between Mafia as culture and Mafia as organization; and there have been several other good pieces done on organized crime from an anthropological perspective.[2] Little has been written about organized crime as a political system and much exploration needs to be done. The writings of Thomas Schelling and others provide promising avenues to explore in the study of organized crime as an economic system and should be pursued.[3]

To speak of organized crime as a political system and an economic system raises as many questions as it answers. What are systems? What are the concepts used to describe the systems? How do we define *political*? Or *economic*? As students of economics and politics know, these questions lead to endless debate and discussion; for instance, David Easton's book *The Political System* is taken up completely with definition of politics and the political.[4] It is hoped here to bypass these arguments by worrying less about a precise rendering of definitions and dealing more with the substantive concerns of social scientists, working with the concepts they have formulated, and formulating some of my own.

Functions of Large Criminal Organizations

To consider organized crime as an economic system is not new or original. For instance, Henry Barrett Chamberlain, director of the Chicago Crime Commission, suggests: "Organized crime is a manifestation of economic movement. In its present form it is the result of increasing intelligence on the part of the criminal class—the application of this capitalistic system by the predators who are not openly protected by the forms of law."[5] Modern analysts are also aware of the economic arrangements in organized crime and the utility of using economic concepts to describe organization. For instance, in *Task Force Report: Organized Crime* the economic concept *cartel* is used in conveying a good detail of information about organized crime. Task force members recognized that the structure of organized crimes are to a great extent shaped by economic arrangements and transactions.[6] It is Thomas Schelling, however, who has asked the most penetrating and suggestive questions about organized crime as an economic system. According to Schelling, some crimes are organized and others are not, depending on a variety of economic concerns which he details.[7] Schelling begins by asking why some activities organized by criminals and others remain unorganized. For instance, why don't we find organized groups of pick-pockets, while we do find organized groups of gamblers?[8] I will ask the question from a different perspective. What kinds of services can a large organization provide for organized criminals?

A primary function of a large criminal organization is the provision of protection for its economic interests; the organization keeps competitors or detractors away from its businesses or the business of friends. For instance, "Sam warned Jack Brennan about his drinking. He said that unless Jack cut it out he would stop associating with him, and reminded Brennan that one week before Sam withdrew his protection from Pickles (Angelo Piccololla) he was murdered. Sam forecast a similar fate for Jack if Sam dropped him."[9] Protection is provided against two classes of detractors, other criminals and the law. Since laws are not going to protect an illegal establishment from illegal encroachments by a competitor, protection against other criminals comes by way of threat or actual use of force. In the early days of gambling this protection from the lawless was necessary; "as gamblers are inhibited from coming into court in order to settle disputes with respect to their property rights, there has grown up within the last twenty-five years a systematic terrorism."[10] Hank Messick suggests that in the early days of bootlegging, there was a good deal of kidnapping and ransoming of the big shots in the bootlegging enterprise. Without legitimate authorities to intervene, the only guarantee of an illegitimate business or enterprise is the threat or use of force.[11]

The bigger and more powerful the organization, the more protection it can afford to members. It can guarantee territory and mediate disputes for their members; it did in the early days of Prohibition and still does today. Ralph Salerno provides an interesting example of the settlement of a dispute over the location of a gambling operation. A group within the Joseph Profaci family in Brooklyn decided to extend their gambling operation into an adjoining neighborhood, one already served by members of the de Cavalcante family.

> The dispute was settled when the two bosses sat down face to face. It so happened that Profaci owned a hunting lodge in New Jersey so he could go across the river and into de Cavalcante's territory without loss of face. The two met at the lodge with great cordiality and only after the dinner was the gambling problem mentioned. . . . Eventually they came to an agreement: the Gowanus Canal which bisected the area in question was designated as the demarcation line between the two groups. The next day the word was passed down to the troops and open conflict was avoided.[12]

Unless a business can be secured from the view of other criminals it is subject to takeover, or must pay tribute to the larger organizations. In other words, these large organizations can not only protect their own interests, but take tribute from others. Vincent Siciliano speaks of his small group's attempt to "organize" whorehouses (make them pay tribute) in Queens, New York; to his surprise nobody had attempted to organize them before.

> The really funny thing about those whorehouses we picked on was that except for a few punks in the neighborhood, nobody had ever organized them. None of the official mobs, the really important ones, had even begun to do any organizing. Maybe we just

picked the right whorehouses, but we never heard a word of complaint from anybody. When we started knocking over crap games, it was different.[13]

He ran into trouble when he robbed crap games run by an organization more powerful than his own.

The other form of protection which is offered by a large criminal organization is from the law, and this may be served in one of two ways. First, by mobilization, expertise, and elaborate financial arrangements, large organizations make their operation more difficult to detect than operations of smaller, less sophisticated organizations. Second, and more interestingly, large criminal organizations, on the basis of capital and political connections, are able to influence authorities to differentially enforce the law (stop one illegitimate enterprise while allowing another to go on) or to ignore illegitimate activities altogether. Henry Barrett Chamberlain suggests that in the early days of gambling there were differential police raids. Some establishments which had paid off the police were allowed to exist while others were systematically closed down.[14] The Kefauver Committee uncovered a very interesting example of selective enforcement by police officials. In Miami there was a very efficient gambling operation called the S & G Enterprise. It became so profitable that it aroused the curiosity of gamblers from Chicago. The S & G people didn't want anyone to move in on them. As the Kefauver Committee suggests, nothing crude or violent transpired, but a number of things began to happen. A rival syndicate, with bookies of its own, began to appear on the scene in a number of plush hotels dominated by the Chicago group.

> Next, Governor Warren's crime investigator, the previously mentioned W. O. Crosby, known as Bing, appeared in Miami Beach. . . . Russell, [Harry Russell, a Chicago gambler] Crosby admitted, started feeding him a lot of information on various bookie joints that he might raid, and Crosby started raiding them. The Committee was not surprised to learn that these were all places operated by S & G bookies, who of course began screaming loudly over the infringement upon the immunity they had long paid for and enjoyed. . . . Finally came the crusher: S & G was buying its wire service from the local distributor of the same Continental Press that had already undergone the experience of being squeezed by Guzik and Accardo [Chicago organized criminals]. This service was abruptly shut off one day, leaving S & G paralyzed. For a few days it managed to bootleg a little news from a rash Continental Press customer in New Orleans, but it speedily became apparent to all parties concerned that this was an unhealthy thing to be doing.[15]

Here is, then, a very interesting example of the differential political protection a large organization can provide.

The risks of being an "outlaw" (not receiving protection from an organized criminal group) is succinctly summed up by Vincent Siciliano: "An outlaw is just that. Unlike the regular organization and the police, he doesn't have any law on his side. The organization has its own law, plus the law it can buy from the other side. . . . But the outlaws are fair game for everybody."[16] He goes on to explain that police must make arrests, and policemen go after the outlaw. "Most of the stories you read about arrests are stories of outlaws getting arrested."[17] Protection is an important service provided by criminal organizations. Financial operations sometimes resembling restaurant franchises in their methods and relationships to the large organization are run under their protective umbrella, sometimes by their own people and other times by people paying protection to the larger organization. They pay for the rights to stay in business and literally for using the name of the larger organization in business transactions.

Large organizations also provide capital and labor to carry out complex activities. If one is going to set up a gambling casino, he needs skilled managers and workers, labor only a large organization with previous experience can provide. Other forms of activities also involve a good deal of skilled labor. For instance, if you want to sell stolen securities, the problem is not the theft itself, as many brokerage houses leave the stocks around and they are easily taken. The problem is the disposal of the securities and this facet of the operation involves many men with specialized talents. The disposal of any goods requires a certain degree of contacts and skilled labor, something which large organized criminal groups can provide.

Capital, as well as labor, may also be needed to provide for organized criminal activity and large organizations can fulfill this need. For instance, it takes a great deal of capital to buy a shipment of narcotics and the independent criminal is not able to raise large amounts of capital. If you want to build casinos, invest in legitimate business, or start any complex operation, you can best procure capital if you are part of a large organization. Finally, given the pressures of enforcement officials on organized crime, capital is needed for diversification of business to prevent complete loss; capital is needed to recover from severe business losses, and capital is needed to innovate (find new business opportunities) to stay in business.

A large economic concern can provide "social services" for its members that smaller concerns can not afford. Some analysts claim that, much like the government in England which provides social services "from the cradle to the grave," organized crime handles all activities involving insurance, old age assistance, and so on. Gordon Hawkins in "God and The Mafia" claims that criminal organizations do little if anything to aid the individual in organized crime. To illustrate his point, Hawkins cites the following transcript from the Valachi hearings:

> SENATOR JAVITS: Were you represented, for example, by lawyers in that time you were picked up?
>
> MR. VALACHI: When you're picked up, sometimes yes; sometimes no. Sometimes you don't even require a lawyer.
>
> SENATOR JAVITS: How did you seek the help of your family when you were picked up?
>
> MR. VALACHI: I used to get my own help. What family do you mean?
>
> SENATOR JAVITS: The family to which you belonged, the Genovese family.
>
> MR. VALACHI: I never bothered them. If I got picked up, I got myself out, I got my own lawyers.
>
> SENATOR JAVITS: Did they give you any protection in the 35 years?
>
> MR. VALACHI: No.
>
> SENATOR JAVITS: Did they furnish lawyers?
>
> MR. VALACHI: Never.
>
> SENATOR JAVITS: Or bondsmen?
>
> MR. VALACHI: Never. I got my own bondsmen, my own lawyers.[18]

In the area of social service, help is sporadic and intermittent, but some help from the larger organization is given. It is not clear whether or not this is done on the basis of status in the organization; perhaps more important people on the level of *capo* or captain would get this aid while Valachi did not. Ralph Salerno suggests that status may play a part in the aid which people receive and he illustrates this with the story of Tom, an apprentice in organized crime. It was arranged that Tom could work as a dispatcher for a trucking company while he waited for trial. Salerno points out that "if Tom had been a higher ranking or more important member, an attempt could have been made to influence one of the jury. Failing that, several of the jurors might have gotten sick and one of the two alternates, say, would have had an accident in the middle of the case, causing a mistrial and delay. . . . None of these things were done for Tom, but he did get a first class lawyer who worked zealously for him."[19]

Perhaps criminal organizations may provide some forms of compensation and not others; for instance, the elderly of organized crime are given some form of assistance. Joseph Profaci, as suggested earlier, was very loyal to his older friends, giving them important work in the organization. It was noted that Sam de Cavalcante indicated a desire to set up one of his lieutenants in a legitimate business so that in his old age, this lieutenant would have sufficient income and security. Meyer Lansky's chauffeur is an individual who could no longer do the muscle work he once performed for Lansky.[20]

The example that Ralph Salerno gives above is one indication that legal aid is furnished by organized criminals. In the early months of 1963, the FBI put a bug in the office of a company owned by Raymond Patriarca, purported boss of the Cosa Nostra in the New England area. From the airtels there is ample evidence that bail as well as other legal help was provided for individuals in organized crime. "Patriarca instructed him that, when arranging bail for any individual, he should make sure that the bondsmen does not know his [Sciara's] identity as he believes that all bondsmen are stool pigeons."[21] Another example is found later on the FBI text. "Another Unman [the FBI identification of an unknown caller] requested Patriarca's help in a case involving an unknown individual who is facing a jail sentence for a crime committed by him. The defendant still has $18,000 from the results of the crime. Patriarca will assist this individual, provided he gets half of the money or $9,000. He did not indicate in what way he would help the defendant. Unman would contact him later when he discussed the details with the defendant."[22]

Finally, money may be used to aid families of individuals who are in jail or waiting trial. De Cavalcante mentioned that he was paying a widow a pension and that her children don't take care of her even though they can afford it; he thought he was giving money to too many people.[23] It seems that the provision of social services is based somewhat on the beneficence and calculations of the heads of the families and not based on any guaranteed pay scale. In the area of social services, the large criminal organization does provide help in some areas, but I would be reluctant to agree with those who suggest that they rival either the United States Army or the British civil service with regard to providing services from the cradle to the grave.

Large criminal organizations can minimize economic risk for the members involved. They can share investments in certain enterprises; for example, if you build a casino you can get other individuals to put up the money. Another way to provide a minimal economic risk is in the area of betting. The larger organization prevents losses of a great deal of money by individual bookies through the process of "laying off" bets. Let us propose as an example a baseball game between the Oakland Athletics and the Cincinnati Reds. In Oakland, nearly everyone who bets on this game will bet on the Athletics. The local bookies will then need the services of a lay-off bettor to take their bets on the Reds and the Athletics, so that if the Athletics win, not every bookie in Oakland will be wiped out. Thus there is a good deal of minimizing of economic risk within large criminal organizations.

The large organization can also provide one other service—insulation. That is, the individual in organized crime can designate other persons to do work which is difficult and dangerous. And because of the sanctions against talking, he can be well assured that his subordinates will not place the blame where it belongs even if caught. Some of the very conditions mentioned place a great deal of strain by impairing organized crime's cohesiveness. These economic arrangements do provide a much needed function for the criminal by making it worthwhile in dollars and cents to belong to the organization. However, there are certain strains away from the absolute discipline, loyalty, and commitment one might expect of organized criminals when business takes precedence over concerns of cohesion and loyalty.

Profits and Losses in Organized Crime

The estimated income figures of criminal societies and matrices are usually astronomically high and are based upon guesses. For instance, Max Singer in *The Public Interest* suggests that "mythical numbers may be more mythical and have more vitality in the area of crime than in most areas. In the early 1950s the Kefauver Committee published a $20 billion estimate for the annual quotations taken for gambling in the United States. The figure actually was 'picked from the hat.' One staff member said, 'We had no real idea of the money spent. The California Crime Commission says $12 billion. Virgil Peterson of Chicago said $30 billion. We picked $20 billion as the balance of the two.' "[24] Estimates of individual wealth are equally astronomical. Donald R. Cressey suggests that "the $6 or $7 billion going into organized criminals each year is not all profit. From this amount must be deducted the costs of doing business. . . . But the profits are huge enough to make understandable the fact that any given member of the Cosa Nostra is more likely to be a millionaire than not."[25] The profit and loss figures quoted tend to give the picture of an organization collecting income in some centralized accounting office and having a payroll department, much like Standard Oil or General Motors. However, individual businesses take in the money and break it down among their business associates. Most members do not receive a salary from the boss and are not paid according to a fixed schedule. As Ianni suggests, "A number of other businesses, operated independently by members of the Lupullo family or their relatives, may be classified as family-related on the basis of their publicly declared control by members of the central family or their relatives, although we have no evidence that the proceeds flow into the central family coffers."[26] There is no evidence either to suggest that one family would share profits with another unless they were involved in a joint enterprise. Annual profits of organized crime will not be estimated here, but some of the categories of costs of doing business and some of the categories of expenditures will be discussed. I will begin with the assumption garnered from the literature that organized crime is accumulating a tremendous amount of wealth. Afterwards, the problem of just what individuals include in calculating the amount of net profit in organized crime will be discussed.

There are two ways often used to estimate the wealth of a business concern; one is to decide on the total assets of a corporation, and the second is to estimate its net income. When Meyer Lansky says, "We are bigger than United States Steel," he appears to be talking about total net assets.[27] The measures of net assets of organized crime used here are crude. One can make some crude estimates of some of the assets of illegitimate enterprises by betting slips that may be found, tax cases made against organized criminals, and informants. Even if organized crime were bigger than United States Steel, it would still be a very small segment of the gross national product. Ramsey Clark, for instance, suggests that the amount of business which organized crime is involved with is minor. "It is easy, however, to exaggerate this movement into major business. The occasions of control of large enterprises is sort of rare. The vested—and usable—wealth and power of organized crime are not that great. Most of the top leaders of organized crime maintain some legitimate business activities; they do not touch one-tenth of one percent of American business."[28] Donald R. Cressey who usually sees organized crime as a very powerful menace, as indicated by the title of his book, *The Theft of a Nation*, is very guarded when he talks about the wealth of organized criminals. "While organized criminals do not yet have control of all the legitimate economic and political activities in any metropolitan or other geographic area of America, they do have control of *some* of those activities in many areas."[29] It suffices here to suggest that probably most analysts overestimate the assets of organized criminals.

According to most analysts, the profits of organized crime are astronomical. Organized criminals continue to reinvest profits and the organizations continue to grow. These hypotheses are subject to question. In the family of Sam the Plumber, individuals are not as wealthy as we might expect. In a taped conversation between Sam de Cavalcante and Joe Bayonne, a member of the Joe Bonanno family, the discussion concerns Joe Notaro, a *capo* of long standing in the Bonanno family. "Bayonne interrupted: Joe Notaro owes me money. He owes me money and he can't pay. He hasn't got a quarter!"[30] The suggestion is made in the follow up of the conversation that Joe Bonanno, the boss of the family, is much better with his money than Notaro. "He [Bonanno] could have $2 million and still grab more. He's got one-way pockets. When that goes down, it never comes back up. Everybody ain't like us . . . well, than I guess it's all said."[31] One must take Donald Cressey's statement that organized criminals are likely to be millionaires with a grain of salt. Certainly, Joe Valachi's activities show that a lot of money ran through his hands, but when it came to settling his estate he had nothing left but royalties from his book. Perhaps Joe Valachi had money in other accounts which were secretly passed on to others. However, from most of the literature one gets the impression that wealth is not steadily compounded but many fortunes are made and lost. The following is a conversation between a man named Pussy Rizzo and de Cavalcante:

> PUSSY: Do you know how many guys in Chicago are peeling [safe cracking]? Do you know how many friends of ours in New York that are peeling? . . . What are the poor suckers going to do? Do you know how many dead-heads that we take for them [the New York bosses]? Two guys with Mike Sabella are running a zingarette game in New Jersey, pretty soon we'll have all the mob here [in New Jersey]. Guys are coming to me, asking to be put on [to work gambling games] and they're friends of ours, and so I put them on because I can't let them starve to death.
>
> SAM: Pretty soon I may have to say no to them, because I gotta look after myself. I'll help your boys whenever I can.[32]

It's not just the small family of Sam the Plumber that has financial problems, but other families as well.

Analysts of organized crime often concentrate on profits of organized crime while neglecting to talk about considerable business and personal expenses. First of all, there are many kinds of expensive overhead in organized crime. Organized criminals do not have to pay taxes; however, non-payment of taxes is offset by other income they must pay to the government, such as protection money to keep their enterprises afloat. In John Gardiner's study, *The Politics of Corruption*, he suggests some of the dollar amounts paid:

> Records from the numbers bank listed payments totalling $2,400 each week to some local elected officials, state legislators, the police chief, a captain in charge of detectives and persons mysteriously labeled 'county' and 'state'. While the list of persons to be paid remained fairly constant, the amounts paid varied according to the gambling activities in operation at the time; payoff figures dropped sharply when the FBI put the dice game out of business. When the dice game was running, one official received $750 per week, the chief $100 and a few captains, lieutenants and detectives lesser amounts.[33]

The Knapp Commission (established in May 1970 to investigate police corruption in New York City) indicates that in the five plainclothes divisions they investigated, plainclothesmen took large amounts of money from gambling establishments for "protection." "Plainclothesmen, participating in what is known in police parlance as a 'pad', collected regular bi-weekly or monthly payments amounting to as much as $3,500 from each of the gambling establishments in the area under their jurisdiction and divided it into equal shares. The monthly share per man (called the 'nut') ranged from $300 and $400 in midtown Manhattan to $1,500 in Harlem."[34] Policemen have developed ingenious schemes for getting money from organized crime. William White in his classic sociological study of Italians in Boston describes the following racket promulgated by policemen. In certain areas of the town, "there are a number of policemen who learn to recognize racketeers and stop them to demand protection money. An agent who covers a lot of territory in soliciting his numbers would have the same difficulty. His boss cannot pay off all the policemen with whom each agent might come in contact."[35] The goal is to pay off the policemen well enough so that they can convince their colleagues to stay away from one another's rackets. White writes, "In Cornerville, it is well established that one policeman does not interfere with the graft of another. In other sections, I am told, these financial and personal relations have not been worked out so systematically. Racketeers must still deal with the problem of the avaricious officer who will not abide by the rules of the business."[36]

There are other kinds of payoffs to the police which are not necessarily part of the recurring costs of doing business. In the tapes made in the bugging of Raymond P. Patriarca's establishment, we hear that a criminal must pay off authorities because there is a witness to a gangland murder. "While . . . (Mr. X) was given another order to kill the murderer, he was observed by a witness. Later, on another job, probably murder, he was picked up and identified by the witness in the first murder. A payoff of $5,000 was necessary to 'square the rap away.' [This payoff] was furnished to a Lt. Dunn (ph) for this purpose and the charge was dropped. The individual was released and the following day he was also murdered."[37]

Many of the activities of organized criminal groups call for large numbers of participants, and this cuts into the profits of organized criminals. In gambling and loan-sharking, for instance, there are a good number of individuals involved such as collectors, numbers runners, bankers, and lay-off bettors. In describing gambling activities, Donald Cressey suggests that "there are at least six levels of operating personnel in such enterprises, and each of these levels except the lowest one is occupied by persons with a corresponding status in the 'family' structure of Cosa Nostra."[38]

The social services provided by organized crime, such as bail, lawyers, and retirement income, can cost an organization a good deal of money. Organized criminals hire some of the finest legal and accounting personnel, and their services do not come cheaply. For instance, in the Patriarca tapes, "Anguilo stated that he had contacted attorney Francis D'Mento, a former assistant United States attorney, and requested him to defend him. D'Mento asked for $25,000 plus an additional $5,000 in the event it went to the Supreme Court. Anguilo refused but subsequently agreed on a fee of $10,000 plus $5,000 in the event the case went to the Supreme Court."[39] Sam Giancana hired six lawyers in his attempt to keep the FBI from harassing him. Legal services do not come cheaply.[40]

Another class of expenses worth mentioning involves extraordinary business losses rather than day-to-day expenditures. Organized crime has good times and bad times just like any other business. For instance, many enterprises owned by organized criminals are made worthless by passing of new laws or enforcement of existing laws. In speaking about "Wincanton," John Gardiner suggests that a new government took office and that

> within six weeks after taking office, Craig and District Attorney Henry Weise had raided enough of Stern's gambling parlors and had seized enough of Braun's slot machines to convince both men that this was over—for four years at least. The Internal Revenue Service was able to convict Braun and Stern's nephew, Dave Fineman, on tax evasion charges; both were sent to jail. From 1952 to 1955, it was still possible to place a bet or find a girl. But you had to know someone to do it and no one was getting very rich in the process.[41]

Hank Messick is very much enamored with the genius of Meyer Lansky, the so-called financial wizard of organized crime. Even though Messick tries to de-emphasize Lansky's failures and turn them into victories, the reader is still aware that Lansky is not always on the winning side. For instance, the "coordinated war on organized crime launched by Bob Kennedy meant the end of wide-open gambling in such remaining stateside centers as Newport, Ky., and Hot Springs, Ark. Lansky's enterprises in Cuba came to even a more swift and abrupt end. Yet the end came more abruptly than anyone anticipated, and Lansky flew out of Cuba on Batista's heels. . . . While he had not written Cuba off as a loss in view of Castro's promises, he began immediately to plot his next move."[42] Thus Meyer Lansky, a wealthy and successful entrepreneur, suffers his business reversals.

Organized criminal occupations are very sensitive to the vicissitudes of the economy. Wars, depressions, and recessions have significant impact on organized crime. For instance, Joe Valachi suggests the numbers are good only when times are bad. "It's poor people who play the numbers, and if you want the truth, most of them play because they are desperate for money and they don't have no other way to get it."[43] With respect to gambling in the Carribean and in the clubs of London, recessions or depressions have the opposite effect and business decreases when they occur.

Organized criminals suffer a good number of losses in their routine businesses operations irrespective of interference by legitimate governments or variable economic cycles. In the airtels, it is suggested that many individuals have shares in the Berkshire Downs Racetrack. "On 10-27-64, John Baborian and Patriarca discussed Berkshire Downs Racetrack. This track lost $140,000 last year and Baborian requested Patriarca's intervention with Lou Smith, owner of Rockingham Racetrack, Salem, N. H., and the Green Mountain Racetrack in Vermont. The reason was to make sure that Smith would not request the same dates at Green Mountain Racetrack as those requested by Berkshire Downs Racetrack."[44] There are many other examples of day-to-day losses: loss is endured when stolen merchandise cannot be fenced; losses are endured in the numbers racket when certain numbers which are heavily bet upon continue to win. Unlike legitimate businesses, one can not take out insurance against loss in illegitimate businesses.

Personal expenditures also cut down on the accumulation of capital available as savings or for investment. Organized criminals fall prey to the same vices which they provide for their customers. In other words, they gamble, they drink, they have expensive hobbies, they travel, and they keep women. Sometimes organized criminals win at gambling and other times they lose. For instance, Valachi relates that

> now the word gets around among the boys that Joe Cago—meaning me—is doing okay at the track, and one day Tony Bender calls me and says to meet him that night at Duke's in New Jersey. . . . It don't take no genius to figure out what *Mr.* Bender wants. Tony was a real sucker with the horses. If my grandmother told Tony about some horse in the sixth race the only sure thing is that Tony would bet on the horse. A lot of mob guys are like that. We're supposed to be so tough and smart, and they act like the biggest squares in the world when they get a tip—it don't matter from where—on a race.[45]

Nor do gambling losses affect only people on the lower echelons. "Sam [de Cavalcante] and Frank Majuri [underboss of the family] informed Lou Larasso [a *capo* in the family] that they had discovered that he was doing some heavy betting at the Yonkers Racetrack.

They told him to cut it out."[46] Hobbies can also turn out to be expensive, as Valachi learned when he undertook the costs of owning three racehorses.[47] Travel, either for personal or business purposes, takes up a good deal of money of organized criminals. We find, for instance, that Sam de Cavalcante made several trips during the year to Florida and Las Vegas.[48]

There is one strong incentive for savings among organized criminals and this is a byproduct of pressures from the Internal Revenue Service to balance reported income with expenditures. Many IRS indictments have been handed down on individuals who obviously spend more than they have been taking in. Expenditures on horses, real property, and other tangible assets must be kept down; thus we find, for example, many organized criminals living in modest upper and middle class homes. If criminals are forced to live modest lives by the Internal Revenue Service, then, like the early Protestants, they have more to spend.

Technical problems must be raised before completing the discussion of the assets and profits of organized criminals and their organizations. Do we consider as organized criminals six thousand "card-carrying" Cosa Nostra members when we estimate income, or do we include them and all of the people they associate with? Is the income of a former bootlegger to be included in estimates? I would suggest that future estimates be made in line with the criteria listed in Chapter 1, and be broken down in several categories. A lump sum estimate for all activities or one activity for all of organized crime conveys the erroneous impression of a monolithic organization with a central accounting office as well as making no useful distinctions as to membership in the organizations. We would want to know the relative wealth of retirees, recruits, and professionals as well as how much a society of "card-carrying" members makes compared with a matrix of narcotics dealers or gamblers.

Organized Crime as a Political System

Organized criminal societies and matrices will be analyzed in the same way social scientists investigate the internal structure of any group, whether it is a political party, trade union, professional association, or radical student group. Behavior is governed by formal rules or informal norms, institutions are set up, and the processes are at work through which power is allocated. Knowledge of the internal power configurations of organized crime tells us what kind of a threat or influence organized crime is on the political structures of this country. The Task Force on Organized Crime described organized crime as monolithic, totalitarian, and out to seize the reins of legitimate government.[49] It will be determined here if actual influence relationships are far more complex than the images the task force's analysis conjures up, and in fact bear only a passing resemblance to them. First, intra-group ("family") relationships will be explored to see how internal control of members is attained. Is the boss all-powerful? Does he rely primarily on violence to maintain his position and hold the group together? Does the family resemble a totalitarian organization? Second, the relationships between various criminal societies and matrices in American society will be discussed. Is there one monolithic organization? Are organized criminals out to destroy American government?

Intra-family Relationships

Many analysts begin their definition of a political unit or state by suggesting the unit has a monopoly of force at its disposal. Talcott Parsons rightfully says that most states prefer not to use force to promote their decisions. Force is somewhat akin to gold bullion in the foreign trade between nations.[50] It is there to back up transactions, but is rarely used. In organized crime, force is one of many factors that lead to organizational cohesion and discipline. Any matrix or society which is pushed to utilize force in every situation is in a state of instability and perhaps insurrection. The following incident exemplifies the stereotyped image of organized crime in which every relationship stems from the barrel of a gun and the idiosyncratic whims of the leaders. Dutch Schultz, a notorious gangster in the 1930s, got into an argument with one of his lieutenants, Jules Martin.

> He had his face stuck out in front of him, arguing with his boss in that loud, blustering voice of his, and Schultz was up close to him, blustering too.

Schultz pulled out a gun tucked inside his pants.

> All in the same quick motion he swung it up, stuck it in Jules Martin's mouth and pulled the trigger. It was as simple and undramatic as that—just one quick motion of the hand. . . . Jules Martin didn't even have time to look surprised.[51]

Witnesses to this event all agreed this was manifestation of Schultz's insanity. Such random, unsystematic, non-functional violence is the exception rather than the rule. Violence, when applied, is carefully thought out and rationalized in terms of the group goals. Also, violence is a double-edged sword and a great equalizer. It is available to subordinates as well as superordinates. Consider, for instance, the executions of the two "bosses of all bosses," Masseria and Maranzano, by subordinates, and the shootings of Joe Colombo, Albert Anastasia, and Dutch Schultz, all purported heads of criminal societies, as examples of the equalizing effects of violence.

If organized crime is to survive, means of control other than force must be at work to bind the organization together. Force can be used as a threat to maintain internal cohesion and external position, but it cannot be used in every situation or it would prove costly. In *Sam the Plumber* we have an example of a threat used to gain compliance coupled with a desire to avoid violence. "Sam told Bobby a debtor was beginning to test his patience, and he thought it might prove necessary to send Frank Cochiarro or Corky (Vastola) to see the delinquent. Sam suggested they might up payments by shooting a few blanks at the debtor. Bobby said that Carmine had already swatted him around, trying to collect, but that Carmine was not skilled at this work and did not get any money. Bobby was afraid that Carmine might end up killing the debtor."[52]

In popular lore or fiction, the awesome power of organized criminals is emphasized. For instance, in *The Godfather*, one gets the feeling that the godfather can do virtually anything he pleases. This is best illustrated when the godfather arranges to have the head severed from the race horse owned by a famous Hollywood producer, and to have the horse's head placed in the producer's bed.[53] However, it is understood by men in leadership positions, whether they are the dons of organized crime, the heads of corporations, or the president of the United States, the use of the power of persuasion is preferable to continual utilization of force, because force can be costly in terms of resources. An interesting example of this is in the attempted coverup of the deeds of Murder Incorporated in the late thirties and early forties. After Lefty Buchalter (a purported Murder Incorporated chief) was indicted, there was some indication that a purge was ordered so that nobody would be left to talk about the murders. After a while it became a bit too costly for organized crime to clear Buchalter by killing all possible witnesses for the prosecution. Violence abated and Buchalter finally went to the electric chair. Earlier Dutch Schultz, a New York racketeer, decided that Thomas E. Dewey must be killed. His friends and acquaintances in organized crime debated the question and decided that Dewey must not be killed, because the risks of reprisal by enforcement agencies would be too great. Schultz went ahead with his plans to kill Dewey, and for his disobedience, among other reasons, he was murdered.[54] Perhaps this idea of the economy of force is best exemplified by an example that turns upside down the fictional view of an organized criminal. Larry Wolfson, Sam de Cavalcante's partner in the plumbing business, tends to go to extremes in using violence. Sam, the head of a Cosa Nostra family, suggests to him that he curtail his violence. "Well, I won't go to extremes unless it's necessary," Larry said, perhaps recalling Sam's warning to lay off the rough stuff.[55]

Violence is institutionalized in the process of being kept to a minimum. Gilbert Geis indicates "violence is not random and sporadic. Rather the violence of organized crime is usually inexorable, stark and businesslike, an enterprise deriving its rationale from the exigencies of the immediate situation." He further suggests that "organized crime represents a system of institutionalized violence."[56] There are informal rules for the employment of violence; one, for instance, is what organized criminals call the "no-hands rule."[57] In speaking of rules, Joe Valachi says: "The most important one is that you can't put your hands in anger on another member. This is to keep one thing from leading to another."[58] As in the case of other secret organizations, violence, with few exceptions, is kept out of family business. In a Senate investigation into the Ku Klux Klan in 1871, the oath of initiation was disclosed. Rule 4 is "Female friends, widows, and their households, shall be the special objects of our regard and protection," a hint that no member should do violence to them.[59]

There are other informal norms involving the use of violence. One is to keep outsiders out of the organized crime disputes. Another concerning violence seems to be the idea of "keeping cool." We see a working example of both of these norms in the interactions of the de Cavalcante family. Sam's lieutenant, Joe Sferra, had acted imprudently in several situations, and Sam had been thinking of taking his title away from him. When called into account for his activities, Joe refused to tell Sam how he broke his leg. Withholding information from the boss is a sin. But the greater sin was the incident Sferra was involved in, and explained why he was willing to incur the costs of withholding information. Joe Sferra was driving his daughter and three other girls home from school. He cut off the driver of another car and an argument ensued. " 'Joe berates the kid and words are exchanged until Joe pushes the kid. The kid went after him like a tiger and pushed Joe off his period. When he fell he broke his leg. Is this any way for an *amico nos* and a *caporegime* to act?' 'No,' Louis said."[60] Violence should be minimized, and used in an intelligent way consonant with the goals of the organization. Violence is even institutionalized between organization members and "clients":

> Bobby told Sam (de Cavalcante) that Bernie Firth and Frank Cochiarro were trying to build themselves a reputation as 'tough guys' and had given a builder named Silverman a beating, and then went around bragging about it. Silverman, when he heard they were bragging, was infuriated; he said he had taken the beating in good grace and not gone to the cops, but was damned if he would let them brag about it and was about to go out looking for them with a pistol until he was dissuaded by other mob characters. Bobby feared that Frank and Bernie would get them all in trouble by acting in this high-handed manner.[61]

As Gilbert Geis states, "Today, there is some consensus that violence in the ranks of organized crime is diminishing."[62] When violence was much more in vogue, there are indications that it was more often than not dysfunctional for the stability and prosperity of organized criminals and their organizations. For instance, in Italy, where honor and respect were of overriding importance, many individuals in the organizations were killed or forced to go underground and curtail their economic activities. In the past in the United States, if there were a breach of etiquette or honor, the individual might have gotten killed. Today these matters are settled more subtly. Sam de Cavalcante became very upset when a member of the Black Muslims beat the son of a Cosa Nostra member, Frank Cochiarro. Frank tells his underboss, Frank Majuri, that he has "conferred with Carlo Gambino [a New York family head] about this case. Gambino said that while a Cosa Nostra member may demand satisfaction in such a matter, it may be denied if there is any danger that such action will destroy *bogarta* [family]. Gambino recommended that any retaliatory measure be delayed for from two to three months."[63] Violence is not indiscriminate and loyalty to the organization now may play a greater role than matters of personal honor. Individuals cannot indiscriminately avenge their honor at the expense of the organization.

Besides force, there are other cements binding the organization together. For example, organized crime is perceived by its members as a legitimate operation. Crime is an accepted way of life in certain sub-cultures and criminals even serve as role models for individuals. In the Illinois Crime Survey of 1929, "when a youthful criminal with a long history of offenses from earliest boyhood was asked his opinion about the causes of his own criminality, he was baffled at first. But later he came out with the answer, 'Who around here hasn't a record?' "[64] The report also suggested, "It is not until the gangster comes in contact with persons outside the underworld that he gets first sense of the necessity of justifying his behavior."[65]

In comparing himself with others in society, such as politicians, the criminal may even see himself as morally superior. Al Capone said, "There is one thing worse than a crook and that is a crooked man in a political job. A man that pretends he is enforcing the law and is really taking 'dough' out of someone breaking it, even a self-respecting hood hasn't any use for that kind of fellow. He buys them like he would any other article necessary for aid, but he hates them with his heart."[66] Besides perceiving organized crime as morally acceptable by those in his circles, the participant also sees it as a profitable venture and a way to step up from relative poverty. Given the incomes that some criminals make, in contradistinction to their education, one can measure them in terms of material values so prevalent in our society as successes.

The dispensing of favors (a reciprocity among members) leads to a great deal of organizational unity. Many commentators have noted the importance of friendships and reciprocity in dealings of organized crime. "There is a drift to the mercenary yet the feudal political system interlocks with the gangs which are organized on a feudal basis, organized upon loyalties, friendships and dependability."[67] Finally, family relationships bind the organizations. Frederic Sondern in *The Brotherhood of Evil* does a good job in detailing the intermarriages and extended families in organized criminal groups.[68] According to Ianni, in the family he studied, kinship is an extremely important variable and even determines one's position in the power structure of a family. "There is no question, however, that as far as the Lupullo family is concerned membership in the organizational hierarchy is determined by blood and marriage and is not an option for outsiders."[69] One is led to conclude that along with force many other norms and sanctions make for a cohesive organization. This is not to deny that the threat of violence isn't important or doesn't add cohesion to the organization, but the feeling that organized crime is a proper and profitable occupation, as well as strong friendship and family ties, effectively add to organizational cohesion. No organization can endure indefinitely on the threat of violence alone.

Most analysts agree that the norms of organized crime are unwritten, but several individuals have been fairly successful in deciphering them. Donald R. Cressey looks at the society of prisoners and infers norms from their behavior which he feels must be exhibited by organized criminals. Don't cheat, be a "stand-up guy," be silent in the face of opposition—these express some of the norms which govern prisoners and hence organized criminals.[70] Ralph Salerno extrapolates the norms from the behavior of members of actual organizations and many of the norms he finds in force are very similar to those listed by Cressey.[71] Ianni finds in his study that there are three basic components to the Lupullo family code of conduct: loyalty to the family, acting like a man (being a stand-up guy), and secrecy.[72]

A rather excellent discussion of norms governing the behavior of organized criminals is in the testimony of Joe Valachi. Valachi suggests that there were two main rules: keep the initiation process secret, and make sure you do not violate the family relationship of a Cosa Nostra member. There is a good deal of evidence that people are still "made" members of the organization. In the FBI tape placed in Raymond Patriarca's place of business, we find out that "Patriarca is going to New York with Henry Tameleo and they are going to make Nick or Chick a member of the 'family' Wednesday night, 9/25/63, at the Roma. The reason they are going to make Nick on Wednesday night is 'in case they want to make peace Thursday.' "[73] The following day "Patriarca instructed Tameleo to go to Boston and tell Jerry Anguilo what is going on and the commission has okayed the making of this kid (Nick)."[74] In reminiscing about the past, Sam de Cavalcante also talks about initiation. "Now the conversation turned to their organization and what it meant. Tony Boiardo said to Sam, 'My father said you must be made 25 to 30 years ago.' 'No,' Sam replied. 'Twenty years. About the same time as you.' "[75] Certain rules, although unwritten, are understood: There is an initiation ceremony and few people have broken the rule of silence to talk about the ceremony.

The norms that have been ascribed to criminal societies are remarkably similar to one another. Many of the elements, rituals, reciprocity, and secrecy are part and parcel of any secret society. What has been neglected in discussions of these norms are the structural dilemmas built into them. In a close examination of the norms Ianni ascribes to the Lupullo family we will see organizational problems that come from adherence to them.

Loyalty to the extended family as opposed to the nuclear family or individual lineage is used to differentiate the criminal group from all others. "The basic rule of loyalty to the family over all else and the subsidiary rules which define the way to use the rule to one's best advantage give the family a group solidarity against anyone or anything outside the family."[76] Needless to say, this leads to organizational loyalty and cohesion, strengthening and reinforcing common bonds while breaking and keeping severed ties with outside groups. However, this effectively discourages a superordinate organization that could guide the destinies of several families and allow them to pool their resources in a concerted effort. It effectively limits recruitment possibilities, and stresses ascribed (as opposed to achievement-oriented) criteria for inclusion in the group. Expansion and growth of the organization is curbed by the requisites of loyalty, for expansion may mean a loss of solidarity and control.

Ianni also suggests that to act like a man, "to have balls," is a norm in the Lupullo family.[77] Ianni, Salerno, and Cressey all agree that the phrases "stand-up guy" or "being a man" are important in defining the way a member of the organization should act. Each has slightly different characteristics that define a stand-up guy. Salerno says "A 'stand-up guy' is by definition a man who lives by the rules and, if necessary, will die for them. He keeps his mouth shut to the police, he puts the organization ahead of himself, he respects the families of others."[78] Cressey suggests that a stand-up guy "shows courage and heart." He does not whine or complain in the face of adversity, including punishment.[79] Ianni sees the stand-up guy as being willing to accept decisions and also suggests that "the behavior involved is similar to the Chinese or Oriental concept of 'face.' "[80] One can lose his reputation as a stand-up guy if he ceases to exhibit such behavior or if outsiders perceive him as no longer a stand-up guy. The similar strand that runs through all of these definitions is the self-consciousness among organized criminals about the importance of being perceived by peers and others as a right guy. Reputations can rise and fall rather quickly and may be dependent on single events.

The norm of being a stand-up guy is useful to organizations, for it forces individuals, regardless of the respective formal roles they play in the organization, to continually exemplify standards of behavior useful to organized criminal groups. Those who do not hold to such behavior lose their positions in the organization. On the negative side, the need to save face and thoughts about individual honor can interefere in negotiations with others and lead to unnecessary conflict. This was even truer in the days when saving face and honor superceded notions about profit in organized crime. When role and respect are not synonymous in an organization, instability is usually the rule. Those in power are continually in danger of losing their position through internal revolt.

All of the authors include secrecy as a necessary norm in organized criminal groups. Ianni explains that this means keeping one's distance from outsiders and from other families.[81] It was mentioned previously that this differentiation is necessary, yet it inhibits growth of the organization and does nothing to facilitate communication. Ianni also suggests that "secrecy serves as a means of establishing and maintaining dominance and social distance not only between family members and nonmembers but within the family as well. Some secrets are more secret than others, and are shared by only some members of the group."[82] This is an important insight, one that is neglected even by Simmel in his treatment of secret societies. It allows for keeping secrets among those who have (in the army's terms) a "need to know." At the same time, however, such secrecy breeds hostility and suspicion among members of the organization. Even on university faculties when affinity groups (individuals who get together to share information on a continuing basis along lines of mutual interest, not in terms of formal positions) form, mistrust begins to build and overall communication breaks down. In organized crime, where the stakes are higher than in academia, a justifiable paranoia begins to build up. Members of the organization suffer a tremendous psychological toll, not because of fear from the law, but from each other. One only has to follow the intrigue in *The Valachi Papers* to understand this problem. Kinship does not cut down on intrigue appreciably and if one is not assured on this point, one has only to read about the history of monarchies, or listen to the jokes about mothers-in-law.

From the introductory discussion on the limitations of force, it is obvious that some deviation from the norms does occur and when individuals are caught, punishment for deviation is not necessarily death. Just as in foreign policy, force is not effective in all instances. The United States may be able to destroy any small power on the globe, but it does not always get its way in foreign affairs. The same process takes place in organized crime; one does not destroy another organization or individual just because one has the physical means to do so. Even if there is the possibility of a death sentence, individuals do take risks and break the rules. For instance, Joe Valachi said that when he described the giving of the oath that he was a dead man; he was risking his life to violate a particular rule. In most situations, organized criminals know the death penalty is too costly to be used on every occasion. There are examples of many lesser penalties meted out. When Joe Sferra, a *caporegime* in Sam's family, has committed a great number of indiscretions, Sam suggests "I am throwing Joe Sferra out. Out of the union and no more *caporegime*. He asked for it."[83] He will still be a member of the organization; demotion, not death, is his punishment. Ralph Salerno gives another illustration of punishment other than death. A *capo* in Vito Genovese's family commits a good number of indiscretions, one of which is punching an FBI man at his brother's funeral. He is also demoted rather than expelled from the organization or killed.[84]

If the norms of the organization are to be effectively enforced, information in the hands of the leaders (as in totalitarian organizations) must be complete. The heads of the organization must be, in that sense, "big brother" to the rest of the organization. Again we look to Sam de Cavalcante's organization and find that very often information is concealed from the boss. "If they can be concealed from police, they can also be concealed at least for a while, from the boss. And of course, such concealment is desirable, for the bosses are liable to demand a cut for any activity he hears about."[85] In another conversation, Zeigler, the editor of *Sam the Plumber*, says that "he, Sam, said again, as he has said so many times before and will say so many times in the future, that he wants to know everything that everyone is doing."[86] Finally, one can more easily tolerate the money maker who violates the political rule than one can tolerate the individual who is not making money for the organization. One of the sins of Joe Sferra, besides creating incidents and acting in a reckless manner, was that he was not performing his economic duties as convincingly as possible. It appears then that there are norms in force in criminal organizations but there are many violations of these norms and many of these violations go unpunished.

Since the thrust of the *Task Force Report* is that criminal organizations are totalitarian, one would expect to see a rigid hierarchy of rank, one which describes the actual distribution of influence in the organization. In the *Task Force Report*, a chart designates a chain of command from head of the family, to underboss, to lieutenants, to soldiers. The titles given to individuals like *caporegime*, buttonman, and *consiglieri* are used by organized criminals, and as a result we do not have to infer their existence from other organizations as Donald Cressey does when he observes these roles played in prison populations and assumes that these exist as formal positions in organized criminal groups.[87] As when looking at any other table of organization, the reader may get the feeling that here there is a formal, hierarchial distribution of influence. However, both the *Task Force Report* chart and Cressey's propensity to assume that a role always represents a formal position may be misleading. In most organizations, if a person holds a formal position we expect him to manifest influence in accordance with his position. However, in organized crime, as mentioned previously, position and respect are not one and the same thing, and respect does not automatically accord to position.

The designation of formal positions and titles to criminal groups was grafted onto an already existing organizational structure. According to Valachi, long after families were in existence, Salvatore Maranzano modeled the organizational structure along Roman lines, not after existing lines of authority in the family. Valachi recalled, "I didn't know until later that he [Maranzano] was a nut about Julius Caesar and even had a room in the house full of nothing but books about him. That's where he got the idea for the new organization. . . . Each Family would have a boss and an under-boss. Beneath them there would also be lieutenants or *caporegimes*."[88]

One would suspect that familial and friendship patterns that long existed would negate or supercede the formal title given to an individual. If he holds a measure of influence he does so out of respect, not out of a member's respect for a formal title or position. Ianni has found the formal roles to be insignificant in the family he researched:

> These two roles, Joe as boss and Charley in a role which seems to combine elements of the *sottocapo* and *consiglieri* described by

FIGURE 1: AN ORGANIZED CRIME FAMILY

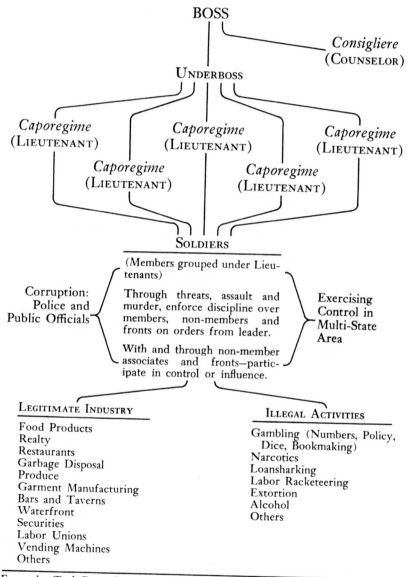

From the *Task Force Report: Organized Crime* (Washington, D.C.: Government Printing Office, 1967).

experts as hierarchical roles in *Cosa Nostra*, and a little of the buffer role described by Cressey, are the only offices we observed (although we found a number of other roles). Some other members of the family do command more authority than the rest, but it appears to us that these differentials develop not from office, but rather through operation of the three ranking rules (loyalty, stand-up guy and secrecy) we described earlier.[89]

In *Street Corner Society*, Whyte suggests that the best way to view the authority structure in Italian street corner groups is by their performance at a bowling match (the leaders always seem to win and the followers always manage to lose) rather than by formal positions they hold in an organization.[90]

The disparity between position and respect has often led to internal revolt in organized criminal groups. Those in positions of authority often lose favor and their positions are not guaranteed by any constitutional authority or legitimacy. Indications are that some of the current chieftains in organized crime do not have as much respect as the older members and their power is not as great. All of these instances involve a disparity between position and respect. There is constant possibility of turmoil caused by the disparity between position and respect, and it makes the leaders wary and at times almost paranoid about their positions. It also makes them attentive to the views of their members. One would not claim that organized crime is a guided democracy, but certainly the views of the members by necessity must be taken into consideration.

Not only is position not identical to respect, but there are situations and contexts in which the formal structure may increase and decrease in importance. Studies of power in other contexts will show this. For instance, in studying power in local communities, analysts find that formal governmental relationships are most important when informal structures are not invoked. Formal structure becomes most important in high-risk operations. Insulation through hierarchy tends to be much more important than in low-risk operations. In case of murder, for example, the boss always goes through a chain of command to insure his insulation. In less risky operations, it appears that various people run to the bosses directly to do business.

Other factors seem to indicate that position is not all-important in organized criminal matrices and societies. The network of communications is very informal and a sociogram of their conversations would not necessarily point to individuals holding formal leadership positions as the center of communications. Sam de Cavalcante speaks most often with Larry Wolfson, his partner in the plumbing business, and Bobby Basile, his non-member relative. He deals directly with soldiers and communicates infrequently with his *caporegimes.* Positions also seem to reflect little of the relationships that exist between individuals in economic activities. Sam, for instance, has a non-member for a business partner, and is dealing with many soldiers directly in economic activities.[91]

In sum, it appears that a description of influence in organized crime as attached to formal positions hierarchially organized does not adequately reflect the actual dispersion of influence in these groups. For example, "Italian geographers" always assume that those paid respect at weddings and funerals hold some formal title in the organization, whereas these gatherings often serve the function of testing, irrespective of formal position, one's own status *vis-à-vis* others in the organization. Such rituals at family gatherings is often a recognition by criminals that formal position may not be of overriding importance in their organization.

It may be, however, that if families grow larger, formal positions will become more important. Or, as business relationships become more complex, if criminal organizations pattern themselves after corporate entities, formal position may become synonymous with power. This, of course, poses a dilemma for the organizations because much would be lost in terms of loyalty and even efficiency if formal roles become more important, and bureaucracy instead of familism becomes the rule of the day.

In sum, it appears that the internal structure of criminal groups does not follow a formal hierarchical pattern. A description of criminal groups as totalitarian is inadequate, for these groups resemble the structure of clans and other secret societies, not the systematic apparatus we associate with totalitarian regimes. Furthermore, violence is not the only means of social control, leaders do not have complete control of information, the formal hierarchy is often irrelevant, and the leaders do not have a monopoly of force. For all of the reasons stated, it may not be a particularly desirable organization to belong to from our perspective, but totalitarian is the wrong label to affix to it.

Inter-family Relationships

In this section the structural arrangements governing organized criminal groups will be explored, especially the nature of the ruling group or groups, the conflict between economic and political organization, and the nature of territory in organized crime. Emphasis will be on the structural dilemmas posed by these arrangements.

Three analysts, Hank Messick, Donald Cressey, and Gordon Hawkins, have interesting theories about the nature of the ruling group or groups in organized crime. Each has something to teach us, even though their views often contradict one another, and from them a clearer description of inter-group relationships will emerge.

Hank Messick in *Lansky* states there is a confederation of crime, but the composition of the confederation is different than the Mafia or the Cosa Nostra; there is a "national crime syndicate" made up of both Italians and non-Italians that dominates organized crime today. "Ironically, the National Crime Syndicate has benefited by the emphasis on La Cosa Nostra. The real leaders of crime have remained hidden while the nation's law enforcement agencies have chased minor punks."[92] The first inclination when faced with this hypothesis is to wish it away for it complicates a hitherto uncomplicated picture of organized crime as Italian crime. Donald R. Cressey indicates that Messick took his thesis from a book by Turkus and Feder called *Murder Inc.* "Messick's information about the 'national association' seems to have come from the book by Turkus who reports that in 1934, at a meeting in a New York hotel, an Italian leader from Chicago proposed to leaders of both Italian and non-Italian groups that they all make up one 'big outfit' or 'one big combination.' " Cressey says that perhaps the meetings took place, but "it is conceivable, however, that what Turkus calls 'a board or panel' is what today is called 'the Commission,' and that what he calls 'the confederacy' is today called 'Cosa Nostra.' "[93] Cressey goes on to say that since 1934, all high-level "arbitration" meetings uncovered by enforcement agents were attended by Italians only. Non-Italians are represented on the commission by Italians, and his proof is that non-Italians have not attended gangland conferences in recent years.

Messick believes the interaction of high-ranking organized criminals indicates an unreported form of superordinate organization. Meyer Lansky, according to Messick, regularly interacts with major criminals and has had a hand in every major action that has occurred in organized crime. "He has been the key man in almost every situation involving other top hoods, and he has pulled the strings in every important move made by the National Crime Syndicate."[94]

122

Messick deduces from mob interactions that Lansky holds formal power in organized crime. For instance, he says that "from the activities of the Bugs and Meyer [Lansky] Mob eventually developed Murder, Inc."[95] However, nowhere in Turkus and Feder's book, *Murder Inc.*, is there any indication of formal or informal ties between the two organizations. If Messick meant to suggest that one group consciously or unconsciously copied the style of operation of the other gang, he did not say so. If this were the case, the implications would be different; Lansky might be a style setter, not a leader, in Murder Incorporated. Murder Incorporated might be a carbon copy, but not a satellite, as Messick implies. Often Lansky does not attend important gangland meetings, but his emissaries are there. We have Messick's word (with no hint of how he gathered evidence) that Lansky's views are made known through others. Perhaps this is true and Messick must protect his sources, but the reader is left far from satisfied.

Messick does not convince this reader or himself that there is a national crime syndicate or that Lansky is the boss. His own ambiguity on the questions seeps through when he is describing the relationship between Lansky and organized crime. "While there is, unhappily, no such thing as Mr. Big controlling all crime, Lansky has been for years the Chairman of the Board. Crime is too large, too sophisticated for a single man to control, but more than anyone else, Lansky has shaped and guided it."[96]

Messick is trying to write history around one individual, Lansky, and for the most part he tends to exaggerate Lansky's role in organized crime, much as the biographies of Caesar, Napoleon, or any other important historical figure overemphasize the importance of their main character. For instance, Messick becomes blind to obvious contradictions when he tries to describe Lansky in control of the situation. Luciano says to Lansky, "Take that crazy kid, Siegel, for instance. He worships you."[97] Then Messick sees Lansky later on scheming to move ahead as if guided by some foreordained plan. "The next step was obvious, and provided the basis for the formation of the Bugs and Meyer Mob."[98] The reader is puzzled as to why the "obvious" brains and leader of the outfit has his name come second in the designation of the group. There may be some explanation, such as the order of the names having been inverted by the police or by ignorant gangsters, but the real point is that such inconsistencies don't bother Messick.

Messick does manage to convey the impression that Lansky does know top Italian gangsters, that he has much interest in successful gambling establishments, and that he has considerable political connections. Even Messick remains unconvinced at times of a national confederation, but he has established the important role of a non-Italian in organized crime. This tends to confirm the notions of Turkus and Feder in *Murder, Inc.*, and to make sense of the Kefauver Committee hearings which found many non-Italians such as Longie Zwillman, Frank Erickson, and Owney Madden involved in important roles in organized crime.[99] His error may be the mistaking of a matrix of activity for a formal organizational structure. Although Messick tends to exaggerate his case, he does leave us with two interesting thoughts. First, non-Italians may play a significant role in organized crime and not just in subordinate positions. Throughout the book we have supported the position which suggests that identification of organized crime with Italian crime is a definitional trick. Even in New York City where much has been written about the "five families," independents exist. Nicholas Pileggi observes that

> It is, of course, unrealistic to think that all organized crime in New York is controlled by the Mafia. Independents are involved in everything from numbers to narcotics. They share boroughs, neighborhoods and crooked cops. In the South Bronx and parts of Brooklyn, there are the Jewish Schlitten brothers. In Bedford-Stuyvesant and Harlem there are independent Black bosses like Peter Mooney and Chick Evans. In the city's Puerto Rican and Spanish-speaking communities, Raymond Marquez has controlled the operations in upper Manhattan, the Bronx and Queens for years, taking it over from his father who had it before him. There are even non-Mafia Italians, such as Vincent (Jimmy Napp) Napoli, who is believed to run the single largest policy bank in the city.[100]

Second, Messick is accurately describing a matrix of activity that occurs in organized crime and takes in both Italians and non-Italians. Many people tend to see Italian societies as isolated forces, set apart from and rarely doing business with others, but Messick has adequately countered this notion. His shortcoming is to assume that this matrix of activity must represent a society when in fact these interactions may represent business transactions, peace talks, and attempted alliances between shifting coalitions of individuals.

Analysis of Cressey's thoughts on the subject are equally unsettling. He suggests that if non-Italians have influence, they are represented through Italians at meetings of organized criminals because no evidence of large-scale meetings of Italians and non-Italians has been discovered since 1934.[101] Non-Italians may be tolerated but not accepted as equals. These are plausible hypotheses, even though he gives no evidence other than his statement about meetings being dominated by Italians to suggest they are accurate. His problem seems to come from an inferential leap he makes: "For some reason, non-Italian groups are tolerated by an organization so strong and ruthless that it could within twenty-four hours dispose of all the non-Italian operators in the United States." They may be tolerated because they (1) have done favors for La Cosa Nostra; (2) have proper political connections; (3) are smart financiers, a hypothesis which Cressey suggests is dubious; (4) possess certain skills which could be used profitably by the organization.[102]

The hypothesis that these other groups could be disposed of within twenty-four hours is empirically false. Italian criminals were involved in a protracted war of extermination with Irish criminals in Boston. The transcripts in the de Cavalcante papers show an abject fear of blacks by the Italian population. In Detroit, as well as other cities, there are rival ethnic groups competing for power. Where actual fighting has taken place, there is no twenty-four-hour eradication of existing groups.

Cressey's statement also leaves the reader with a set of misleading assumptions about political power. In contrast to Cressey's notion, power is a reciprocal relationship and even the slave has some power over his master. Many books were written in the antebellum era to suggest how more work may be obtained from slaves who subtly resist work and feign obedience. Even if non-Italians could physically be removed in twenty-four hours because Italians have superior manpower and weaponry, it does not follow that in day-to-day transactions Italians could completely dominate all other ethnic groups. Even Ecuadorians can negotiate from a favorable position with the United States on fishing rights in spite of our overwhelming military strength. The exercise of power can be costly, even for a great nation. Knowledge of this increases the underdog's power.

In *The Honest Politician's Guide to Crime Control*, Gordon Hawkins suggests that organized crime is a myth perpetuated in much the same way and with much the same logic as arguments for the existence of God.[103] We create it because we need it. He cites evidence to support his claim that there is no national organizational structure. He makes the point that government witness Joseph Valachi's testimony before a congressional committee is fraught with discrepancies, and cites the discordant details of the meeting of criminal leaders in Apalachin, New York, as reported in newspaper accounts.

Despite his claim, there is evidence overlooked which refutes or at least weakens his arguments. For instance, the FBI has produced transcripts of eavesdropping in court which tell of the meetings and business of the ruling "commission."[104] Also, there are many names, places, and dates which recur in various investigations by law enforcement agents.[105] Finally, Gay Talese in his *Honor Thy Father* writes of commission business based on the evidence he gathered from long talks with the son of a purported commission member, Bill Bonanno.[106]

Hawkins's views are interesting, for they suggest the public's need to create conspiracies even where there might not be any. He had the courage to speak up when others were claiming a fully rationalized, national conspiracy. However, as was suggested, evidence has been turned up which indicates the existence of a commission as well as data suggesting frequent interaction between the New York families. The commission is made up of Italians from some of the larger cities in the United States, mainly those on the East Coast. Families may be represented through other families and votes at the commission are not given equal weight; it depends upon the prestige of the family and the family's political connections. The task force indicated that "according to current information, there are presently nine families represented, five from New York City and one each from Philadelphia, Buffalo, Detroit, and Chicago."[107]

The problem with setting forth this picture of the inter-group relationships is the same one which occurs when detailing the organization chart of the family to describe intra-family relationships. It conveys the impression that this is the picture organized criminals have of their organization, when in fact it is the reconstruction by the task force. The task force's picture is too neat and too pat. It downplays the importance of matrices of activities and the role of other ethnics in organized crime. The "family" does not mean the same thing to Italians everywhere. In Chicago, other ethnics joined in the outfit at an early juncture, while in other cities other ethnics couldn't break in. John M. Seidl in *Upon The Hip*, a superb doctoral thesis, describes the different forms and degrees of dominance Italian groups may have in cities. In New York he suggests that five families joined in an oligopoly to control criminal activities.[108] Detroit's underworld "is probably the most tightly organized and controlled in the United States."[109] It functions as a cartel and controls prices, yet some independents do operate in Detroit. According to Seidl, Italians do not predominate in Philadelphia and Cleveland: "Criminal organizations are ethnic in character and service specific neighborhoods and areas. In each city, the largest criminal organization is the Italian organization. In fact, the 'Italian' organizations are criminal cartels within the Italian areas of their respective cities—but only in those areas."[110] One of the biggest mistakes the analyst could make is to assume uniformity of criminal societies or matrices throughout the country.

My objections to organization charts and listings of merely Italian crime families have been articulated throughout the book. Here it is only necessary to state objections to their depiction of a commission. First, it meets infrequently, suggesting that it can not govern on many issues. Second, the shifting number of members on the commission may indicate the particular concerns the commission may presently be involved with. Those groups most intensely involved in a dispute may be asked to attend.

In conclusion, there is a commission made up of Italians and, as Messick suggests, there may even be an overriding organization called the national crime syndicate. However, if this syndicate exists as a formal, on-going institution, no one claims it is any stronger than a confederation. In addition, there are powerful non-Italian groups that cannot be eradicated, nor would it be in the best interests of Italians to do away with them. They are not merely represented in all their affairs by Italians at a council, but presumably have some independence of their own. Finally, and most importantly, no claim stronger than that of a confederation is made for either Italian or mixed groups.

My basic hypothesis is that a confederation by its very structure is limited in terms of the power it has to control its internal affairs and to influence, direct, and dominate events in a political and social system. Power in a confederation resides with the willing compliance of the constituent organizations. One of the first organized criminals who failed to realize this lesson was Salvatore Maranzano, the man who proclaimed himself to be the boss of all bosses. He tried to form an independent family or palace guard to control all of the other organized criminal families. Influence resided with and still resides with the families and did not gravitate to an executive or boss of all bosses. Maranzano was killed by a conspiracy of family heads.[111] Any attempt to form a strong federation with an enforcement arm with control over all of the families was doomed to failure for the base of power is the family.

In *The Godfather*, one of the memorable incidents occurs when Don Vito Corleone, a powerful family head, tries to stop the flow of narcotics in organized crime. A great deal of blood is spilled before the don goes to a meeting of the commission, and finally agrees to go along with the other families' decision to deal in narcotics.[112] The commission does no more than serve as a mediating board, not as an authoritative decision-maker. The families have already fought among themselves to decide whether traffic in narcotics is to be continued. More interesting is the actual sequence of the narcotics ban in organized crime. Frank Costello purportedly got families and their members to cease traffic in narcotics, and to do so, some families paid compensation to their members for withdrawing their participation in the traffic.[113] However, the ban by the bosses flew in the faces of the individual families' and family members' greed, and the agreement was broken. This is typical of the limits of the power of a confederation. It can guarantee compliance where there is an overwhelming consensus of the powerful members, but is powerless in the face of much opposition. Their function is less to provide leadership than to mediate and bargain.

The ban on narcotics deals illustrates the leaders' attempts to present a unified policy to the broader social system. What we want to look at now is how effectively a commission can mediate in disputes and policy questions which come from within the confines of a family. It appears that the commission cannot do much to settle inter-family disputes. Although the commission could have interfered in the Gallo-Profaci war (which took place between two factions of the same family), they chose not to. It appears to have been the policy of the commission to let them settle it between themselves. Ralph Salerno indicates that "with the wisdom of Solomons who were really most interested in protecting their own domains, the Commission finally ruled that the problem would have to be worked out as an intra-family dispute."[114] Their only real decision was that all of the other families were to stay out of the situation.

Even where the commission tries to intervene we may find defiance and nullification of their edicts. In the so-called Bonanno wars, the authority of Joe Bonanno to preside over his own family was questioned because of inter-family and intra-family norms he alledgedly violated. The commission tried to get Bonanno to testify on the dispute but he refused to comply, indicating it was an internal family matter.[115] The commission apparently did not like to take sides as a body for fear their authority and respect would be eroded if the wrong side won. The commission is willing and able to arbitrate some disputes. If there is a conflict between two bosses who are willing to let third parties settle the dispute, then the commission will operate. Very often, if members of two different families have disagreements, the bosses of the families and others will sit down and try to arbitrate the dispute. However, this is different than suggesting the commission has power in case of fundamental disagreements involving equals or the case of a majority against a powerful minority.

One function a confederation can serve is to keep peace among groups *vis-à-vis* outsiders, even if they cannot decide crucial issues or provide active leadership. There is much to show that the desire to stop costly wars provided the impetus for setting up cooperation among groups. Peace enhances the power of organized crime, for war does not bring economic benefits to any group and calls the police in upon them. Keeping the peace appears to strengthen criminal societies and matrices. However, the methods of maintaining the peace any also serve to weaken the organization. Since 1930, families have only been allowed to recruit members periodically and replace older members when vacancies become available. This has prevented any one family from becoming too powerful. It does prevent expansion of membership and causes them to rely on, or abdicate to others, income-producing activities in which they might like to engage. Hence, the goals of profit and growth conflict with the maintenance of stability within the organization, an important structural dilemma.

It is now clear how analysts can come up with a succession of people they claim are "Mr. Big." Anyone who comes into the public eye, either through a gang war, exposure of a commission meeting, or testimony before a congressional committee, becomes a candidate. It is also understandable how the largest organized crime family has put up the most candidates for office: Genovese, Luciano, and Costello. This is because power resides with the family.

Further, it was suggested that organized crime was at best a confederation. A confederation usually has its legislative body meet regularly and with all members present. In organized crime, the body of the whole rarely meets. Rather, many business affairs are settled by the interested parties with the help of a few intermediaries. The New York families may meet far more often to transact business than any national commission. It is better to talk about inter-group relationships in organized crime as a series of interlocking communications and alliances rather than as a confederation. Members of a confederation get together more than once every few years for a couple of days. Thus, the machinery for a confederation is there, but rarely utilized. This may explain the kinds of fluid relationships that exist between all organized criminal groups, Italian and non-Italian—interlocking alliances formed on the basis of common business concerns and often cemented by common ethnic bonds and marital ties. This may be why authorities have such trouble looking for those who govern; alliances are fluid, and conferences represent arbitration over disputes and not necessarily formal constitutional bodies.

Finally, although a confederation or a series of alliances may not lead to concerted action, or a takeover of government, this form of organization may be in some sense useful or functional for organized criminal groups. Operating under the pressure of harassment of law enforcement agencies, a confederation or series of alliances can run smoothly in the absence of a central leader. This is why organized criminal groups can survive even with a succession of "Mr. Bigs"—Capone, Luciano, Buchalter, Genovese, Costello—who die, get deported, or go to jail. The decentralization inherent in a confederation or alliances makes it easy to operate in the absence of formal meetings. For instance, the Apalachin meeting was not an interruption of a continuing congress in session, but evidently the kind of session which is generated periodically by special problems. Criminals get together more often to arbitrate disputes than to legislate. This also suggests another function of a series of alliances or a confederation. Each group can best deal with local problems which may be very different in one community than in another. Not only is decentralization a necessary fact of life in organized crime, but perhaps a functional one as well.

A major structural dilemma is caused by the increasing lack of coincidence between the economic and the political structure of organized crime, the conflict of matrices with societies. The organization follows a certain organizational arrangement for economic activities but internal political matters may follow different structural arrangements. The conflict between the two causes a great deal of aggravation and strain within organized crime as we can see by a look at historical events. Since the Castellamarese War and the Americanization of organized crime, profit may be increasingly significant to organized criminals, and power and respect have declined somewhat in terms of their importance. It is difficult to tell whether the relationships between economic and political arrangements have been increasing in the direction of the economic relationships, or whether the economic structures have always predominated. I suspect that from the very beginning when organized crime first took hold in this country, economic arrangements played an important role in organization.

An explanation can be provided for this lack of coincidence between economic and political organization, not in historical terms, but by stating it as an abstract proposition about economics and politics. The needs for capital, labor, and protection from government and other criminal groups have caused organized criminals to broaden the scope of their economic activities beyond the confines of the family. Thus the family, which may seem an ideal arrangement for social control, has become increasingly less descriptive of the pattern of economic relationships. There are a good number of economic alliances with members of one family and non-Italian individuals. Joe Valachi, in dialogue with Senator Javits, is describing some of Vito Genovese's economic activities:

> SENATOR JAVITS: As far as you know, is Vito Genovese still in Las Vegas gambling?
> MR. VALACHI: Yes.
> SENATOR JAVITS: What is his outfit there, do you know?
> MR. VALACHI: Anywhere Meyer Lansky is, Vito Genovese is."[116]

Sam de Cavalcante provides us with another illustration. Sam's partner in the plumbing business, Larry Wolfson, is kept somewhat aloof from illegal enterprises, but Sam is very willing to share the plumbing business with Larry even though it is of questionable legitimacy.[117] Ziegler, the editor of *Sam the Plumber*, suggests that "Jack Brennan, a close associate of Sam's (although not a Cosa Nostra member because of his non-Italian origin), came in and got some advice about what to do with his young son."[118] Close personal relationships between the two carry into business affairs.

There are economic alliances between members of different crime families, as well as economic alliances with non-members. In discussing the sanctions which should be put on the Bonanno family, the commission "decided that Bonanno was no longer a capo boss or commission member. They also put out the word that nobody is to have any business dealings or association with any members of the Bonanno group."[119] Elsewhere in the transcript, the FBI officer reports that Angelo Bruno of Philadelphia is one of the persons issuing franchises for various states.[120] He was talking about Bruno's issuance of franchises for juke boxes equipped with TV-type screens. Allegiance can often rest with those with whom you interact most frequently and who are your business partners, and they need not be members of the family.

One of the major reasons for conflict in the Profaci family was that in the beginning profits seemed to be split among family members on the basis of rank. The individuals in the organizations all had to pay tribute to the boss, and perhaps he did not redistribute this in an equitable manner. Nevertheless, individuals were all indebted to the boss and had to pay a certain amount of dues. There are some indications that dues, as opposed to giving the boss a percentage of your business, is looked upon as old-fashioned. "Long after other families had stopped collecting formal dues, [Joseph Profaci] continued to exact $25 a month from every member."[121] In *Sam the Plumber* we find that most of the other individuals split their profits with the boss on a percentage basis.[122] This means that there is a possible disparity between what might be called political rank or status in the family and economic wealth. This produces great strains if, for instance, a lieutenant would be wealthier than the boss himself, or if various soldiers have disproportionate wealth among themselves and want commensurate influence on family affairs.

Finally, there is a great diversification of family business. Ramsey Clark, for example, suggests in *Crime in America* that "diversification is important to organized crime."[123] There are many activities the criminal may enter and few organizational restraints keeping him from them. When one's business is risky, diversification is important to guarantee some modicum of income. If a person is not making money in his gambling enterprises, then he must rely on his other businesses, as in the case of Sam de Cavalcante, who supports himself from his plumbing business. He is not only in plumbing and unions, but he is even in the business of sponsoring a singer.[124] Typical of the diversity of mob businesses is the empire of Raymond Patriarca that Ed Reid describes in *The Grim Reapers.* In 1956 Patriarca went into the vending machine business. "He followed this up with juke boxes, cleaning-and-dyeing stores, linen services, auto agencies, drugstores, and garbage-collecting firms. He now controls numerous nightclubs and restaurants. . . . His mob owns cemeteries, dude ranches, a New Hampshire ski resort, and a country club north of Boston."[125] Except for trade in narcotics, there seem to be few restraints on members of organized crime who wish to develop new business. This leads to a great deal of entrepreneurial activity and organizational flexibility. However, it makes it very difficult for bosses in the family to keep track of what other members are involved with. As the enterprises of organized crime diversify, the political structure tends to become weaker and more decentralized.

Diversification in organized crime allows maximum flexibility for economic enterprises; it allows people to be rewarded somewhat in accordance with their ability to produce, rather than on a salary schedule fixed by the boss. However, in the political realm, there tends to be less contact or dependence on the boss of the family for friendship, income, and services. Dissension, as suggested, may follow when political power is not commensurate with wealth or because individuals may be keeping their economic activities a secret from their superiors.

Although most people suspect that one organized crime society or matrix operates in one geographical area, and another group in a different area, in fact the quest for income has meant that the groups have become spatially separated at times, and the territories are often non-contiguous. There are indications that some large territories, including parts of California, Nevada, the Bahamas, and Florida, are open territories and offshoots of many societies and matrices are in business there. Territory is not contiguous even within the five-family structure in New York City. Senator Curtis of Nebraska wanted to know how territory was divided and asked Joseph Valachi at a Senate meeting. Valachi responded:

> "You see, Senator, you take Harlem, for instance. We have about four families all mixed up there. There isn't any territory. You find Brooklyn guys in New York and New York guys in Brooklyn. They all get along very well. If anything, you have in Brooklyn, in fact they help protect it for you. I would not say there's territories. You take, for instance, Harlem, we have about three

families bumping into one another. You have the Gambino family, the Luchese family, and you have the Genovese family right in Harlem."[126]

It is also evident that families have their favorite hangouts and tend to cluster in certain geographical areas. When matrices and societies first form, territoriality is much more important. Today when we speak of territoriality in established groups, it is evident that business opportunities cross territorial lines. Even in the early days of rum running, groups joined together and their activities didn't necessarily coincide with territorial boundaries.

Perhaps a distinction can be made that will suggest which businesses follow geographical boundaries and which ones do not. Cottage industries like gambling, distillery of alcohol, and prostitution might be expected to follow geographical lines, at least at their inception. Formed in slum areas, each gang supplies its own territory. In territories controlled by other ethnics such as Harlem, or cities where gambling or prostitution is the major transplanted industry, open territories are declared and the businesses may pay protection to several different families. Non-cottage industries, such as the infiltration of unions, theft of securities, hijacking at airports, and ownership of legitimate business, may be less fixed to a particular location. Finally, organized criminals may no longer have their place of residence in the area in which they do business. Like other businessmen, they show a distinct preference for the suburbs.

Certain areas of cities are controlled by criminal matrices or societies, or at least these groups appear to have the monopoly over crime in the area. As a by-product, such areas may be free of street crime. As the groups expanded and diversified into non-cottage economic enterprises, territoriality in terms of physical location became less important, for territoriality is as much of a concept of domination over an activity as of domination of territory. As was the case with the economic forces mentioned earlier, territoriality invites economic opportunity but weakens political control, thus causing a structural dilemma. Physical absence doesn't necessarily make the heart grow fonder, but accelerates other splits in the political structure and decreases surveillance of members by their overlords.

Finally, as Ralph Salerno suggests, Italian crime families developed in Eastern urban centers where large Italian populations live. Many of the Western states became open territories or independent families were allowed to form. Nevertheless, of the twenty-four crime families, nine are reported to be on the commission at any one time and all five New York family bosses are members. Buffalo, Pittsburgh and Philadelphia are usually also represented. There is no doubt that this causes strains in the organizational structure, yet none so serious has arisen to lead to open warfare as in the early 1930s.[127] One can only speculate why.

First, the New York City groups are quite large, and just as New York tends to be the center of legitimate trade, so it is for illegitimate trade. Explanation of this hypothesis does not rest with the native corruption of the people, or depravity of the rulers. New York is the financial and commercial center of the country and provides opportunity for a good deal of security and airport theft. In the narcotics trade, addicts come to New York City where it is more readily available. All of the opportunities of a waterfront are available to organized crime, as well as the terrible poverty that organized criminals prey on. It is not my intention to explain organized crime in New York City, but to suggest why the City can rightfully retain an important place in a nation-wide coalition. A second reason why the composition of the membership might not lead to a great deal of friction are its limited powers. If the organization is primarily the arbitrator of disputes, membership is not at a premium. Other groups when in conflict can independently get together and bargain.

Finally, in cities outside of New York, other ethnic groups are more powerful than Italians, given the smaller Italian populations. This last factor becomes very important in tailoring the analysts' views of organized crime and it works much like Spiro Agnew's criticism of the media and their New York bias. Analysts in Houston, Philadelphia, or Miami, for example, would not see the hegemony of Italians in organized crime as much as reporters from New York.

Conclusion

Two separate goals have been accomplished in the book thus far. First, the social and psychological characteristics of criminals as well as the characteristics of criminal organizations have been examined to adequately describe the workings of these organizations. Along the way many myths have been examined, elaborated upon, and punctured, providing new avenues of inquiry for any thoughtful analyst. Little more will be said about this line of inquiry. Second, structural dilemmas that criminal organizations face were pointed out. "If we conceive of social systems as being confronted by dilemmas, that is, by choices between alternatives in which any choice must sacrifice some valued objective in the interest of another, the implicit assumption is that problems are endemic and, therefore, serve as a continual internal source of change in the system."[128]

In the study of many organizations, the inevitable dilemmas have already been uncovered and the approach would not yield many surprises to the analyst. In the study of organized crime, however, most analysts give us an idealized picture of organized crime, hinting that organized criminals have certain goals, and without incurring costs, move inexorably towards them. These idealized versions needed to be contrasted with other goals the organization deems important to suggest the conflicts and choice situations facing organized criminal groups. Thus, from the perspective of structural dilemmas, organized crime is viewed as an activity rather than a meaningless cliché or set of rational organizational goals.

The first step in this work was to modify certain stereotyped notions so that discussion of dilemmas could proceed. The *Task Force Report* definition of organized crime was reworked, for it blocked the way to inquiry. The analyst was expected to assume a certain organizational structure, one which resembles the totalitarian ideal type, rather than one which leaves the nature of the organizational structure open for investigation. Next, any notion that organized criminals, as opposed to the rest of the citizenry, are supermen had to be dispelled. It was shown how the structures of the organization made it impossible for them to be efficient at every juncture. The distruction of these two stereotypes, superorganization and supermen, began the inquiry into the structural dilemmas of criminal matrices and societies.

The first part of the book has uncovered various dilemmas and the intention is not to repeat and summarize all of them here. What will be done is to suggest a variety of ways the analyst may organize these dilemmas to analyze organized crime. In a discussion of dilemmas the analyst can begin with any value that is prominent in an organization and suggest how others conflict with it. In the study of organized crime, three perspectives, each suggesting the dominance of one or more values, have been promoted. The *Task Force Report* suggests that organized crime is a monolithic, totalitarian society seeking to take over the country. Everything is organized to maximize control over members and the rest of the citizenry. In the

Task Force Report and in the writings of others, organized crime is conceived of as an illegal business where the basic value is profit. In Ianni's *Family Business*, organized crime is conceptualized as an activity that promotes values of loyalty and cohesion which stem from familial loyalties, not organizational requisites.

The study began by suggesting that the organization was not monolithic, totalitarian, and out to destroy free society. The major conflict is with the economic goals of the organization. To make profits, society members entered a variety of businesses which pulled loyalties away from the nuclear families, led to non-contiguous territories which led to a breakdown of communications, and caused status anxiety when there was a difference between political status within the organization and wealth.

The nature of the ethnic-based family also limited the inter-organizational, state, and national political control exercised by nuclear groups, while promoting secrecy and cohesion. The organization could not expand without breaking down some of the cohesion based upon ethnic loyalties, which included recruitment based on nepotism and favoritism rather than on expertise. The organizations could not have a dictator (as opposed to a set of alliances or a confederation) because loyalty is based upon the primacy of the nuclear group.

By the same token, an analyst can begin with any other set of values such as family cohesion or profit, and examine organizational dilemmas. For instance, strong family ties limit growth of an organization while promoting loyalty and secrecy. Business opportunities are lost because of anti-expansionist policies of family groups. For example, it took the Castellamarese War to convince ethnics to allow other ethnics into business.

A variety of other dilemmas stem from the status of members in their organizations to the age of members of the group. There are any number of perspectives from which to view these dilemmas, some which were specifically articulated and others obvious from the analysis. Pointing out these dilemmas leads to viewing organized crime as an ongoing activity as opposed to a set of national goals. All of these approaches tell us something, yet in themselves do not tell us everything. From the dilemmas we are able to see potential changes in the organization in the future.

At this juncture a picture of organized crime is complete with two basic exceptions. First, in concentrating on societies, we have neglected the day-to-day activities that criminals are involved in. This will be remedied in the next chapter where spheres of activities are examined irrespective of societies. This will bring us to the second missing item, a discussion about public policy. How should enforcement agents react to criminal societies and matrices? One alternative would be to suggest that enforcement officials work on organizational dilemmas to help destroy criminal organizations. Organized criminals could use the same blueprint to improve their own organizations. This alternative will not be chosen because these strategies become obvious from reading the first half of the book. The policy approach taken here will be to suggest alternatives that flow from two basic perspectives: organized crime as a matrix and organized crime as a society. Hopefully, based on the information gathered in the book thus far, this approach will cast a new light on the debate on public policy toward organized crime.

Chapter 5

Activities and Society

Violence

One activity of organized crime that intrigues individuals is the committing of murder. It will suffice here to summarize our earlier comments about murder and to try to unravel a curious paradox about violence. If violence in organized crime is decreasing, why have the late sixties and early seventies experienced a resurgence of violence in some aspects of organized criminal activity?

Among organized criminals, violence is institutionalized; that is, there are rules that govern its use, and random, indiscriminate violence is frowned upon. Also, the threat of violence often serves the same function as the committing of the violent act itself. For instance, in Indianapolis in the early summer of 1972, three business-men were killed, and it is unlikely the killers will be apprehended. Every loan shark in the area will allude to that event as part of his own handiwork when he tries to collect a loan from a client.[1]

Violence, as was suggested, is a by-product of other activities and not the *raison d'être* of organized crime. Murder Incorporated, a matrix of criminals erroneously dubbed a society by a newspaper reporter, has most often been associated with murder in organized crime.[2] However, for this group as well as for other criminal matrices and societies, activities such as gambling were the main sources of income and violence was a lower-paying sideline.

It has almost become a cliché that organized criminals today have been using less and less violence in achieving their goals. They are supposedly moving with finesse into legitimate businesses. Ralph

Salerno suggests that "as they increase in entrepreneurial skills, the men rising to power in organized crime will probably be more subtle in the use of violence than are many of those now in control."[3] Data from the Chicago Crime Commission show that from 1919 to 1971, there were 1,008 murders attributed to organized crime in that city. From 1919 to 1930, there were 599 murders; from 1931 to 1940, 226 murders; but in the last three decades, only 70, 52, and 61, respectively.[4] Yet in the late sixties and early seventies in New York, Detroit, and Gary, Indiana, there have been a rash of gangland killings.

If violence is classified according to the relationship between the deliverer and the recipient, not only will we find out why violence still occurs in organized crime, and towards what ends, but enforcement policy toward murder might be straightened out.

Violence that takes place between organized criminals who are producers and those who are consumers is called "client-centered" violence. It may arise out of a loan-sharking transaction or an attempt to muscle into another man's business to establish a monopoly in a given field.[5] When Salerno speaks of organized criminals becoming more subtle in their use of violence, he appears to be referring to client-centered violence. It was shocking to most people when they found out that a sales agency purportedly had tried to force the A & P to buy a detergent that had been rejected by them because it did not meet the A & P standards. Queens District Attorney Thomas J. Mackell revealed that the murder of two A & P store managers and sixteen fires were connected with the attempt to have the A & P buy the detergent.[6] This type of client-centered violence was the order of the day in the twenties and thirties when organized criminals tried to establish a monopoly of businesses or infiltrate a labor union. Today the A & P incident stands out because although this type of violence still exists, it is usually less overt and carried on to a lesser extent.

"Inter-organizational" violence takes place when one organized crime family is at odds with another. During the Castellamarese War, families were fighting one another for control of the organization. The wars in Gary and Detroit appear to be between blacks and established gangs over the control of narcotics.[7] Inter-organizational violence is similar to inter-ethnic violence; indeed the Castellamarese War was fought partially on the basis of perceived differences between Neapolitans and Sicilians. Nonetheless, it is still useful to distinguish between wars that take place between Italian groups or black groups and those which are inter-ethnic in nature. Both types of violence indicate a shift in power relationships between dominant groups or the free market situation in new activities. These types of violence do not decrease on a linear basis, but occur sporadically and presage major changes in organized crime. Some of the violence in the late 1960s and early seventies has been of this nature.

Finally, there is "intra-organizational" violence, which is character-ized by factional disputes among family members. The Gallo-Profaci war and the Bonanno wars are examples of intra-organizational feuds which revolve around influence relationships in the nuclear groups. Much of the fighting in New York appears to be an outcropping of the Gallo-Profaci wars.[8]

Most of society finds murder both illegitimate and illegal and hence strongly urges enforcement agents to seek out killers. Yet the distinctions above allow us to suggest that the public and agencies show more outrage at client-centered violence than they do when organized criminals appear to be killing each other. Few would disagree that client-centered violence should be stopped. However, Ralph Salerno suggests that in dealing with organized criminals, "The idea is to take advantage of the inherent suspicion and greed to cause internal disorganization."[9] It may be advantageous to pro-mote violence among family members. This, Salerno says, can be done in ways that are "legal but not pretty," and he gives examples, some of which we have cited.[10] "Arrangements might be made with frequent hijacking victims and their insurance companies to issue inflated figures to the press on an amount stolen."[11] The thief's cohorts might feel they were being cheated on the percentage of the take. Thus with murder, depending on the relationship between victim and killer, enforcement agents might want to promote violence.

Finally, where a premeditated murder takes place and alibis can be secured, witnesses can be intimidated and the best lawyers can be obtained even if the individual is apprehended. The chances of solving a murder, no less obtaining convictions, are slim.[12] More frequently, they remain unsolved.[13] None of the murders done by Murder Incorporated were solved and convictions obtained until, by chance, one of the members, Abe Reles, began talking about his participation.

Legitimate Businesses

The term *legitimate business* seems to refer to businesses which are run by individuals who are not organized criminals. The implication is that they are legal businesses run with legal means and legitimate in the eyes of the public. However, businesses run by organized criminals often are legal businesses run by illegal means. They may be legitimate in the eyes of the public, as in the case of restaurants, bar and grilles, and gambling establishments in Nevada, or illegitimate in the eyes of the public, as in the case of adult book stores.[14] A discussion of legitimate business will include both legal businesses conducted through legal means and legal businesses run by illegal means.

Organized criminals run a wide variety of legitimate businesses and we can get some idea of this by looking at the businesses of the participants at the Apalachin conference in 1957. At least nine owned or operated coin-operated machine (slot machine) manufacturing or distributing companies; sixteen were associated with the garment manufacturing or trucking industries; seventeen owned taverns or restaurants; eleven were in the olive oil and cheese importing business, and nine were in building and heavy construction. Other businesses were funeral homes, auto agencies, horses and race tracks, linen services, and entertainment services. In addition, most of the participants had connections with unions.[15] As with other activities of organized crime, income from legitimate businesses is difficult to estimate. Even if we knew of all of the businesses, the income reported to the Internal Revenue Service would be grossly understated, for very often organized criminals operate businesses that deal in easily siphoned-off cash.[16] Even the United States Chamber of Commerce, which wants to alert businessmen to the dangers of organized crime, quotes Lyndon B. Johnson as suggesting that the core of organized crime is supplying illegal goods and services, "but organized crime is also extensively and deeply involved in legitimate business and in labor unions."[17] If we are to believe certain estimates, the volume of business and income is very large. "In a single midwestern city, leading racketeers controlled, or had large interests in, eighty-nine businesses with total assets of over $800 million and annual income in excess of $900 million."[18] As with most estimates of income in organized crime, the reader must be wary. He might ask: Is this the largest city in the Midwest? Is this income before taxes? Is it shared with non-criminal partners? Are all of the owners professionals or are some retirees?

It is interesting to speculate as to why organized criminals engage in certain legitimate businesses and not others. Thomas Schelling suggests that illegal rather than legal businesses are most often the targets of organized criminals because they are much more amenable to extortion, the characteristic operating procedure of organized crime.[19] In the twenties, when violence was more flagrant, businesses were often forced to pay tribute to organized criminals, or were taken over by them. According to John Kobler, author of *Capone*, "During the twenties, some 700 bombs destroyed millions of dollars' worth of Chicago property. The contractors established a price list:

Black powder bombs—$100

Dynamite bombs—$500 or $1000 (depending on the risk)

Guaranteed contracts—$1,000 and up."[20]

Today extortion may be a bit more subtle, but the extortion victim has not changed. Normally, it would be a family-type business, not a corporation, where one man can be prevailed upon to pay tribute, or can be moved out of the business in default of a payment to a loan shark.

Businesses that are sensitive to public opinion are also subject to extortion. For instance, restaurants, motels, and other businesses dealing in customer services are vulnerable. The methods are more subtle—little bombing, except for the A & P incident a few years ago —but often are as effective. A group recently threatened exclusive beauty parlors in New York by suggesting that black women would be hired by the gangsters to frequent the parlors and drive the other clients away. Racism can replace violence as a weapon of extortion.

Another characteristic of businesses preferred as targets by organized crime is that they do a large cash business. Restaurants, casinos in Las Vegas, slot machines, race tracks, bar and grilles, and grocery stores all do such a business and money can be skimmed off the top before payment of taxes.

Larger concerns with corporate ownership are more difficult to infiltrate, although this has not been unheard of. Organized criminals can also have the competitive advantage in concerns where they must compete for government contracts, such as construction firms. Here they can gain advantages by manipulating sweetheart contracts with the unions (where payoffs are made to union leaders to keep wages low). This has happened in the trucking and garment industries.

One speculation about organized crime might be that instead of gaining a larger and larger share of the gross national product through purchase of legitimate business, it has lagged behind the rest of the economy. The small, entrepreneurial enterprises are profitable, but show little growth potential.

It is easy to understand now why organized criminals move into legitimate businesses. Profits can be made from these businesses, and in certain ones, where organized criminals can establish a monopoly, gain a labor advantage, get preferential treatment from the government, or skim cash off the top of the business, they have a competitive advantage over the businessman who does not resort to these practices. Legitimate business can also be a cover for tax purposes. If organized criminals own a reasonably profitable business, they can account for their spending on consumer goods, travel, and other personal items. Finally, they move into legitimate activities to convey an aura of respectability, to differentiate themselves from ordinary criminals. There are two explanations of this hypothesis, each conveying a different notion about human motivation. Daniel Bell would suggest respectability is part of the American dream, part of advancement up the queer ladder of social mobility. Others are less charitable to organized criminals. They suggest that an alliance with respectables takes place. Organized criminals can do business with unsuspecting businessmen and government officials. This can work in business deals as well as providing character witnesses for the criminals if they ever go on trial. In other words, the aura of respectability is just plain good business for organized criminals. There is no doubt that both motivations are at work in moving organized criminals to participate in legitimate businesses.

There are a variety of ways in which organized criminals acquire businesses. One, obviously, is to make a legitimate purchase of a business establishment. This can be done in the individual's own name or under a fictitious name by men who "front" for the real owner. The extortion practices described earlier are also utilized to gain control of a business or to exact tribute from its owner. Very often a gambling debt or a loan from a loan shark will lead to a takeover of a business by an organized criminal. The businessman will either explicitly or implicitly put up his business as collateral for a loan and when he defaults in his payments his business is taken over.

Ownership is not necessary for the criminal to reap profits from legitimate businesses. He may own the business outright and manage it himself, or he may allow the old owner to manage it. The organized criminal may not own the concern but may exact tribute from the business at a certain percentage per month. Or, tribute may be paid in the form of compensation for products or services that the business is forced to accept from criminal groups. A restaurant owner might have to use a hatcheck girl, linen service, *maitre d'*, parking lot attendants, or entertainment supplied by organized crime.

There are a few other methods designed to make money quickly that should be mentioned. One way is to sell off all of the disposable assets of a particular business and set fire to the premises to collect insurance money on the premises and inventory. This is very simple to pull off and hard to detect. Only Jimmy Breslin's characters could fail. Kid Sally Palumbo was given the job of burning down a nightclub that was losing money. "This made the nightclub a candidate for the usual restaurant fire, a grease fire in the kitchen, helped along by fifteen gallons of gasoline."[21] Kid Sally made the only mistake he possibly could have. "The next day fire marshals found four gas cans in the embers. 'If Eisenhower owned the place we wouldn't pay,' an insurance adjuster said."[22]

Another way to make money quickly is known as a "bust-out" or "scam." The idea is to build up a good credit rating in a wholesale or retail business and then order excessive quantities of merchandise just before a busy season, for example, Christmas. The goods are hidden away or sold at bargain prices and with the inventory depleted the business declares bankruptcy. The operators either vanish, or stay and blame the bankruptcy on theft, fire in the warehouse, or an urge to gamble.[23] Credit rating is established in several ways. A criminal group can get hold of a company that already has a good business rating. Or it can open a business and pay creditors in full at the beginning, gradually lengthening the time between receipt of merchandise and payments.[24] Finally, a company may be formed with a name almost identical to that of a reputable firm in operation. For instance, criminals may form the Rapito Scrap and Paper Company when the Rapito Scrap-Paper Company already exists.[25] The company than uses the similarity in names to order excessive merchandise prior to declaring bankruptcy.

Gambling

There is substantial agreement that gambling is the most lucrative activity in which organized criminal groups are engaged.[26] Donald

Cressey suggests that people spend about $5 billion annually placing bets at race tracks.[27] Estimates on profits and gross on gambling receipts and amounts wagered vary greatly. The *Task Force Report* settles on at least $20 billion in wagers and $6 billion to $7 billion in profit, but the commission admits it cannot judge the accuracy of the figures.[28] Even though estimates vary widely, there are other indications of the scope and pervasiveness of illegal gambling in this country. Talk to people in factories and those who work on the waterfront, to union members, to people who live in large cities, to those who frequent social clubs in rural communities, and you will find they are engaged in an extensive amount of gambling.[29] John Gardiner in *The Politics of Corruption* gives an excellent description of the scope and extent of gambling in one city.[30]

Games of chance have been played since ancient times and lotteries were utilized to raise money for the colonies. There is now a wide variety of ways to gamble, all which have been exploited by criminals. "The gambling industry's chief source of revenue is from wagering on horse racing. But professional gamblers also control many other forms of betting, including that on sport events, the numbers game, lotteries and sweepstakes of various types, slot machines, and professionally operated dice, poker, blackjack, roulette, and other games."[31]

Depending on the type of activity, it may be run by a small or a very large matrix. Crap games, for example, may be run on street corners by a few individuals. But most gambling, including crap games, tends to be run on a larger scale because large organizations are at an advantage. They can provide capital, customers, and protection from other criminal groups and the law that small groups cannot provide for themselves. Independents and outlaws lead shaky lives even in running crap games which do not need the manpower or capital necessary to run a horse parlor or to buy gaming machines.

Horsebetting, especially, needs a large organization to sustain its operations. William J. Duffy of the Chicago Police Intelligence Division suggests that there are six levels in a bookmaking operation.[32] At the lowest level is the solicitor, who takes the bets by phone from a central location, or walks to a factory or union headquarters so the individuals can place their bets. At the next level is the bookmaker, who has several solicitors working for him, or who might be serving in both capacities at the same time. He works just as the legitimate operators at the track do by paying off only after deducting his cut and expenses. Almost everyone has seen films in which a person goes in to a bookie and bets an exorbitant amount on one particular horse which happens to be a long shot. The bookie can protect himself by paying off at no higher than 20:1 odds, but he may still take a loss. This necessitates a lay-off man with whom the bookies can place a bet to hedge against losing too much money in any one race. According to Duffy, there are four levels for lay-off man—local neighborhood, community or county, inter-state, and nationwide.[33]

Essentially the same description is found in Donald Cressey's *Theft of a Nation*.[34] Cressey again makes no distinction between the activities of organized crime and the power structure of criminal societies. To him, they are one and the same. "There are at least six levels of operating personnel in such (gambling) enterprises, and each of these levels except the lowest one is occupied by persons with a corresponding status in the 'family' structure of the Cosa Nostra."[35] He gives no evidence for this other than to suggest he knows that one large lay-off man works in Chicago and others are in Las Vegas and other cities, but does not suggest their rank or names.[36] It is unlikely that status as a lay-off man corresponds strictly to political rank, for gambling is a business, one of many developed by criminal societies, and it is doubtful that the largest lay-off bettors are dons and their lieutenants are capos. There are differential sizes in families and other ethnic groups involved. The lay-off bettor may not be a member of a criminal society, but may pay tribute to it. Again, the growth of families and the matrix of gambling did not necessarily coincide. I suspect that Cressey is making an inference and does not have evidence to back up his hypothesis. Duffy confirms my suspicions when he asks rhetorically, "Who occupies these various lay-off positions? Does the lay-off operation which is indispensible to bookmaking specifically function in the manner (six levels) just described? Quite frankly, we don't know the answers to these questions."[37] Thus we are left with inferences and no data, and I would contend that there is nothing in the literature to indicate that the activity hierarchies in organized crime are isomorphic with rank in the criminal societies.

Lotteries are also large money-makers in organized crime. "Projections made from records seized by the Intelligence Division of the Internal Revenue Service reveal that the volume of business conducted by major numbers banks in Pennsylvania totals over $240 million per year."[38] In every state or city there is a different way of picking the winning number. It may be a sequence of numbers in parimutuel betting, the totals of the daily transactions of the stock exchange, the number that results from spinning a wheel, or the final digits of the United States Treasury cash balance.

One way of betting is on a three-digit number. If a player bets on a three-digit number, and it hits, he gets paid off at 600:1 odds, giving the house a substantial cut in the proceeds. If one digit is bet on, the odds may vary from 5:1 to 8:1. The same problem arises as with horsebetting; that is, the bookie stands to lose a substantial amount of money if one number is heavily played whether by one or a hundred individuals. One way of preventing this is to limit the amount bet on any one number by a single individual. However, if too many people bet on the same number, the bookie stands to take a substantial loss. Valachi tells of the time there was a payroll robbery in Brooklyn and $427,000 was stolen. "Now everybody has to play 427. We must have had around $100 on it. [Bets beginning at 25 cents were accepted then. Most common were $1 bets and some larger operations took $10 bets.] If it hits, that means we get banged for $60,000."[39] Valachi tried to lay off the bets with a friend, but all over the city bookies were running into the same problem, and the friend could lay off only $44. Luckily for Valachi, the number was not hit.[40]

Gambling is an activity that all social classes participate in, but its legal status may differ for each class. In the abstract, anyone can go to the Bahamas, England, or Las Vegas to gamble where it is legal. But, unfortunately, it is quite expensive to maintain a hotel room, eat your meals out, and pay for transportation. Consequently, it is sport for the rich. Middle and upper middle class individuals can go to these islands of legalized gambling, or they may belong to private or fraternal clubs where gambling is allowed.[41] For the lower class, gambling is an activity that is confined to neighborhood areas and places of work. The question to be raised, of course, is whether or not there is differential enforcement of the laws. It is obvious that for one set of individuals gambling is illegal and for others it is legal.

What causes the biggest stir in society is not the day-to-day gambling that takes place, but rather the news that a sporting event has been fixed. Day-to-day operations are rarely reported by customers or neighborhood residents and are often ignored by the police. Perhaps the most famous attempt to fix a sporting event involved the 1919 World Series. Each of eight Chicago White Sox players was to get $10,000 for fixing the series, and the White Sox did lose the first game to Cincinnati. After that game the story broke. The players had arranged the scheme and tried to sell it to gamblers. After the first game, the players tried to collect from the gambler who had agreed to the deal, but the man said he didn't have the money. They got nothing for their efforts.[42]

In 1950, a scandal broke that implicated basketball teams at CCNY, LIU, Kentucky, Bradley, and other schools. Players on these teams and others had been given money to "shave" points in a game, winning by less than they were expected to so the gamblers could win their bets. If a team was expected to win by thirteen points, the gambler would bet that it would win by less. The rationale was easy for the players to accept: "We're not asking you to throw the game, but just to win by a few points."[43] History repeated itself, and from 1956 to 1961, "twenty college basketball players were paid $44,500 in bribe money to fix forty-four games, according to indictments and statements by prosecutors in New York and North Carolina."[44]

The case is interesting for several reasons. First, the explanations of the events selected data that suggest that if bad apples had not been chosen for college, the scandals would have been at a minimum. In an article called "Irresponsible Recruiting is the Chief Reason Behind the Basketball Scandal," Tim Cohane argues that "if the academic qualifications and general backgrounds of all the twenty-six players had been screened thoroughly by the colleges, many of these players would have been rejected."[45] Again we have a version of the queer ladder theory that the educated person will shy away from crime. Second, the players I knew who were implicated came from a variety of backgrounds. What they all shared was knowledge of the interrelationship between gambling and sports. Lou Brown, one of the players implicated in the scandals as arranging some of the fixed games, recalls his childhood: "Placing a bet on a horse or playing the numbers was part of living. After school, I shot craps or played cards."[46] Even those who came from different environs were aware of gambling when they played summer league basketball on their playgrounds or for the Catskill resorts.[47] Third, the climate around the universities—where money is given out under the table and players are treated like commodities—does not help, either. Scandals of this type must be looked at as part of a broader spectrum of corruption in American society, not something to be caused by a lack of education.

In the seventies it has been revealed that many horse races have been fixed. The technique is to drug the front runners so the long shots can win. Although some disagree, it appears this practice is fairly wide-spread.[48] Several interesting points come up when discussing the fixing of sporting events. Such activities usually spread indignation throughout the public about gambling and gambling practices. Also, the fixing is not necessarily done by producers in organized crime. They get a regular share of the profits regardless of who is to win or lose. The consumer often will arrange the fix and then spread his bets over several bookie joints so as not to arouse suspicion. Aaron Wagman, a key figure in the basketball scandals of the late fifties and early sixties, bet very little himself, but "he'd have as many as three or four games going on a Saturday night, with as much as $300,000 to $500,000 involved for big gamblers."[49] Fixing of games is also a manifestation of the emphasis in this country on sports, winning, and the spirit of competition. Whether or not gambling was legal in this country, there would be attempts to fix athletic competition.

Narcotics

Perhaps the most written-about activity organized criminals are involved in is the manufacture, sale, and distribution of narcotics. Yet, experts are still not agreed upon some fundamental issues. First, there is not just one "narcotics problem," for there are different types of drugs with very different distribution systems. There is not even a settled definition of addiction that sets off narcotics from the category of dangerous drugs. Most frequently, the word *addiction* refers to a physical dependence upon drugs; however, this is not satisfactory because alcohol is physically addictive and yet not a considered part of the drug problem.[50] The word *narcotic* refers to a substance which "induces sleep, dulls the senses, or relieves pain."[51] In law, the term *narcotics* is applied to include the opiates, cocaine, and even marijuana. The Illinois Legislative Investigating Commission indicates that "the term 'narcotic' generally refers to opium and drugs made from opium, such as heroin, codeine, and morphine."[52] Under the rubric of dangerous drugs, it classifies stimulants, such as amphetamines; depressants, such as barbituates; and hallucinogens, such as

LSD, peyote, and mescaline.[53] These distinctions are important because the seriousness of the effects of drugs to the health of individuals and society may vary. The so-called marijuana problem may call for different solutions than heroin addiction. Matrices to deliver the drugs from farm or factory to people on the streets may also involve different groups of people.

Somehow we tend to think of the narcotics problem as one of comparatively recent vintage. It is surprising to learn that in the 1890s opium was a familiar basis for household tonics and elixirs which people could obtain without prescription. Much as some tonics today with a high percentage of alcohol hook their users, the opiate drugs created numerous addicts. "It has been estimated that in the year that marked the beginning of the present century, one American out of every 400 was addicted to an opiate. Thus, we begin this century with almost 190,000 American drug addicts, a figure which nearly matches many estimates of the number of heroin addicts in the United States today."[54]

In 1914, President Wilson signed the Harrison Act, which required physicians to keep careful records of narcotics sales, prohibited sale or possession of drugs without proper registration or prescription, and taxed importers and manufacturers of the drugs. Enforcement was placed under the jurisdiction of the Treasury Department, and by 1920 addiction switched from a medical to an enforcement problem.[55] Later, other drugs were treated in the same way by federal law. The Marijuana Tax Act was passed in 1937 with the express propose of limiting use of marijuana, and all amphetamines and barbituates were covered by the Drug Abuse Control Amendments of 1965.[56]

A problem has been whether drugs such as marijuana should be permitted on a discretionary basis. On the other side of the spectrum, there has also been controversy as to whether the strict penalties for possession, sale, and distribution of heroin should apply to marijuana and similar drugs as well.[57]

It is difficult to find a typical process of distribution of narcotics or dangerous drugs, but it might be useful to describe the various stages in a possible process. The description will pertain to heroin traffic; although still the favorite process, government efforts have hampered it a bit recently. Turkish farmers for many years supplied up to 80 percent of the opium to be processed into heroin and morphine for United States addicts.[58] Most often the heroin enters the port of Marseilles in France for processing. The French, until recently, had no drug problem of their own, and the conversion laboratories are well hidden in the Marseilles area. The laboratories and traffic in and out of the city is run by Corsicans. Secrecy abounds and, as is the case with many organized criminal groups in the United States, the Corsican milieu is based upon "clan, village, and valley loyalties."[59] The Corsicans operate in a series of independent groups that unite from time to time. They process the drug for a fee, and then movements to and from the lab are handled by *La Gache*. "*La Gache* is a large, indolent male population of petty truants" who carry trunks and suitcases from one end of the city to the other.[60] When the shipment arrives in the United States, the wholesalers break it down to others and, after going through several levels, it is in the hands of street peddlers. When they get the shipment, it has been diluted at every stage and contains only a fraction of pure heroin. This is the "usual" pattern of distribution on the East Coast of the United States. "The importers, top members of the criminal cartels . . . do not handle and probably do not ever see a shipment of heroin. Their role is supervisory and financial."[61]

This is a description of one particular matrix of narcotics activity in organized crime, the distribution of heroin to the East Coast. The matrix is made up of people of perhaps five nationalities each working on a different phase of the process; the farmers, refiners, wholesalers, street peddlers, and addicts. If there is a society or societies involved, they may each be in only one aspect of the process. "On the West Coast, the traffic is in heroin of Mexican origin and is carried on by large independent operators."[62] The same is true of marijuana distribution and appears to be true of traffic in stimulant and depressant drugs.[63]

It is foolish to think of these patterns as static, and to maintain that once they are broken and key figures arrested, the traffic in drugs will dry up. The Turkish government, in return for $35 million in aid from the Nixon Administration, agreed to halt legal farming of opium after the fall of 1971 crop was harvested and to increase enforcement efforts. But there are indications that Afghanistan, Pakistan, an area known as The Triangle (a remote mountainous region bordering on Thailand, Burma, and Laos), and other countries will pick up the slack.[64] Also, cocaine production is likely to increase.[65]

When pressure is put on manufacturing or distribution points, locations and individuals involved change. For instance, stepped-up enforcement in New York City, a prime port of entry, forced "enterprising Frenchmen, South Americans, Puerto Ricans, and Cuban refugees" to turn to southern Florida as their new point of entry.[66] Thus, it makes no sense to speak of the traffic in narcotics and dangerous drugs purely from the perspective of a criminal society, nor does it make any sense to discount these matrices as not being part of organized crime.

One point that should be made refers to our whole discussion of activity matrices. There is a great deal of overlap in matrices; the same individuals may be involved in running a bookie joint and fencing merchandise. On the consumer level, there is also a good deal of interrelated activity; the addict may be a prostitute to support the habit, or may gamble and take money from loan sharks. Finally, it is easy to see why large matrices are needed to traffic in drugs, whether they be cocaine, heroin, or amphetamines. The same kind of organization is needed as with the manufacture and distribution of any dangerous drug.

Loan-sharking

Another major activity of organized crime is loan-sharking, the process of lending money at usurous rates. The practice is centuries old; we are all familiar with *The Merchant of Venice*, in which Shylock says to a loan applicant: "This kindness will I show— Go with me to a notary, seal me there your single bond. . . . If you repay me not on such a day, in such a place, such sum or sums as are exprest in the condition, let the forfeit be nominated for an equal pound of yours fair flesh, to be cut off and taken in what part of your body pleaseth me."[67] Those who lend money at usurous rates today are often called shylocks or loan sharks, *shark* being a corruption of the word *Shylock*.[68] The process which will be described is the same, but the actors, of course, have changed.

According to the *Task Force Report* on organized crime, "In the view of most law enforcement officials, loan-sharking, the lending of money at higher rates than the legally prescribed limit, is the second largest source of revenue for organized crime."[69] There is no doubt that there is substantial activity in this area. The *Task Force Report* goes on to say that "gambling profits provide the initial capital for loan-shark operations."[70] No doubt gambling and the loan-shark

153

racket itself, along with other illegal activities, are sources of funds for loan-sharking activity. Other sources of funds are friends, relatives, acquaintances, and other lending institutions.[71] Money borrowed at normal bank rates can generate a good deal of profit when circulated through customers willing to pay usurous rates. Loans may be obtained legally or by posting stolen securities as collateral, by borrowing through a third party, or through collusion with lending officials.

According to John Seidl, an analyst with excellent insights into the loan-shark process, "Interest charges which borrowers pay for loan-shark funds are not a function of supply and demand or marginal cost and marginal revenue relationships. Rather they are traditional prices which have been established over time."[72] In the twenties and the thirties, loan-sharking was known as the 6-for-5 racket. Seidl indicates that 20 percent still remains the key figure in small loans. "Even in cases where charges vary from city to city, the small-loan rate usually includes the number 20—20 percent per week, 20 percent for six weeks, or 20 percent for ten weeks."[73]

Customers come from all social classes and for a variety of reasons. Rich and poor alike come to loan sharks because they have gambled and do not have enough money to pay their debts. Rarely is it the intention of the individual to get himself into this kind of mess. Mort Golden, a man who describes himself as a typically middle-class salesman with a nice family and a home in the suburbs, relates how he fell into the hands of a loan shark after doctors told him his newborn son would probably be blind for the rest of his life. "It sounds funny now, but I was drowning my sorrow in a bowl of chicken noodle soup when I saw this friend. He suggested this crap game. I was glad to be with someone."[74] Golden doesn't remember what happened that night (he might have been drugged) but he woke up terribly in debt. He borrowed from everyone he knew, but the time finally came when he had to come up with three thousand dollars by the next day or his business and reputation would be ruined. Another friend said he knew Mafia people. Golden rationalized his involvement and still does. "Mafia loan sharks do serve a purpose. They are there when a man who needs money has exhausted banks, friends—all other 'legitimate' possibilities to obtain loans."[75] The pattern was familiar: he took out a three thousand dollar loan and after he'd repaid several installments, the loan added up to twelve thousand dollars still owed. He went to Las Vegas in a desperate attempt to win the money back and lost even more. Before he called in the FBI, his business had been lost, his self-respect was gone, and his wife had divorced him.[76]

Golden got into trouble by gambling, but others go to a loan shark because of sporadic unemployment or to cover business losses. Loan sharks thrive in unions where work is seasonal, such as the construction business, and on the docks, where daily work is not guaranteed. People in ghetto areas or in the working class often must turn to loan sharks out of necessity at the end of the month or in a layoff period, for their credit might not be high with regular lending institutions.[77] As Ralph Salerno points out, loans to these individuals rarely exceed two hundred dollars.[78] Businessmen go to loan sharks when loans they have made through legitimate institutions have become due and they cannot borrow from a legitimate source to pay them off. The loan shark may never recoup all of his money, but will loan the businessman more money than a factory worker, for he will take over the individual's business upon non-payment.[79] In sum, all economic classes provide fertile fields for the loan shark.

People who do not pay their debts to loan sharks are subjected to a variety of tactics. First may come a warning and then a severe beating. Murder is rare, because a dead man pays no debts. Most often, the individual is asked to pay the interest if he cannot pay off on the principal as well. The debt mounts and finally the principals may sit down to a settlement. In a conversation, Sam de Cavalcante talks about arrangements to allow a man to pay off his debt.

> SAM: He owes me—
> BOB: Seven hundred.
> SAM: Plus about a year's interest. The interest is twenty dollars a week. So he owes seven hundred legitimately and a thousand dollars interest. So give a break.
> BOB: Charge him fifteen hundred.[80]

Or, the organized criminals can take over the individual's business as settlement.

The matrix of the loan shark is meshed with the other activities of organized crime, both for the loan shark who gets his funds from other businesses or acquaintances and for the consumer who often needs money because of debts incurred through gambling or taking narcotics. More than one or two individuals are usually involved in loan-sharking operations because of the need for capital, contacts who get customers (often bartenders, office workers, etc.), collectors, and enforcers. Charles Siragusa suggests that there may be four levels of operation—financiers, juice men, collectors, and enforcers.[81] These do not have to correspond with rank in an organized crime family, for many of the participants—enforcers and financiers, especially—may be fellow travelers, recruits, or the like in the organization.

Theft, Fraud, and Extortion

Usually we do not associate theft with organized crime, but view it as the work of individual criminals. Although Ralph Salerno does not dwell at length on particular examples of theft, he does try to determine the degree of organized crime involvement. "A really complete family chart would reveal that organized crime is actually responsible for much crime against property—burglary, automobile theft, bank robbery, arson. . . ."[82] He goes on to say that although Cosa Nostra members may not be involved in actual theft, they could set up jobs and fence the merchandise.[83] Salerno is straining to include such thieves under the rubric of the family, but we can more easily speak of such groups as matrices of crime. Our emphasis is different, because matrices of jewel thieves or car thieves do not become organized criminals only if associated with La Cosa Nostra. If these matrices fulfill the tenets of the definition, such as a sufficient number of individuals involved in illegal activity over a period of time, they are organized criminals regardless of their association with La Cosa Nostra or any "name" society.

One of the ways to see how theft is organized is to look at the process of theft. The simplest act is the theft of cash or usable merchandise by an individual. It involves no second parties to fence the merchandise. At times, such theft as robbing a bank may require no fence, but have more than one person involved. In this category we would include such crimes as embezzlement, employees' theft, and shoplifting. Mary Cameron in *The Booster and the Snitch* found, for example, that most shoplifters have no contract with the criminal subculture and "the small value of merchandise taken by pilferers implies that it could hardly have been stolen for sale to 'fences' through recognized criminal channels."[84] The activities above would be considered part of organized crime only if the thief were part of a criminal society.

The crime becomes a bit more complex when the thief disposes of the goods to people acting as his own middleman or to friends or relatives. Often people who work for manufacturing concerns, grocery stores, or other retail stores will supply relatives with goods. Almost everyone who has used the railroad to commute to New York at one time or another has been approached by someone who wanted to sell a watch or a bracelet cheaply. Again, we would not consider this theft as organized unless the thief were a member of a society, a highly unlikely prospect.

Theft becomes even more complicated when disposed-of goods become a problem. Professional shoplifters sell to the fence but "store protection officials of large retail stores believe that only a minority of commercial thieves market their stolen merchandise through regular criminal channels."[85] Most sell them to small retail shops, the majority of them legitimate. "Photographic supply store owners, jewelers, neighborhood women's and men's wear stores, electrical appliance shops, and the like are also suspected of acquiring considerable proportions of their stock in implicit collusion with people they actually know to be thieves."[86] Disposal gets more complex and difficult when thieves are disposing of truckloads of watches rather than dozens, or diamonds or stolen securities rather than wallets or key chains. There are at least four parties involved in complex thefts—victim, thief, fence, and consumer. Often all parties may know of the theft, as when someone buys a brand new Cadillac for three thousand dollars from a dealer.[87]

There is no limit to the kinds of theft; for instance, groups steal guns, automobiles, leopard pelts, diamonds, treasury bonds, air cargo, truck cargo, paintings, and fur coats. It appears that the greater the volume or scarcity of the merchandise stolen (making it more difficult to dispose of), the greater the chance that a large number of individuals and perhaps large criminal societies are involved. More people are involved in the process of stealing and disposing of leopard pelts or automobiles than in individual items stolen from a store. And in major endeavors, large organizations can provide protection from police, pay off customs, and furnish necessary financing.

Theft of securities, which has recently troubled authorities, provides an interesting means of illustrating the complexity of the theft process. There are several ways stocks and treasury bonds are procured. Matrices may have people working for brokerage houses or may have leverage on employees through gambling debts, and these individuals steal the securities. The thieves depend upon loose audits, loose checkups, and a backlog of transactions in brokerage houses to allow them to steal.[88] Stocks and bonds can also be stolen from other institutions or at other junctions in transactions. For instance, in August 1970, FBI agents apprehended seven Americans in London in connection with the theft of $30 million in securities. The FBI reported that a truck "owned by Mark IV Freight Co. of Chicago was hijacked . . . while transporting 18,000 blank stock certificates from a printing plant to a transfer agent."[89] Theft of mail at airports is another way of obtaining securities and, finally, securities may be counterfeited.[90]

The process becomes complicated when it comes time to dispose of the securities. George White (an alias) testified before a congressional committee about his involvement in illegal security transactions and explained that the ordinary thief does not know what to do with securities. He contacts a "catalyst" who is often a member of a criminal society. The society frequently "controls the production of counterfeit securities, they control the theft of the securities; by the same token, when they advance a few dollars to the thief, the thief turns over the stolen securities to them."[91] The take for the thief is never very great. James Schaeffer, a participant in airport thefts, admitted that he and other thieves only got a small percentage: "$19 million in common stocks. I don't believe there is a real big market for them. There was 2 million some-odd dollars in bearer bonds, (easier to dispose of) of which I understand you can get 15 points for, 15 percent."[92] Schaeffer said the thieves managed to pick up extra money by passing counterfeit money. The easiest place to pass it was at church bazaars, "because at a bazaar you have 50 different stands and mostly inexperienced people are there, inexperienced in handling money."[93]

The securities are disposed of in a variety of ways; one of the most common is placing them with banks as collateral for loans.[94] In foreign countries, stocks are sold to the government at a discount and "there is a device where trusts are established, major trusts, you see, and the assets of the trusts are stolen securities nobody looks. If you have entry to a bank or an institution, and you carry $10 million worth of securities, auditors in general don't check to see whether each security is stolen."[95]

There is no end to the kinds of manipulation that goes on in the securities business. George White tells of acquiring almost worthless stock in a company called Seaboard Airlines Railroad Stock because the name was almost identical with Seaboard Airlines Railways, Inc. and he believed that bankers would not notice the difference. He used the stock as collateral for loans. "I estimate that the total amount of loans made with these worthless securities was between $300,000 and $500,000."[96] Another time, White took over an inactive brokerage firm and through it aggressively sold stock in the Ben Franklin Oil and Gas Company, a company that needed capital to develop. By controlling the sale of stock through a single brokerage firm, he was able to increase the price. The owner wanted both to own a significant share in case the stock was successful and to sell a huge chunk at a large profit. In such a case, if the stock is successful everyone is happy, but if the property turns out to be worthless, George White still makes money.[97]

Theft and fraud can become very complex and a multitude of schemes are devised. They take a degree of sophistication and manpower. Men like White work in matrices of crime and sometimes their cohorts are members of criminal societies. White and members of the matrices he worked in were not necessarily members of organized criminal societies and White was in no way a salaried employee nor did he perceive of himself as one. Often, however, he would be involved in matrices in which society members were principals. "The principal person in organized crime [society] with whom I was involved in the Red-O-Lier expansion was Peter LaPlaca, whom I met in Lewisburg Penitentiary in 1960."[98]

In addition to bringing out the magnitude and complexity of certain transactions, this example illustrates the myriad opportunities, not only theft, but fraud, embezzlement, and extortion, that may be associated with a particular industry or activity. No particular activity seems to be immune to exploitation. Regularly book stores take unsold books and ship only their covers back (to decrease shipping costs) to the publishers. They are then reimbursed for the unsold copies. Counterfeiters now sell book covers to stores so the stores can ship the counterfeit covers back to the publisher and get reimbursed.

"Counterfeiters charge between 10 and 20 cents for each forged cover, which is often printed by the hundreds of thousands. Because paperbacks generally retail at 95 cents to $2.50, the distributor could command up to $1.25 from the publisher for each returned cover."[99]

Theft is not totally frowned upon, nor was it ever completely frowned upon in society. Jewel thieves are looked upon with amusement, bank robbers in the thirties were folk heroes, and one merely has to remember the Robin Hood legend to see that the thief is not always a villain. Thus, crimes and criminals that prey on the rich often receive acceptance in society. Personal theft has always been rejected when one person steals from another and the victim suffers an economic loss. In this category are the purse snatcher and the thief who steals from small uninsured businessmen. Moral strictures come down less heavily today because of what I will call institutional crime, that is, crime against large institutions that are insured or receive favorable tax write-offs in theft. Mary Cameron suggests that shoplifting is not easily explained as the product of psychological disturbance.[100] The individual does not think of himself as a thief. "Although pilferers often have guilt feelings about their thefts, it still seems to them less wrong to steal from a rich store than to take from the family budget."[101] The same is true with the public's perception of theft. According to this perception, it is less wrong to steal from the wealthy or the large than it is to steal from the humble or the small.

Thus far we have been talking about moral arguments given pro and con for stealing, but there are implicit economic arguments that large firms may give that do little to discourage theft. One argument is that a certain amount of theft is going to occur regardless of security precautions, and that the firm must therefore balance the cost of increased security with the cost of continuing theft. All big department stores have made the decision that open counters, although they encourage shoplifting, are more profitable than closed glass cases and tighter security measures. More recently, it has been disclosed that theft adds excitment and interest to boring jobs. Lawrence R. Zeitlen found job enrichment to be the chief motive behind employee theft in a large Midwestern department store.[102] Some employers are determining permissible levels of theft. In a large Eastern city, the port authority did not have a difficult time keeping toll takers on the job even though it was a boring one. But by 1950, an elaborate security system reduced drastically chances for employee theft, and turnover of personnel reached a new high. The cost of reducing theft was excessive because of the turnover of personnel, so the port authority determined it could tolerate theft of up to ten dollars a week per man.[103]

The growth of corporations and disparities of wealth give people differential perceptions about what kinds of theft are acceptable. The strictness of enforcement may also vary according to who is taking the losses. For instance, thefts of securities that appear to threaten the structure of capitalism are the subject of intense enforcement drives.

So far we have talked about theft and fraud, which may or may not be perpetrated by society members or may or may not be of such magnitude as to involve a matrix of crime. It has been suggested that while many of these crimes are committed by organized criminals, numerous others are the work of persons we would consider ordinary citizens. In talking about extortion—the process of wresting something from a person by violence, intimidation, or abuse of authority—the same kind of distinction is made. Not all who are involved in such activities are necessarily part of criminal matrices or societies.

Thomas Schelling suggests the establishment of monopoly and extortion are the main businesses of organized crime.[104] Gambling concerns, he points out, pay tribute to large organizations, and organized criminals sell slot machines and dream books (astrology books to help customers pick a number to bet on) to gamblers at their prices. It is an interesting approach to looking at the activities of organized crime, and no doubt a lot of money comes from what were previously called tribute and franchises. But the fact remains that criminal societies own and operate their own legitimate and illegitimate operations as well as extorting from others.

There have been several recent cases in which extortion has been flagrant. As mentioned earlier, criminals tried to force the A&P to buy a particular detergent. These days, if extortion involves physical coercion, it often shades into activities that involve cash transactions rather than the exchange of violence or threat of violence for services. For instance, "the American Telephone and Telegraph Co. testified . . . that two employees accepted gifts from a detergent distributor whose secret owner has been identified as a 'soldier' in the Vito Genovese organized crime family."[105] Perhaps we would want to call this activity "private corruption" when extortion shades into non-violent persuasion, the payment of employees or management of a private firm by an independent source for services explicitly discouraged by company policy. This might entail a payoff to AT&T for use of a particular detergent or a payment by truckers to unions for the right to load and unload quickly on the docks. In many areas of the country, this is not viewed as private corruption, but as accepted "costs of doing business," not only by organized criminals but other employers and employees as well. What encourages tolerance of extortion and private corruption is its pervasiveness in American society.

This section on the activities of organized crime has not been exhaustive since every new business creates new possibilities for criminal activities, and one business often can foster several illegal activities. Nonetheless, we have covered major activities that are of current interest to enforcement officials and the public.

Patronage, Corruption, and Ideology

It is unusual to include corruption in a section on activities, and yet it is one of the activities carried on by criminal societies and matrices. The danger of its inclusion here is that it will be considered an end in itself rather than a by-product of other activities. Corruption of legal governments is certainly not the *raison d'être* of organized crime; rather, the necessity for corruption arises from the ordinary pursuit of their business. "The criminals would have much more difficulty eroding the process of law enforcement if it weren't for official corruption."[106] It is part and parcel of doing business and many criminal groups engage in such activities.

James Q. Wilson, in his article "Corruption Is Not Always Scandalous," suggests the difficulties of clearly arriving at a concept of corruption. According to Wilson, "in general, corruption occurs whenever a person, in exchange for some private advantage, acts other than as his duty requires."[107] Wilson notes that by this definition, almost all politicians are corrupt.[108] If you offer a union leader a place in your cabinet in exchange for his endorsement in an election, you are corrupt. J. S. Nye wishes to make clear that corruption differs from acceptable behavior in that a legal norm must be breached. In general, he writes, "corruption is political behavior which deviates from the formal duties of a public role because of private-regarding (personal, close family, private clique) primary or status gains, or violates rules against certain types of private-regarding influence."[109] This might represent a failure to act as well as willfully making some action occur.[110] This definition of corruption is narrower in scope than Wilson's.

Wilson's view is that corruption is an exchange of considerations

162

or services, and Nye's is that we must distinguish between legal and illegal activities. Most acts of politicians and police are not illegal *per se*. Politicians may award contracts to one firm over another, influence zoning boards to change their rulings in favor of commercial interests, get private and non-civil service jobs for their employees, and pardon criminals. In each case, they would be within the law. Similarly, judges cannot be arrested for bad judgment in a murder case, nor policeman for concentrating on one form of crime over another. The distinction between legal and illegal comes in when the private citizen gives consideration for services on the part of these officials. Hence, we can distinguish three distinct relationships: public interest, patronage, and corruption. The ideological relationship is rare, but it occurs when a politician gives out favors solely on the basis of his perception of the public interest. It might be seen in an action that costs him votes in the next election. "The ideological approach to politics and government is encouraged by politicians, who would much rather portray themselves as motivated by principle than by power or personal profit."[111] Patronage, on the other hand, is "the allocation of the discretionary favors of government in exchange for political support."[112] (By political support, I mean cash contributions to public officials and the delivery of votes on election day.) Corruption, as indicated previously, involves the giving of government services and the receipt of private-regarding primary or status gains. It may be, in the words of George Washington Plunkitt, a turn-of-the-century Tammany ward boss, "honest" or "dishonest." "Dishonest" corruption may involve bribery or blackmail, while "honest" corruption (Plunkitt uses the term "graft,'" not "corruption") may bring the politician additional business for his law firm, advanced information on the fortunes of a corporation on the stock market, or a promised job in private industry after retirement.[113]

Organized criminals obtain favors from politicians primarily on the basis of patronage and corruption. In the 1930s, organized criminals took an active part in machine politics and helped to deliver the vote through coercion and campaign contributions. Al Capone's organization was under pressure from Judge Dever's reform administration in Chicago, so Capone backed Bill Thompson's campaign for mayor. Thompson, a former mayor, had left Capone and the rest of organized crime to its own devices. "The prospect [of Thompson back in office] was so attractive to Capone that he contributed $260,000 to Thompson's campaign chest and applied every technique of bribery and terrorism in his behalf. Capone was credited with the slogan, 'Vote early and vote often.' "[114] Today, organized criminals still use coercion and money as a lever to influence politicians, though rarely as flagrantly as in Capone's day. Joe Colombo's attempt to lobby to get the FBI to stop hounding Italian-Americans also served as a subtle cue to politicians to leave Italian-American criminals alone if they wanted to continue receiving the Italian vote.

It goes without saying that organized criminals use bribery and intimidation to corrupt public officials as well. The process of corruption, as we said before, involves an interaction between private individuals and public officials. Donald Cressy refers to one party as the corruptor and the other as corruptee.[115] Unfortunately, most people look at the process as one in which a few bad apples are influenced and tainted by their association with criminals; their role is passive, they are corrupted. But there is evidence to suggest that far from being passive, public officials seek such association with criminals and even organize themselves to promote it. William White, in his study of an Italian neighborhood in Boston in the late 1930s, came across just such an organization. "In the language of the corner, the policeman was trying to shake down the racketeer."[116] The shakedown came in a variety of ways. Numbers runners moved from one part of town to the other and police officers learned to recognize their cars. Policemen then stopped these cars and demanded protection money. Also, "some arrests are made on the initiative of individual policeman for the purposes of securing themselves more favorable financial relations with the racketeers."[117] After the men were released, the officer persuaded them to put him back on the payroll. In Boston at this time, it was not the rookie, the uninitiated, who cooked up such schemes. On the contrary, "the racketeers fear the rookies. It is hard to do business with them. Their actions are unpredictable."[118] In 1971 and 1972, a commission headed by Whitman Knapp conducted an investigation in New York City and found the same kind of pervasive atmosphere of corruption and self-seeking on the part of the police. The commission uses a distinction between "meat eaters," those who "aggressively misuse their police powers for personal gain," and "grass eaters," who "simply accept the payoffs that the happenstances of police work throw their way." It suggests that the "grass eaters" exist in far greater numbers. "Their great numbers tend to make corruption respectable. They also tend to encourage the code of silence that brands anyone who exposes corruption a traitor."[119] It is therefore easier for the rookie to become corrupt than it is to stay honest, assuming they are honest to start with. Thus corruption is an interaction process in which police often actively seek and accept renumeration, and the policeman who is honest faces great social pressures to conform.

The assumption is often made that organized crime is coexistent with corruption, but the relationship between the two is a bit more complex. First, different activities require cooperation of public officials to a greater or lesser extent. Most experts agree that gambling involves a significant degree of corruption, as does prostitution. The locations of their places of business are known to a large number of clients and are certainly common knowledge to the police. Police and politicians are not adverse to taking money to look the other way and can rationalize so doing by saying that the public wants these services. Also, it may be that policing these activities takes low priority not because of bribery, but merely because the public gives no outcry to do away with them. In John Gardiner's study of Reading, Pennsylvania (Wincanton), he concludes on the basis of a survey of community attitudes towards gambling that "while the Wincantonites' rejection of current gambling laws provides support for the thesis that corruption facilitates the realization of popular values —that the . . . mayors and policemen [bribed by Stern, the head of the organization] were simply giving Wincantonites the gambling they wanted—the survey clearly shows that the residents of Wincanton did not tolerate corruption *per se*."[120] Thus when gambling is brought to the public attention, it is condoned, but when corruption is the issue raised, most citizens opt for public norms of morality.[121]

In the past, there was even less public and police acceptance of corruption connected with the sale and distribution of narcotics. But there now are indications that police have been corrupted in this area and that, in a perverse way, larger payoffs are granted because of the moral qualms people have about accepting the sale and distribution of narcotics. The *New York Times* reports that the Knapp Commission found that "though narcotics corruption appeared less well-organized than the corruption found in gambling, individual scores or 'bribes' were commonly received and could be staggering in amount."[122] One payoff was for $80,000.[123] In the sale of narcotics, quite a few people may need to be paid off. Customs inspectors and judges who must rule in narcotics cases are prime targets. Nevertheless, large organizations that deal at the upper echelons in the business would not necessarily be concerned about the safety and livelihood of the street peddler and would not pay for his protection. And many theft-related enterprises that may require corruption if members of the matrices are caught can perform their acts without resorting to corruption. Thus, different activities will be dependent on corruption and others not, and with some activities, corruption may come with more reluctance on the part of public officials and at a higher price.

Corruption, when it appears, takes place at a variety of levels of government and in a variety of agencies. Gamblers may deal with policemen, and narcotics peddlers may want to corrupt customs agents. It depends on which agency has jurisdiction in a particular activity. As a rule of thumb, the higher up in government organized criminals reach, the easier it is to operate. A politician can develop priorities for his police force and the police sergeant can discipline his men The authors of the *Task Force Report* on organized crime concur when they say that "organized crime currently is directing its efforts to corrupt law enforcement at the chief or at least middle-level supervisory officials."[124] For street activity, there is no need to get senators or representatives on your side. They may play some part in attempting to make federal legislation, but the task of corrupting a majority in Congress is slim and the payoffs too indirect. Besides, until recently, most enforcement responsibility lay at the local level.

Interactions based upon corruption can come about in a variety of ways. Criminal societies or matrices may put friends in positions of public authority, or they may bribe or blackmail those already in these positions. The cloak of respectability facilitates interactions between criminals and politicians, and the politician in need of money may turn to his "respectable" friend. However, in many communities, all the participants have their eyes open and corruption is part of the way of doing business, so there is little differentiation between government and the public in terms of role or function.

The rewards for the actions of public officials with respect to organized crime vary from the delivery of votes to the payment of cash. Sometimes these payments are open or outright, such as in Chicago in the twenties when policemen were paid off in cash, or in many situations today. In Reading, Pennsylvania, payments were also made in cash. "While the dice game was running, the mayor was reportedly receiving $1,500 per week; the chief, $100, and a few policemen, lesser amounts."[125] Sometimes payments are more subtle, especially when the public officials are not being asked to do anything extraordinary. "Certainly no more than ten of the 155 members of the Wincanton police force were on Irv Stern's payroll (although many of them accepted petty Christmas presents—turkeys or liquor)."[126] This is enough sometimes to tell the patrolman on the beat that it is foolish to break up a gambling game which all the participants enjoy, and which is run by the nice man who provides him with a big bird every Christmas. This brings us to the point that targets of corruption are asked to perform in a variety of ways, some involving positive action and others the turning of official heads. Customs officials may not check the bags of a traveler, a judge may let someone off free, or a mayor may tell his police force to go easy on gambling.

It is difficult to estimate the extent of corruption and patronage that stems from organized groups and matrices. These activities are not limited to criminal groups, and also may involve other individuals and groups out for private gain. Also, corruption does not control every activity of a public official. The policeman on the "take" may perform poorly in cleaning up gambling, but be exemplary in every other function. The politician "controlled" by organized crime is not directed on how to vote on every issue, but just the ones that affect the maintenance and enhancement of his benefactor's business. Take-over of government is not the goal of organized criminal groups, merely the byproduct of their activities, and their intention in corrupting officials is to allow themselves to operate freely. Restraints in their power lie as much in the nature of their organization as in the pressure put on for law enforcement. A total take-over of government by organized criminals would not be functional for them. "If there were no untouchables on the force, police-racketeer relations would develop to such an extent that, when finally a crisis arose to bring this condition to public notice, the department would lack the men necessary to bring about an apparent reversal of policy. The resulting scandal might assume such proportions as to threaten the prevailing police organization with destruction."[127] This is an outcome neither the police nor organized criminals desire. Thus, as Whyte suggests, public outrage is the last resort in keeping at least

167

some government activity free of corruption. There also is no reason to believe that corruption need be elitist in nature. A plurality of groups, only one of which may be an organized criminal group, may be receiving patronage and corrupting a single government.

Another point is that it is unrealistic to talk about take-over of American government for, as Robert Dahl points out, there are ninety thousand governments in this country.[128] Corruption varies from region to region and city to city. The federated nature of organized criminal groups makes it difficult to envision their assuming total control of government.

Chapter 6

Policy Perspectives

Matrices vs. Societies

The distinction between matrix and society set forth in the definition of organized crime differentiates between two kinds of organizations, one which describes a network of activity and the other which designates a self-conscious group of people who perceive of themselves as belonging to an organization. Matrix and society, as I suggested, are also two different perspectives from which the public and law enforcement officials may view organized crime. Looking at the same social setting, one analyst may see matrices of crime and another may see criminal societies. Neither analyst need have an incorrect view of reality, for a criminal society is usually going to be involved in a matrix of activity. What is important is that each perspective, if held by the public and/or enforcement officials, tailors actual or potential institutional response to organized crime. Depending upon whether organized crime is perceived as a matrix or a society, different processes for dealing with it are stressed and developed.

It is not the purpose here to set out specific proposals for legal and institutional changes in the fashion of a governmental report. Those who deal more closely with specific aspects of the policy process or have done intensive study on a single facet of the process (such as laws on immunity, wiretap, or legalized gambling) are in a better position to do so. The goal here is to articulate the hidden and scattered behavior maxims present in the debate on policy-making in the area of organized crime. If these maxims are made clear, debate on the policy issues can be carried out with more clarity and directness. In the end, the "wrong" viewpoints may prevail, but critics will be able to point with their minds as well as with their hearts to the shortcomings of policy.

It might help to recount briefly how the perceptions of organized crime as society reflect historical trends and their interpretation, so we may treat this perspective in more detail. The disclosure of the Apalachin meeting of criminal leaders led the public and enforcement officials to think of organized crime as a secret ethnic society of criminals. The Valachi hearings and Valachi's subsequent biography reinforced this impression. The organization was given a name, La Cosa Nostra, and there even was an initiation oath taken which members were not to reveal under penalty of death.[1] Valachi recalled, "I took a piece of paper, and the piece of paper is burning, and it is lighted and then in your hand, you say—well, again, they give you words in Italian but I knew what it meant. . . . This is the way I burn if I expose the organization."[2] When enforcement agents were called in to verify Valachi's testimony, they identified many of the individuals designated by Valachi as family members, but often did not have knowledge of the exact structures or family arrangements. The publishing of *The Godfather* also reinforced the public's view of organized crime as a society. This perspective of organized crime is firmly fixed in the minds of both enforcement agents and the public.

This perspective was reflected in the pronouncements of public officials. John McClellan wanted to devise legislation to make it illegal to belong to a criminal organization, and the *Task Force Report* described the family structure in organized crime and saw it as a purposeful, tough enemy of society. In recent years, federal strike forces against organized crime have been formed in eighteen areas of the country to deal with criminal societies. The forces are staffed with men from different backgrounds and agencies. For instance, in the eastern district of New York the staff "includes seven attorneys and thirteen agents from the Federal Bureau of Investigation, the Internal Revenue Service, the Bureau of Narcotics and Dangerous Drugs, and the Bureau of Customs."[3]

The singling out of societies for enforcement action is not limited to organized criminal groups. The Black Panthers have complained in the past that they were singled out for extinction by enforcement officials and subjected to legal and illegal harassment.[4] Of course police agencies, if guilty, were not going to publicly acknowledge

170

this policy. The government, however, has been more open in acknowledging its internal enemies in other situations, J. Edgar Hoover made no effort to conceal his attempts to diminish the influence of the Communist party in the United States. Similarly, Robert F. Kennedy as attorney general launched an attack on the Teamsters Union and its officials. Cloaked as an attack on union corruption, it was directed primarily at the teamsters and James Hoffa, the union leader, a purpose well known to the American public. Walter Sheridan, a former FBI man, headed a group of attorneys in the Justice Department. "And when Sheridan's group, variously known as 'the Hoffa Squad,' 'the Get-Hoffa Squad' and 'the Terrible Twenty,' had finished their work on Hoffa, he [Kennedy] dispatched them to Mississippi to see what might be done about the Klan."[5] Thus, the perspective of societies within the American spectrum that need to be attacked by law enforcement agencies is common not only in the fight against organized crime, but also in campaigns against other groups looked upon as subversive to American life.

Societal Perspective

Identification of Societies

The existence of the societal perspective and its impact on enforcement policy need to be examined in greatest detail to determine the implications of this approach. The initial problem is to identify and single out societies which merit enforcement attention. Enforcement agencies have a good deal of choice as to which policies to follow or groups to attack. As John Gardiner suggests, "so long as large (and vocal) interests within the community do not believe themselves to be adversely affected by police practices, a 'zone of indifference' exists within which the official can choose to stress certain laws, ignore others, and so forth."[6] Public apathy, indifference, and lack of knowledge about organized crime make it difficult to achieve public input into public policy. Because criminal societies are prone to secrecy, their activities and the magnitude of the threat they pose to society are often assessed by fiction writers and enforcement agencies. For these reasons, agencies are often free to pick and choose among their enemies.

Several criteria may be implicitly or explicitly involved in the singling out of a society for scrutiny and extinction by enforcement agents. First, agencies may find a scapegoat in a single group to explain all of the malaise in the United States or in a particular policy arena. Scapegoating is as old as history itself and tends to provide an economical explanation for a complex phenomenon that might be the result of innumerable societal forces. Organized crime can be economically explained as run by one society, but the consequences of this course of action are often unsatisfactory. As in the case of perceiving organized crime as La Cosa Nostra, Italians, the vast majority of whom are not members, feel discrimination against them. The danger in the scapegoat method, of course, is that in addition to implicating innocent people it involves only one criterion: the need for a victim or group of victims. The societal interpretation reifies the enemy and lets the people choose up sides.

A second criterion for singling out a society is based upon partisan considerations. For instance, on the national level, Democrats may chose to emphasize illegal arrangements between large corporations and large trusts as the area which demands enforcement. They may avoid or deemphasize attacks on societies that operate in large urban areas. Many of their politicians may be indebted to or have been tolerant of these societies in the past and may not want the adverse publicity that would result from their public exposure. Conversely, partisan considerations may drive Republicans to go after one society as opposed to another. Certainly if all of the Chinese in San Francisco voted for the Republican party, the party would not want to expose organized crime in their area. It would embarrass the politicians who had close ties with these societies, and annoy voters who might benefit from the services of the societies, but who wish to avoid the stigma of being identified with them.

A third criterion that may be explicit or implicit in policy-making is the social class to which a given group belongs. White-collar criminal groups may be ignored while ghetto crime and ghetto groups may be singled out for extinction.

A fourth criterion that might be used is whether a group is a secret society, rather than a matrix of crime, which is more loosely organized and appears less purposeful, and therefore less of a threat to society. In other words, the decision is often made to concentrate on the conspiratorial groups. Hank Messick might be wrong about the existence of a national crime syndicate, but he is genuinely worried about organized criminals who do not belong to La Cosa Nostra.

"Ironically, the National Crime Syndicate has benefited by the emphasis on La Cosa Nostra," he writes. "The real leaders of crime have remained hidden while the nation's law enforcement agencies have chased minor punks."[7] Thus matrices, less intriguing, less developed on the basis of readily identifiable common ethnic backgrounds or neighborhood ties, may be more disruptive of the public weal than secret societies. Fears of conspiracy often exaggerate the powers of a group in the eyes of both the public and enforcement agents.[8] Also, concentration on conspiracies make it difficult to change enforcement direction or notice trends in which one conspiracy no longer dominates or for that matter, even exists.

The first four criteria suggested—use of a scapegoat, partisan affiliation, social class, and status as a secret society—all suggest less than noble reasons for singling out a group for enforcement purposes. I do not wish to imply these are the only reasons for picking on a single group. Agencies might decide to go after a particular group on the basis that it threatens the general welfare of a particular state, town, or municipality. As is known from political theory, the general welfare is many different things to many different people. To some, the group that commits the most murders might represent the great threat to the general welfare, and to others it might come from the largest criminal groups, or the ones that deal in narcotics. There will not be a plea here for a stiffer definition of the general welfare, but just the suggestion that one's criteria for choice of the enemy group must be made clear. Until this is done, and it becomes a matter for public debate, agencies will have a great deal of latitude in dealing with whatever group they wish.

Tactics

Even if a society is singled out as a threat to the general welfare on some agreed-upon set of characteristics, problems still lie ahead from this perspective of enforcement. Once a society is designated by officials for extinction, tactics must be devised to destroy it. Following from the societal perspective, the targets become individuals who play key roles in the organization and would be sorely missed. After Thomas Eboli, a purported acting head of a New York crime family, was killed, the police let it be known what their strategy towards him was: "Deputy Commissioner McCarthy is a tight-mouthed sort, but he has let it be known that the best way to fight organized crime is to zero in on certain targets. And such a target was Thomas Eboli and the rackets he operated, principally in lower Manhattan."[9] Certain activities may be singled out for attention, but only because drying-up income sources would put pressure on the man the authorities want to apprehend.

Given the societal perspective, members of criminal societies are prime targets for investigation and non-members take second priority. Danger lies for those within the confines of the secret organization. A distinction made earlier may serve as a criterion for choosing targets in organized crime. Membership in a secret society is not the critical variable, and it was displaced in the analysis by the degree of involvement in organized crime. As viewed by enforcement agents, those more heavily involved in the activity should be apprehended first, if possible. There are two dimensions that distinguish involvement, one which differentiates between producers and consumers, and the other which distinguishes part-timers from full-timers. This allows for the categorization of individuals as professionals, steady customers, apprentices, freelancers, retirees, innocents, and opportunists. Enforcement priorities can be based on this set of categories, and not on membership in a formal organization. The agency might choose to go after a full-time freelancer rather than an organizational retiree. A non-member professional, such as Meyer Lansky as purported, may be a more important cog in organized crime than many member professionals, retirees, or recruits.

The focus on the individual may lead enforcement agents to select certain tools and tactics over others. "Italian geography" becomes the order of the day in surveillance. Attempts are made to determine the key figures in the organization. Agents attend all funerals and wait outside and check license plates at weddings and other functions. Attendance at funerals of Mafia chieftains used to be *de rigeur* for fellow Mafiosi, even though it provided the Federal Bureau of Investigation with a handsome opportunity to take photographs and jot down license plate numbers.[10] Dossiers are kept by the agencies on individuals in organized crime. The Apalachin meetings and the Valachi hearings were unique opportunities to check out assumptions about organizational structures.

The obvious criticism of these tactics is that they entail possible breaches of civil liberties. Surveillance of an individual's activity can put significant pressures on him but often the courts do not go along with such harassment. Several years ago, Sam Giancana, a purported family member from Chicago, contended that he was being harassed by the Federal Bureau of Investigation. Giancana got a court order requiring the FBI agents to play or remain at least two foursomes behind him on the golf course.

Publicity is another form of harassment that falls into the gray area in terms of acceptable practice. In 1972 Frank Sinatra received a subpoena to appear before the House of Representatives Select Committee on Crime. Sinatra claimed this was another attempt to muddy his name in public. Regardless of the claims of guilt or innocence, appearance before one of these committees invariably does cast aspersions on the individual involved. This problem is not new or peculiar only to the case of Sinatra. "The televised hearings of the Kefauver Committee provoked a vigorous debate among lawyers, civil libertarians, and intellectuals generally concerning the possibility of balancing the public's need and right to be informed against the rights of individuals either mentioned in televised proceedings or forced to testify before the cameras."[11]

Electronic surveillance is also used as a weapon to gather information on the activities of organized criminals. No doubt much electronic surveillance is prompted by the desire to know about the family relationships in organized crime and the way secret societies are organized. There is no doubt that it is helpful in ascertaining information about criminal activities and movements. If it is to be used, and I have severe reservations on this point, it shall not be used to invade the whole of one's social life, but only to gather information on his business activities. I am grateful for the publication of the de Cavalcante papers, yet they do represent a remarkable intrusion into the private life of one individual.

There are positive aspects to making policy on the basis of the perception of organized crime as a society. Convincing the public of this perception helps to mobilize the resources of government to fight organized crime. As was stated earlier, the perception of a monolithic, totalitarian organization which threatens the legitimate operations of government is a useful force in mobilizing opinion. The singling out of individuals as targets and the publicity given to certain criminals helps to focus public attention on them and win support of legislators and other elected officials for anti-crime measures. According to Ralph Salerno, "While hounding gangsters is really only designed to get them to move somewhere else, the harassment of public investigation and exposure is supposed to focus public opinion on their activities so that new laws or new strategies will be developed. Exposure by Congressional committee, grand jury, crusading district attorney, or newspaper editor usually does create sentiment in favor of action against organized crime."[12] The question that agencies have to ask themselves is whether they wilfully persist in peddling inaccurate pictures of organized crime in an effort to win citizen and governmental support for anti-crime campaigns. Do they want to perpetrate the "noble lie"?

Emphasis on societies as opposed to matrices is also a tool for securing inter-agency cooperation. The Apalachin meetings prompted the formation of the Attorney General's Special Group on Organized Crime. Formed in April of 1958, this group was to help coordinate the "war" against organized crime.[13] Gerard L. Goettel, deputy chief of the new group, indicates that cooperation of member agencies was not automatic. "It turned out that we were woefully wrong in assuming that various law-enforcement agencies would be eager to cooperate with us," he wrote.[14] Victor Navasky in *Kennedy Justice* suggests that Robert F. Kennedy used the Valachi testimony and the notoriety of La Cosa Nostra to motivate the public to support a drive on organized crime. Simultaneously, he gave priority to the Justice Department's Organized Crime Section. It would, according to Navasky, "do informally what Hoover had prevented him from doing formally (e.g., setting up a National Crime Commission that would coordinate and serve as a national clearinghouse for information on organized crime and racketeers)."[15]

The mobilization of forces at the various levels of government is, of course, a mixed blessing. The sharing of information decreases duplication of effort and, more importantly, allows for more effective apprehension. As publicity spotlights criminal societies, federal agencies are also prompted to become more active in the battle against them. Federal agents are often more indispensible when local units of government, public, and police officials are on the payroll of criminal groups. On the other hand, increasing federal intervention always raises the specter of a national police force, central data banks, and the surveillance by Big Brother.

All the tactics of law enforcement mentioned before—harassment, surveillance, and publicity—are effective in helping to put individual criminals behind bars. It is fruitless here to establish the outer limits of the laws in these areas. It suffices to suggest that the need for law and order must be balanced against the civil liberties of the individual, but only hold if "law and order" means enforcement of all laws—whether or not one cares about them.

A final consequence of the societal perspective on organized crime is that defeating the enemy, the societies, is viewed within the narrow confines of an enforcement problem. From this viewpoint, it would appear that if the agencies have the necessary tools and laws to work with, organized criminals can be taken off the streets. This perspective thus makes it difficult to perceive organized crime as a manifestation of American society, and to consider measures such as the legalization of gambling or loan-sharking as ways of decreasing crime.

In sum, the societal perspective tends to lead individuals to single out a particular society as a target of law enforcement activity. Care must be taken to make the choice of target groups on some basis other than partisan consideration, class affiliation, or desire for a scapegoat. The societal perspective leads agencies to go after particular individuals, choosing them on the basis of their degree of involvement in organized crime. Care must be taken not to breach the individual's rights of privacy. Overall, the societal perspective, from the government's viewpoint, is a proper one if there is an immediate danger to the security of the country (my empirical analysis tells me there is now no threat), and it is also useful for mobilizing governmental resources to fight organized crime. The danger lies in the great latitude agencies possess due to the lack of sophistication on the part of the public. The wrong groups and the wrong individuals may be investigated and unduly harassed.

Matrix Perspective

Like the perception of organized crime as a society, the view of it as matrices of activity is often found in lore and literature. The Kefauver Committee concentrated its efforts on investigating activities of organized crime. For instance, it did a thorough investigation of the Continental Press Service and of all the operations that used the service.[16] It also looked into the activities of selected individuals such as Frank Costello, Meyer Lansky, and Carlos Marcello. The committee would have liked to have understood the inner workings of organized crime as a society, but had to be content to infer organization from the activities of individual criminals and criminal groups For instance, it suggested that "the New York syndicate is headed by Frank Costello, Meyer Lansky and Joe Adonis; Willie Moretti and others, including Abner ('Longie') Zwillman, Vito Genovese, and Joe Profaci, figure in the picture."[17]

This is far from the insider's view given by Valachi years later, but because the committee was forced to perceive organized crime as matrices of activity, it found many groups interacting on various transactions.

In the post-Valachi era, Ramsey Clark, a former attorney general, shares the Kefauver Committee's perception of organized crime as matrices of activity. He suggests that "as with all crime, we over-simplify our definition of organized crime. There is far more to it than La Cosa Nostra. . . . There are hundreds of small operations that engage in organized criminal activity—car theft rings, groups of burglars, safecrackers working together, gangs of armed robbers, combinations that occasionally smuggle and distribute marijuana and dangerous drugs—scattered throughout the nation."[18] He does not suggest that La Cosa Nostra does not exist, but he feels that concentration on a society would distract attention not only from other organized criminal activities, but especially from emphasis on other crimes the public is fretting about. "What does organized crime have to do with street crime—murder, rape, assault, mugging, robbery? Practically nothing."[19]

Norvall Morris and Gordon Hawkins imply by their remedies for organized crime that they do perceive it as a matrix of activity. Their program of enforcement is based upon the opinion that the law is involved in too many activities and is trying to legislate morality, a phenomenon they call the "overreach" of criminal law.[20] In policy-making towards organized crime, their approach is not to attack criminal conspiracies, but to legitimize activities in which criminals may be engaged. They contend that too much manpower is diverted to enforce laws in such areas of private morality as sexual behavior, gambling, and narcotics.[21] The institutional reform they suggest indicates a disregard for attacking organized crime as a society. "All special organized crime units in federal and state justice and police departments shall be disbanded," they write.[22] Thus, they imply that we ought to look at activities of organized crime as opposed to organized crime as a secret society.

They lose credibility with enforcement agents, however, when they stress throughout their chapter on organized crime that Va-

178

lachi's testimony is unreliable, that reporting in the Apalachin meetings was confused, and that on the basis of available evidence La Cosa Nostra and a commission do not exist. This does not sit well with agencies that have seen the de Cavalcante papers or the airtels, listened to the tapes put out by the New York State Joint Committee on Crime, or gathered their own independent evidence. The unfortunate consequence is that Morris and Hawkins are not taken seriously by agency personnel. This could have been avoided, for the implication that there is no large, overarching criminal organization was not necessary to their argument. It would have been sufficient for them to hold to their weaker hypothesis that there is no monolithic nationwide syndicate, or to ignore the question of organized criminal societies altogether.[23] One could still argue that examining the matrices of activities, rather than looking for and attacking societies, would be possible and even intelligent even if societies existed.

Thus there is ample precedent for looking at organized crime as a matrix of activity even though no previous analysts have attempted to articulate the difference between perspectives of matrices and societies or to elaborate upon the rationales for concentrating on matrices. One can also deal with organized crime as a matrix of activity even when criminal societies do exist.

Rationales for Crackdowns on Particular Matrices of Activity

The hope here is to foment discussion and debate on the rationale government agencies use to combat organized crime. Why do they single out gambling, or murder, or theft in their "battle" against organized crime? After explicating the rationale for moving in on a particular activity, I will emphasize specific strategies. Rationales may be explicit or implicit in agency's policies already, or may be possibilities they might want to consider. I am not talking about an "overall" rationale, for there are hundreds of agencies on all levels of government with which coordination would be difficult, if not impossible. Some agencies, such as the Alcohol and Tax Division, the Bureau of Narcotics and Dangerous Drugs, and Customs already have prescribed roles. Yet even within these agencies there is room for debate on priorities; the Bureau of Narcotics and Dangerous Drugs, for example, could emphasize stimulants and depressants and decrease enforcement efforts on hard narcotics. Similarly, Customs could concentrate its manpower in a port where diamonds are being smuggled while de-emphasizing its search for narcotics or marijuana. A few years ago, President Richard Nixon concentrated Customs activity on the border between the United States and Mexico to try to halt the flow of marijuana into this country.

Agencies like the Federal Bureau of Investigation or intelligence divisions of police forces have far more latitude in the activities they choose to concentrate their efforts in, although they may be limited by legal restraints. On the legislative level, debates can also take place, new agencies can be formed, budgets can be approved or disapproved, and agency priorities from time to time can be changed. Thus, the call is for debate on priorities, not massive change that is not politically feasible. Debate could be held along at least six suggested lines.

Chance of Success

This rationale dictates that agencies go after organized crime on a case-by-case basis, with priorities going to cases in which the chance of success is greatest. Given the limited resources of most agencies in terms of the tasks to be done, this rationale insures some modicum of success. Ralph Salerno articulates it well: "The most common active way of fighting organized crime is to chip away at it on a case-by-case basis, prosecuting individual members as they can be caught committing crimes."[24] My conversations with enforcement agents convince me that this is the articulated rationale of many agencies. Information is received from a variety of sources and the agencies go after the individual or activity with which they can make the best case.

This rationale is difficult to apply in reality; moreover, its articulation seems to block further systematic thinking on priorities. With this viewpoint, agencies and enforcement officials do not have to think about definitions of organized crime or priorities because they are picking out the best cases to make. There sometimes is an interaction effect. They become specialists in certain kinds of cases, and these specialties may in the future dictate the kinds of cases they will pursue.

In reality, however, agencies and agents have a great deal of choice in what cases to make. The articulated chance-of-success rationale is equaled in naiveté by the public's view of a policeman as someone whose job is just to enforce the laws as they are broken.

James Q. Wilson notes that "formally, the police are supposed to have almost no discretion: by law in many places and in theory everywhere. . . ."[25] Discretion, however, is inevitable because police can't observe every infraction, many laws require interpretation, and police believe the public might not tolerate enforcement of all laws all of the time.[26] Cases just don't come to the prosecutor or to the patrolman's desk; information comes in on a variety of matters, and the decision to act and investigate is made on very few. Whitman Knapp suggests that his experience in District Attorney Hogan's office in New York indicates that criminal cases are not made by others, but take active seeking and discretion on the part of enforcement officials. "In order to make criminal cases you've got to want to."[27]

Given the latitude enforcement agents have and the active role they must take in gathering evidence to support or make a conviction, the only rationale in fighting organized crime should not be ease of making a case. Often agencies may decide to follow a particular activity for months with no particular payoff. This is especially true in organized crime where cases tend to be elaborate and investigations costly in terms of manpower and other resources. J. Edgar Hoover, in speaking about the benefits of electronic surveillance, also indicates the difficulty in bringing a conviction against organized criminals, and the time and resources it takes. Congress, according to Hoover, has given the federal government the authority to utilize court-approved electronic eavesdropping "and the results of months —and sometimes years—of investigation are beginning to bear fruit in the form of increased arrests, confrontations, and convictions."[28] All one has to do is look at successive FBI bulletins to see policy shifts in terms of the activities that the agency pursues and tries to make cases against. Thus, on both the policy level and the operating level, there is a good deal of discretion as to the types of policies that are made, and the chance-of-success rationale is only one of many that can be and are applied. This rationale most often hides (unintentionally) less articulated, less reasoned policy assumptions. This, however, is not to say that the ease of making cases should play no part in enforcement policy.

Most Pernicious Activities

Under this rationale, priorities are based upon perceptions of which crimes take the greatest human toll as individual acts—theft, murder, loan-sharking, or gambling. There are many arguments that suggest the adoption of this rationale. It is feasible because there is a great deal of public support for it. Support generally means greater enthusiasm on the part of enforcement officials, for ordinarily they share the same values as the citizenry at large as to which crimes take the greatest human toll. If agencies have the support of the public, the public will not jeopardize other public investigations agencies want to make. The policeman who interferes with gambling in an area finds himself shut out of the information system in that area and is hindered in his other work. This same phenomenon is at work between agencies. The state police force that goes after gambling in a local community is likely to get great resistance on any other matters it pursues in that area. Thus it is easier to pursue criminals who commit crimes that all agencies and the public view as pernicious and are hence less likely to be covered up by corrupt officials.

Finally, agencies and personnel respond with more enthusiasm in trying to apprehend and convict individuals who commit pernicious crimes. A strong argument can be made that regardless of success rate, or any other policy considerations, it is justification enough to try to punish or put out of circulation (depending on one's theory of punishment, one or the other is deemed suitable) people who commit murder rather than those who run a bookie joint. Or, putting it another way, crimes against people are accorded greater priority than those against property.

There are, however, several arguments that mitigate against acceptance of the most pernicious activities rationale. Sometimes these crimes may be extraordinarily difficult to solve and may require a tremendous amount of manpower and resources. Murder, for example, is very rarely solved when committed by organized criminals. When indictments are brought against individuals, the state must bear the expense of costly trials and housing of friendly witnesses as well as other expenses in the information-gathering process.[29] Local police forces do not have the means or the authority to track down complex narcotics rings and cannot pursue them effectively without the aid of higher-level government agencies. Without such aid, they can only attack piecemeal on the street-peddler level.

Those enamored of the societal approach will complain that trying to apprehend and convict criminals who commit the most heinous of crimes will not help to alleviate pressures from organized criminal societies. If a society member is apprehended for murder, he is most likely to be a low-ranking figure or a part-timer contracted to do the work. It is almost impossible to apprehend those who ordered the killing.[30] Also, an attack on narcotics distribution often will concentrate in sections of the country where no societies operate, and even in those sections where societies are active, many of the personnel involved do not belong to them. Thus, to those who believe strongly in the societal approach, an attack on the most pernicious activities may not be an attack on organized crime at all.

Other than by societal consensus, how does one decide what the most pernicious crimes are? During Prohibition it was obvious that a great many people condoned bootlegging activities while others viewed them as sins or signs of moral degradation, or at minimum, a violation of the law that should be punished. Police agencies are not about to debate the ultimate justification of murder, narcotics, or gambling, and cite Kant or Bentham as their sources. For this reason, the criterion in the definition of organized crime might serve as a starting point for debate. It is obvious that those activities that are perceived as illegitimate (those that are illegal and pursued by illegal means) are the most pernicious activities. Debate on a hierarchy in terms of the relationship of these crimes and on which should be pursued could follow the lines of the legal-illegal, legitimate-illegitimate classifications in Chapter 1. It must be pointed out again that an activity may fall into different categories depending on the laws of the localities and the public opinion. Even a crime like murder can elicit varying public responses and, to a certain extent, gangland killings, as long as they involve only mob personnel, are viewed as legitimate. People follow the count of who gets killed with the verve of baseball fans reading the box scores. For example, the gangland shootings which have taken place since Joe Colombo was shot on June 28, 1971, in New York (fifteen in the following fourteen months) have been viewed with various degrees of amusement.[31] As suggested earlier, enforcement agents even think of encouraging gangland conflict as enforcement policy. However, on August 16, 1972, two innocent bystanders were shot down and, according to the papers, "New York's 30,000-member police force was under mandate from Mayor John V. Lindsay today to 'run the mobsters out of town.' 'Get out and stay out' was the message the mayor ordered. . . ."[32] Although this may have been nothing more than tough talk, the example illustrates the different effects the same class of crime can have on public opinion.[33]

Another criticism of the most pernicious activity rationale is that it calls merely for public pressure on the authorities in response to individual acts—a murder or movement by a loan shark to collect on sale of heroin to a teenager. But some would view the individual acts as part of a larger matrix or society of crime and as symptoms of the activities of criminal groups. Therefore, this reasoning goes, the way to deal with these activities is indirectly—by drying up their source of income or destroying the society by other means. Many of these other means are embodied in the alternative rationales we will suggest.

It appears then that the most pernicious activity strategy is and can be generated by public pressure. It is feasible and is followed in many cases.

Income-Producing Activities

The rationale for going after activities that produce the most income for organized crime is quite straightforward. If the income of criminal societies or matrices is dried up, they will be hard pressed to pursue other activities financed by the more lucrative ones and will be unable to maintain their present strength. This rationale is elaborated upon in many places and an articulate statement is found in an FBI law enforcement bulletin. "Failure to combat illegal gambling effectively is a definite aid to the business of crime—helping to finance narcotics and vice rings as well as other underworld activities."[34] In the past, bootlegging and related crimes were the most lucrative of criminal activities. Today, that distinction belongs to gambling, followed by loan-sharking.[35]

There are several arguments against this rationale and again, many of them are embodied in justifications for other rationales. First, the question must be raised as to how officials determine the most lucrative activities. They are obviously estimating income of societies and not matrices. Perhaps as we look down the line at other activities, they may be very profitable, but be performed by other matrices. In a particular locale, does each enforcement agent make a determination as to which activity is most profitable in his area, or does he follow the national efforts and get at the largest single operation? This is critical, for if we are right, and groups and matrices function autonomously, each locality should make its own determination as to the main source of income for groups. In New York City it may be numbers, and in southern Indiana it may be slot machines.

Second, the most profitable activity may be difficult to strike at because of pervasive corruption that surrounds it and the prevailing attitude of the citizenry that there is really nothing wrong with it. Third, drying up the main source of income may drive the criminal elements from an activity we deem to do little social harm to activities that are less palatable to us.

But, despite these weakness, the income-producing activities rationale can be a feasible and practicable one, following as it does the maxim that a person hurts most when you hit him in the pocketbook.

Traditional Activities

This rationale is very closely linked to the one just described, hitting the income-producing activities. In that rationale it was assumed that income-producing activities that do not stem from the larger societies would be included in the equation. The strategy of hitting the traditional activities of criminal groups, for instance, gambling and loan-sharking, stems from the perception of organized crime as a society. This rationale may leave many organized criminal groups and matrices untouched and allow enforcement agencies to announce that there is no organized crime in their localities when there are, in fact, evidences of slot machine operations, prostitution, and truck hijacking going on. Often, in talking with enforcement agencies, this seems to be the implicit rationale for special units designed to combat organized crime. In the course of pursuing this strategy, however, the enforcement agencies are hurting organized criminal societies even though they are neglecting significant activities.

Corruption Producers

There are two possible rationales for dealing with corruption in organized crime. One is to attack those activities, like gambling and prostitution, that most require corrupt public officials in order to operate. According to the Knapp Commission, the effort to reduce corruption should be "aimed at reducing the exposure of policemen to potentially corrupting situations—the commission called for the legalizing of additional forms of gambling and the repeal of Sabbath laws controlling the sale of some goods on Sunday."[36] A second way to limit corruption is to strike directly at it by creating special police details or prosecutors to weed it out and by enacting tighter laws making the corrupt relationship a crime.

The justification for both rationales is the same. The existence of corruption undermines the ability of government agencies to perform their proper functions and also undermines proper respect for government. A further justification is that organized crime is taking over government, a hypothesis that was dismissed earlier due to the nature of organized criminal groups and societies.

The first alternative, striking at activities that most give rise to corruption, suffers from many of the pitfalls noted in earlier arguments. The very fact that corruption is part and parcel of certain activities makes police forces reluctant to do anything about it. Part of this attitude is due to the need to protect one's own brethren and part to the community's resistance to enforcement in these areas.

The second alternative—striking directly at corruption—can threaten the privacy and civil rights of public officials. Zealous prosecutors can move too quickly and, in so doing, breach these individuals' liberties. Also, investigations of corruption are inevitably political. The party in power is never the one under investigation. For example, note the apparent reluctance of the Nixon administration to look into the break-ins at the Watergate Hotel and the office of Daniel Ellsberg's psychiatrist, and the reasons for ITT's donation to the Republican party in 1972. At the same time, the Nixon administration and state Republican administrations vigorously prosecuted mayors on the East Coast whose administrations were tainted with corruption. The same patterns emerge when Democrats are in power.

Another argument against attacking corruption is made by social scientists who suggest that corruption is functional; that is, it is a means for supplementing legal patronage and thus helps to oil the wheels of an urban political machine.[37] James C. Scott follows this direction of thought when he views corruption as an integral part of the political process: "Corruption may then be seen as just one of many ways a person can persuade someone who exercises public authority to act as he wishes—that is, as a kind of influence."[38] The tendency, then, is to accept corruption as normal and even beneficial to orderly government. However, acceptance of a functional approach to corruption makes one uneasy because of the implications of acceptance of corruption in any shape or form.

A final criterion directed at attacks on corruption comes from those who see an attack on corruption as diverting resources from the fight against organized crime. Much corruption, they point out, may be perpetrated by business firms to avoid excessive competition, thus speeding up government contracts and freeing them from annoying regulations,[39] or by labor groups, professional societies, or almost any segment of American society.

Differential Enforcement

Unfortunately, law enforcement and the administration of justice are often carried out to the detriment of a particular social class or ethnic group. There may be one set of standards for the rich and another for the poor, one set for native Americans and another for immigrant groups. It is not new to suggest that the hand of justice may fall more heavily upon blacks than whites in this country, or that the rich stand a better chance than the poor to come through our system of justice unscathed. If enforcement agencies do effect such differential justice, it is rarely articulated and at times is less the result of agency policy than of the attitude of individual enforcement officials. But, whatever the reasons, it is suggested here that policy towards organized crime is at times governed by different standards for different groups of people.

There are several ways in which enforcement agencies are harsher on the poor and certain ethnic groups than on the rich. Consensual crimes, such as gambling and prostitution, are legalized in certain regions accessible to the middle and upper classes, but not the poor. For instance, the wealthy can go to England, the Bahamas, or Nevada to gamble and can do so legally.[40] Nevada now has a county option on the legalization of prostitution and there are some indications that it could become a larger industry.[41] The poor who like to gamble have no choice (except in states where certain forms of gambling are legal) but to do so with bookies who are operating illegally. Another example of differential laws for different classes of people is illustrated by the history of laws on the sale and distribution of marijuana. As long as use did not spread to the middle class, penalties remained harsh for usage. The great push for liberalization of the laws has resulted from usage by all segments of the population.

Even if consensual crimes service both rich and poor, there can be a double standard in enforcement practices. For instance, in many private clubs there are slot machines, and gambling goes on constantly. In rare instances, police enforce anti-gambling laws in these types of situations as well as in commercial gambling establishments. The Oakland, California, police department "has been known to raid not only commercial gambling operations but also gambling sponsored by labor unions, Catholic church bazaars, a local Lion's club, and a woman's social club."[42] By and large, however, these activities are usually left alone.

Differential enforcement may also depend upon the political party in office. In most cases, criminal groups try to be non-partisan in the sense that in elections they often give money to both political parties. The top gambler in Reading, Pennsylvania, was a man who hedged his bets in this way. "In some years, he helped several candidates, not caring who won but wanting to guarantee access to all."[43] But reform candidates may win and crack down very hard on the organized criminals in the area, and they may come from either party, usually the party that has been out of power for some time.

On the national level, Republicans have fewer inhibitions about attacking organized crime in the ghetto areas. It was under a Republican administration that indictments were brought against several Democratic mayors in New Jersey. On the other hand, the Republicans may react more quickly to dismiss wrongdoing between groups of businessmen or corporations which may be supportive of Republican politics. The point is that partisanship may play a role in selection of particular societies or activities targeted for attack by the government.

Thus far we have spoken of the ways in which certain groups may be counteracted because of their social class, ethnic group affiliation, or party loyalties. Their activities are the ones chosen for extinction. Certain problems become vital to enforcement agents only when they begin to affect or threaten middle and upper class individuals. As noted previously, the whole problem of addiction was promoted to a more important status when it was perceived as a middle class phenomenon. People do not get upset about gambling until they find out that the games or horse races they are watching are fixed. For most in the middle class, gambling simply remains invisible and there are those who want to keep it that way. For example, Pete Rozelle, the commissioner of the National Football League, bitterly resents schemes to bet on NFL games for he does not want overt manifestations of gambling to detract from the game. For the middle class, the sports scandal, whether it is in basketball, football, or hockey, is a reminder that gambling exists and some people succumb to the temptations of big money.

Crimes of property—the theft of securities, airport thefts, and truck hijackings—do not provide organized crime with a substantial amount of income, but they catch the public eye and seem to be a threat to the economic and social system of the middle and upper class individual. Theft of securities in particular seems to threaten the very foundations of our society. There is no doubt that enforcement agencies spend a good deal of time and resources to investigate these thefts. Thus, loan-sharking or gambling, which provide much more income and whose matrices may be far more complex, draw much less public attention.

Another activity that inspires a mobilization of the middle and upper classes against organized criminals that is all out of proportion to the threat is the infiltration of legitimate businesses. Here again, a broader segment of the population can identify with the threat, and public knowledge brings swift public action.

One of the inequities here is that it is most frequently organized criminals, particularly those from ethnic groups, who are apprehended for carrying on legitimate business through illegal means, despite the fact that such activity is far from the exclusive province of these groups.

Fear is spread only when organized criminals move into respectable businesses, and this is viewed as a threat to society whether they run the businesses by legal or illegal means. The public does not get as upset if a whole industry is involved in price fixing, conspiring to corner markets, or making inferior merchandise. In other words, a public outcry does not occur when a legal business is run by illegal means. Rather, the outcry comes when businesses, legal or illegal, are being run by individuals with a background of involvement in businesses we think of as strictly illegal. However, organized criminals have infiltrated certain family-type industries and may not have kept pace with the rest of the economy. Furthermore, businessmen may be perpetrating crimes just as serious in the furtherance of their own businesses and organized criminals in legitimate businesses may often be retirees.

This concludes the discussion of the various rationales for making policy on the basis of activities engaged in by organized criminals. Some of the rationales may be explicitly stated, while others are implicitly at work. There are other arguments for and against each rationale that I have not mentioned and, certainly, there are other rationales used. Hopefully, this list is relatively complete so that debate may at least begin.

Actual Choice of Rationales

Throughout this discussion of rationales, reference has been made to certain characteristics of enforcement institutions that may inhibit development of a certain rationale. Thus, it may be helpful to look at enforcement activities from an agency's perspective to see what restraints may be built in. The discussion will center on speculation as to why the FBI did not enter into the war against organized crime earlier. Much of this speculation is plausible and illustrates why many enforcement agencies tailor their programs in a particular way. (One point I will not deal with is that if there is corruption in the enforcement organization, there will be few attempts to apprehend criminals. This goes without saying.)

Although one of the usual bureaucratic imperatives is growth, and an organization may have as its whole *raison d'être* the motive of growth, some of the following points suggest why the FBI might not have wanted to expand its jurisdiction.

Until Robert Kennedy's concerted drive in 1961, the FBI remained relatively unconcerned about organized criminal activity. "In 1959, for example, only four agents in its [FBI] New York Office were assigned to this area. On the other hand, upwards of 400 agents in the same office were occupied in foiling domestic Communists."[44] This was two years after the Apalachin conference, at which there was evidence of some criminal conspiracy. Again, it is interesting to suggest why the FBI may have stayed out of the fight so long, for each suggestion illustrates a bureaucratic limitation in the part of enforcement agencies.

First, as suggested by the agent assignments mentioned above, an enforcement agency like the FBI has a variety of responsibilities. It may be that the FBI recognized there were organized criminal groups, but rightly or wrongly felt that the danger to the national interests lay with the Communist party. The bureau might not have recognized organized criminal groups, but when those were brought to its attention, it did move slowly into the fight in a clumsy bureaucratic way.

Second, agencies have a great deal of latitude in terms of which laws they will enforce, but sometimes they may lack proper jurisdiction in an area. The FBI argued that it lacked sufficient jurisdiction in the area of organized crime. Victor Navasky in *Kennedy Justice* suggests that "the Bureau's jurisdiction in the area was not explicit."[45] Kennedy pushed through some explicit legislation on organized crime in 1961, but "until then the implicit organizational truth on the subject was that if it is outside our jurisdiction, as far as we are concerned, it doesn't exist."[46]

A third factor is that one of the imperatives of any bureaucratic organization is that it project the best possible public image. In the past, the Bureau of Narcotics and the Internal Revenue Service have had agents corrupted by organized criminals. It is possible that Hoover wanted to protect his agents from corruption and maintain their reputation as untouchables, and recognized that there is more chance of corruption in dealing with gamblers and gambling than in apprehending kidnappers or car thieves.

Another way to project a favorable image is to build up an impressive record of arrests and convictions. From the top to the bottom levels in enforcement agencies, arrests and convictions are important means for evaluating success. Navasky suggests that "the Bureau's preoccupation with impressive statistical batting averages for display at appropriation time led to the avoidance of the long-drawn-out investigations organized crime requires and concentration instead on such easily quantifiable, open-and-shut crimes as auto thefts and bank robberies."[47] A related hypothesis is that Hoover had other ways of making newspaper copy and one of these was the "ten most wanted men" program. William W. Turner, a former FBI agent, suggests this in his notes from a 1953 lecture by an FBI speaker: "Top Ten—good publicity—Bureau wants to know if certain newspapers' publicity results in apprehension."[48] As Turner indicates, this list gave a distorted view of the crime picture by "elevating to the status of national menace an array of cheap thugs, barroom knifers, psychopathic rapists, wife-beaters, and alcoholic stick-up men—again, the 'few preying on the few.' "[49] The FBI launched this program at the same time Estes Kefauver began his probe of organized crime.

There is some credence to the notion that dealing with organized criminals is not easy and an agency may lose some of its reputation if it attempts to do so. One of the biggest scandals in FBI history occurred in the pursuit of organized criminals. In 1968 the home of Joe Bonanno, a reputed organized crime figure, was bombed. Evidence pointed to the fact that the bombing was planned by an FBI agent named David O. Hale and executed by two individuals he hired.[50] The case received a great deal of publicity, most of it adverse, and had its bizarre aspects. "Convinced that it was Peter Notaro who had shot at Stevens (one of the men who planted the bomb) the night of the Bonanno bombing, Hale approached Dunbar, (one of the three who perpetrated the bombing) with a plan to avenge Stevens' injury by killing Notaro; knowing that Dunbar was a skilled archer, Hale suggested that death by crossbow would be an interesting method. Dunbar refused." Hale resigned from the FBI and was unavailable to the press.[51] Indications are that the bombing was planned in the hope that rival gangland factions would blame each other for it. Needless to say, dealing with organized crime can get rough and even dirty, and this is something the FBI might want to stay away from.

There are other reasons for the FBI's reluctance to become involved in the fight against organized crime. Giving the bureau the benefit of the doubt, and judging from its pronouncements, one may conclude that it fears the formation of a national police force. This, one line of reasoning goes, is why the FBI did not move swiftly into organized crime enforcement. Gerard L. Goettel, a prosecutor for the Department of Justice, said that "Mr. Hoover has indicated that he does not want the FBI to become a national police force, and shows no indication to expand the bureau's functions."[52] Less altruistic reasons also existed for the FBI's reluctance to expand. The bureau's fight on organized crime would overlap with that of other agencies and it might have feared loss of bureaucratic autonomy if it joined an effort others were engaged in. There is some evidence for this structural dilemma the FBI faced. The FBI was the coolest towards the Justice Department in cooperating to gather evidence on the Apalachin meeting. Gerard Goettel suggests that "this performance was consistent with the FBI's rigid policy of refusing to take on any case which does not clearly fall within its jurisdiction; nor will it investigate if another agency has already done so."[53] The FBI carefully maintained and still maintains its autonomy and preserves its mystique in crime fighting. The FBI was finally dragged in to cooperate with other agencies in fighting organized crime and now some of its agents participate on the organized crime strike forces. As would be expected, they had to give up some of their autonomy and are under Justice Department supervision.

Finally, the FBI might have stayed out of the organized crime fight for the same reasons it was reluctant to get into civil rights controversies. Often local authorities were responsible for perpetrating violations of civil rights in cooperation with other citizens. "The FBI didn't want to jeopardize its relationship with local enforcers whose cooperation they needed in non-civil rights areas."[54] There were other reasons, of course, but if they harassed a local sheriff, they would get no cooperation in other matters. The same may be true with regard to organized crime. Many local enforcement agencies are riddled by corruption and FBI crackdown on these agencies may diminish cooperation from them.

This discussion has applied specifically to the FBI, but many of the same structural dilemmas confront other agencies and create a reluctance to get into the fight against organized crime. Local police forces do not want to lose their autonomy, risk corruption, or dim their success rates against other forms of crime in the process of fighting organized crime.

Something must be said for the federated relationship between various agencies responsible for enforcement. The first tendency is to blame corruption and non-enforcement on the local police forces. Very often they are at the mercy of local politicians who are beholden to organized criminals. The leniency of the courts on people who are convicted of gambling and other crimes weakens local forces' resolve to do anything about organized crime. Public opinion, which frequently does little to support the police in this effort, must also be blamed.

Most of the laws to deal with organized criminals, and hence jurisdiction for their apprehension, lie at the local level. Michael Dorman recognizes this fact and suggests in *Payoff* that organized criminals are wasting their money by corrupting federal officials before they have gained influence in local institutions. He also suggests they "try to keep someone with power at each level—or else anyone along the line can put [them] out of business."[55] Recently, especially since passage of the Organized Crime Control Act of 1970, jurisdiction in matters involving organized crime has been given to the federal government. Still these federal agencies account for little more than 1 percent of all enforcement agencies.

Even with more federal help, there still is the problem of promoting interagency cooperation. If an academic suggests he is studying enforcement, most agencies assume he is naively trying to figure out how to promote such cooperation. Unfortunately, much of the conflict is built into the system as suggested before. Agencies jealously guard their prerogatives, and corruption makes an agency reluctant to allow another force in. It is interesting to note that most state police do not have to ask the local sheriff's permission to arrest a speeder or an ordinary thief. But if they are to make a gambling raid, protocol is to get permission of local authorities. Challenges to local authorities can severely hamper the pursuit of other activities in the area by superordinate agencies.

Tactics

Before concluding this discussion of perceiving organized crime as a matrix of activities, it would be helpful to briefly mention some of the tactics that can be employed against these activities.

Sanford Kadish talks about the overcriminalization of the enforcement process, by which he means that in American society we tend to make laws for every moral transgression, and throw an intolerable burden on enforcement agencies that have to police against gambling, bootlegging, drunkenness, abortion, and so forth.[56] Morris and Hawkins feel that we can solve many of our enforcement problems by legalizing these activities.[57] This tactic can apply to some, but not all, of organized criminal activities. One can conceive of legalized gambling, prostitution, and the charging of high interest rates by government to the poor, but not of the legalization of murder, theft, or bribery. A serious problem with this tactic is that public opinion is very often slow to change in regard to gambling, prostitution, and the like, and for the near future, some of these changes remain unlikely. Finally, where experiments in legislation have taken place, the results have been mixed.

A second tactic is to improve the livelihood of all Americans so they will be better educated and less in need of the services of organized crime, and less prone to commit crime. This suggestion follows from implicit or explicit belief in the queer ladder of social mobility. But it has been shown that organized crime is much more than a response to poverty and is endemic to all segments of our society, including both producers and consumers. Another obvious problem with this tactic is that it says nothing about solutions to immediate problems. Often it is a veiled suggestion that we put more weight on righting inequalities and promoting social justice than on the more punitive aspects of criminal justice.

A third tactic is to call upon more and better tactical weapons to deal with organized crime, more extensive use of wiretapping, larger forces, tougher immunity laws, more stringent laws on search and seizure, stronger sentences for habitual defenders, and so forth. There is no need to deal with the pros and cons of each except to say that the debates usually come down to the rights of criminals and other individuals who might be unjustly implicated versus the imperatives of enforcement practices. Unfortunately, there is no easy way to decide what the limits of authority ought to be. Politicians and enforcement agents should not have one set of standards for organized criminals and another for the rest of society. Nobody raises much of a cry when Mayor Lindsay says he is going to have organized criminals followed day and night after the killing of two innocent citizens by mistake. Yet think of the public outcry when congressmen, journalists, entertainment figures, and others were designated as enemies to be investigated.

Finally, there are ways to make sure that illegal services are not a menace to the public health or safety. For instance, during Prohibition Al Capone bragged that the services he provided were better than those of competitors. Nobody was poisoned, blinded, or killed by his liquor. Enforcement agents can go after those illegal businesses that are conducted through illegal means. They might go after the independent narcotics smugglers whose doses are irregular enough to cause death from overdoses in some cases, or the gambler who doesn't pay off, or the house of prostitution in which venereal diseases are rampant. This tactic is very likely to establish as the enemy, not the very large matrices and societies, but independent groups.

I had hoped to draw the lines upon which alternatives for dealing with organized crime can be debated. One law enforcement agent is correct in his assessment of those of my ilk who pompously suggest solutions. "The social scientists and the professorial types like to talk about grand strategies. There is no grand strategy that I know of that promises to wipe out organized crime."[58] I might add, at least none that is feasible. All the social scientist can do is draw up the alternative lines of argument that follow from his perceptions of organized crime.

Notes

Chapter I

1. Nicholas Gage, *The Mafia is not an Equal Opportunity Employer* (New York: McGraw-Hill, 1971), p. 67; *New York Times,* 10 June 1971, pp. 1, 12. After Lansky was ordered to leave Israel, he searched in vain for a country which would give him refuge. He returned finally to the United States to face charges pending against him.

2. See, for example, Fred J. Cook, "The People v. The Mob; Or, Who Rules New Jersey?" *New York Times Magazine,* 1 February 1970, pp. 9, 11, 33, 36.

3. "The Mafia: Back to the Bad Old Days?" *Time,* 12 July 1971, p. 14.

4. Gay Talese, *Honor Thy Father* (New York: World Publishing, 1971).

5. Mario Puzo, *The Godfather* (New York: Fawcett Publications, 1969).

6. C. Wright Mills, *The Power Elite* (New York: Oxford University Press, 1959); Herbert Marcuse, *One-Dimensional Man: Studies in the Ideology of Advanced Industrial Society* (Boston: Beacon Press, 1964); and Theodore Lowi, *The End of Liberalism: Ideology, Policy and the Crisis of Public Authority* (New York: W. W. Norton and Co., 1969).

7. Robert E. Lane, *Political Ideology* (New York: Free Press, 1962), pp. 27-28.

8. The phrases found in quotation marks are titles of books about organized crime and/or phrases often used to describe organized criminals.

9. The President's Commission on Law Enforcement and Administration of Justice, Task Force on Organized Crime, *Task Force Report: Organized Crime* (Washington: United States Government Printing Office, 1967), p. 1.

10. *Combatting Organized Crime: A Report of the Oyster Bay, New York, Conference on Organized Crime* (Albany: Office of the Governor, 1965), p. 19; and see, for instance, use of the definition in the Pennsylvania Crime Commission, *Report on Organized Crime* (Harrisburg: Office of the Attorney General, Commonwealth of Pennsylvania, 1970), p. 10; and Donald Cressey, *Theft of a Nation* (New York: Harper and Row, 1969), pp. 297-324.

11. *Task Force Report: Organized Crime*, p. 1.

12. See Daniel Bell, *The End of Ideology* (Glencoe, Ill.: Free Press, 1960), pp. 133-136; for an extended discussion of this theme see Chapter 3 of this volume.

13. Ramsey Clark, *Crime in America* (New York: Pocket Books, 1971), p. 52.

14. *Task Force Report: Organized Crime*, p. 1.

15. Logs of electronically surveilled conversations of Samuel Rizzo de Cavalcante made by the FBI in 1961-1965 were introduced during proceedings of *United States v. de Cavalcante et al.* (Camden: U.S. District Court, District of New Jersey). These hearings are edited and appear with commentary in Henry A. Ziegler, *Sam The Plumber* (New York: Signet Books, 1970). There is evidence for the hypothesis made in the text on pp. 148, 192, 208, 275.

16. Francis A. J. Ianni, "The Mafia and the Web of Kinship," *Public Interest* 22 (Winter 1971): 91-92.

17. For a brief description of the Gallo-Profaci war see Ralph Salerno and John S. Thompkins, *The Crime Confederation* (New York: Popular Library, 1969), pp. 133-148.

18. Gilbert Geis, "Violence and Organized Crime," *Annals of the American Academy of Political and Social Science* 365 (March 1966): 87, 92.

19. *Task Force Report: Organized Crime*, p. 1.

20. *Ibid.*

21. *Ibid.*

22. Salerno and Thompkins, *Confederation*, pp. 310-320.

23. Hank Messick, *Lansky* (New York: G. P. Putman's Sons, 1971), p. 7.

24. *Ibid.*

25. *Hearings Before the Permanent Subcommittee on Investigation of the Committee on Government Operations* (McClellan Committee), [hereafter referred to in notes as *Hearings* (McClellan)] 88th Cong., 1st Sess., 1963, p. 20.

26. *Ibid.*

27. Organized Crime Control Act of 1970, Public Law 91-452; 84 Stat. 922, p. 4470.

28. *Task Force Report: Organized Crime*, p. 1.

29. *Task Force Report: Crime and Its Impact—An Assessment* (Washington, D.C.: U.S. Government Printing Office, 1967), p. 96.

30. Salerno and Thompkins, *Confederation*, p. 92.

31. Carl T. Curtis, "A Courageous Leader," *New York Times*, 21 June 1973, p. 39.

2. See especially, *Hearings* (McClellan), 88th Cong. 1st Sess. 1963, parts 1-3.

33. Talese, *Honor*, book jacket.

34. *Ibid.*

35. Vincent ("The Cat") Siciliano, *Unless They Kill Me First* (New York: Universal-Award House, Inc., 1970); *Hearings* (McClellan), 92nd Cong., 1971, pp. 772-838; Sidney Slater and Quentin Reynolds "My Life Inside The Mob," *Saturday Evening Post* (29 August 1963).

36. Siciliano, *Unless They Kill*, p. 117.

37. Peter Maas, ed., *The Valachi Papers* (New York: Bantam Books, 1968); Talese, *Honor*.

38. Ziegler, *Plumber*; and Joseph Volz and Peter J. Bridge, eds. *The Mafia Talks* (Greenwich, Conn.: Fawcett Publications, 1969).

39. *Hearings Before the Subcommittee on Criminal Laws and Procedures of the Senate Committee on the Judiciary*, 90th Cong., 1st Sess., 11 July 1967, pp. 942-954.

40. *The Voices of Organized Crime*, an educational tape prepared by the New York State Joint Legislative Committee on Crime, 1968.

41. Ziegler, *Plumber*, p. 28.

42. *Ibid.*

43. Talese, *Honor*, pp. 53-56.

44. *Ibid.*, p. 54.

45. *Voices of Crime.*

46. *Hearings* (McClellan), 88th Cong., 1st Sess., 1963, p. 169.

47. *Ibid.*

48. National Commission on Law Observance and Enforcement (Wickersham Commission), vol. 12, *Report on The Cost of Crime* (Washington: Government Printing Office, 1931).

49. See for example, Gage, *Not Equal*; Talese, *Honor;* Sandy Smith and William Lambert, "The Congressman and The Hoodlum," *Life*, 19 August 1968, pp. 20-27; and Messick, *Lansky.*

50. Nicholas de B. Katzenbach, "Crime Reporting: The Need for Professionals," *Vital Speeches*, 14 February 1966, p. 351.

51. Gage, *Not Equal*, p. 12.

52. *Ibid.*

53. *Ibid.*, pp. 11-16.

54. Paul Weaver, "Is Television Biased?" *Public Interest* (Spring 1972).

55. See for example, *Inside The Mafia*, vol. 1, no. 1 (New York: Swinton Publishing Company, 1972).

56. Jimmy Breslin, *The Gang That Couldn't Shoot Straight* (New York: Bantam Books, 1969), p. 215.

Chapter 2

1. John Heron Lepper, *Famous Secret Societies* (Sampson, Low, Marston Co., Ltd., 1938), p. 196.

2. *Ibid.*, p. 199.

3. *Ibid.*, p. 296.

4. *Ibid.*, pp. 56-60.

5. Norman Mac Kenzie, ed., *Secret Societies* (New York: Collier Books, 1967), p. 93.

6. Arkon Daraul, *A History of Secret Societies* (New York: Citadel Press, 1961), p. 244.

7. Hugh D. Graham and Ted R. Gurr, eds. *Violence in America, A Report to the National Commission on the Causes and Prevention of Violence* (New York: Signet Books, 1969), p. 44.

8. Herbert Asbury, *The Gangs of New York: An Informal History of the Underworld* (New York and London: Alfred A. Knopf, 1928).

9. Johnathan Craig and Richard Posner, *The New York Crime Book* (New York: Pyramid Books, 1972), pp. 14-19.

10. Peter Maas, *The Valachi Papers* (New York: Bantam Books, 1968), pp. 56-57.

11. *Ibid.*, p. 56.

12. Craig and Posner, *Crime Book*, p. 55.

13. Maas, *Valachi*, pp. 66-67.

14. John Kobler, *Capone* (New York: G. P. Putman's Sons, 1971), p. 38.

15. Kenneth Allsop, *The Bootleggers and Their Era* (New York: Doubleday and Co., 1961), p. 33.

16. Kobler, *Capone*, pp. 89-90.

17. Except, for instance, where one company can effectively create a monopoly by patent, excellent product identification such as Kleenex and Hershey bars, or prior technological sophistication in a related field which gives them an edge over customers.

18. Arthur Train, *Courts and Criminals* (New York: Charles Scribner's Sons, 1925), pp. 285-286.

19. Donald R. Cressey, *Theft of a Nation* (New York: Harper and Row, 1969), p. 8.

20. Train, *Courts*, p. 281.

21. Gaetano Mosca, "Mafia" *in* Edwin R. A. Seligman, *Encyclopedia of the Social Sciencies*, vol. 10 (New York: MacMillan Co., 1933); Giovanni Schiavo, *The Truth about The Mafia* (New York: Vigo Press, 1962); and Francis A. J. Ianni, "The Mafia and the Web of Kinship," *Public Interest* 22 (Winter 1971).

22. Ianni, "Web of Kinship," pp. 82-83.

23. *Ibid.,* p. 83.

24. *Hearings Before the Permanent Subcommittee on Investigations of the Committee on Government Operations* (McClellan Committee), 88th Cong., 1st Sess., 1963.

25. Joseph Lopreato, *Italian Americans* (New York: Random House, 1970), pp. 12-13.

26. Mosca, "Mafia," p. 36.

27. Luigi Barzini, *The Italians* (New York: Bantam Books, 1965), p. 264.

28. Ianni, "Web of Kinship," p. 79.

29. J. Richard (Dixie) Davis, "Things I Couldn't Tell Till Now," pt. 3, *Colliers* (5 August 1939): 44.

30. Maas, *Valachi,* p. 103.

31. *Ibid.,* p. 109.

32. *Ibid.,* p. 113.

33. *Ibid.*

34. Ralph Salerno and John S. Thompkins, *The Crime Confederation* (New York: Popular Library, 1969), p. 244.

35. Burton B. Turkus and Sid Feder, *Murder, Inc.* (London: Victor Gollancz, 1953), p. 9.

36. *Ibid.,* p. 79.

37. Joseph Bruce Gorman, *Kefauver* (New York: Oxford University Press, 1971), p. 87.

38. *Second Interim Report of the Special Committee to Investigate Organized Crime in Interstate Commerce* (Washington: U.S. Government Printing Office, 1951), p. 10.

39. Robert F. Kennedy, *The Enemy Within* (New York: Harper and Row, 1960), p. 6.

40. Frederic Sondern, *The Brotherhood of Evil* (New York: Farrar, Straus and Cudahy, 1959), pp. 3-4.

41. Maas, *Valachi,* pp. 260-265.

42. Norvall Morris and Gordon Hawkins in *The Honest Politician's Guide to Crime Control* (Chicago: University of Chicago Press, 1970), pp. 215-224, try to discredit Valachi's testimony by showing discrepancies in his statement. Most important, however, is not his complete accuracy, but the change in perspective his views as an insider in a "society" brought to the study, investigation, and public rendering of organized crime.

43. Salerno and Thompkins, *Confederation,* p. 133.

44. *Ibid.,* pp. 133-142.

45. "Colombo: A Man with Several Roles," *New York Times,* 29 June 1971, p. 20.

46. *Ibid.*

47. "Suspect in Shooting of Colombo Linked to Gambino Family," *New York Times,* 20 July 1971, p. 21.

48. Eric Pace, "Mafia Members Said to be Hiding," *New York Times,* 13 April 1972, p. 40.

49. Gay Talese, *Honor Thy Father* (New York: World Publishing, 1971), p. 165.

50. Henry A. Ziegler, *Sam The Plumber* (New York: Signet Books, 1970), p. 53.

51. Salerno and Thompkins, *Confederation,* p. 125.

52. Talese, *Honor,* p. 22.

53. For further information on these events see "U.S. Investigating Lansky's Crime," *New York Times,* 10 June 1971, pp. 1-12; Lou Brown "I Worked with Basketball's No. 1 Briber," *Look,* 27 February 1962, pp. 71-84, and Sandy Smith and William Lambert, "The Congressman and the Hoodlum," *Life,* 9 August 1968, pp. 20-27.

Chapter 3

1. The choice to study these two dimensions is necessarily arbitrary. For instance, ensuing chapters will explore the questions of whether the organized criminal is a profit maximizer or motivated by considerations of power. Any number of dimensions could be studied.

2. Edwin M. Schur, *Our Criminal Society: The Social and Legal Source of Crime in America* (Englewood Cliffs, N.J.: Prentice-Hall, 1969), pp. 57-73, 82-86.

3. Nicholas Gage, *The Mafia is not an Equal Opportunity Employer* (New York: McGraw-Hill, 1971), pp. 41-42, 60-61.

4. Sidney Slater and Quentin Reynolds, "My Life Inside the Mob," *Saturday Evening Post* 29 (24 August 1963): 40.

5. Francis A. J. Ianni, "The Mafia and the Web of Kinship," *Public Interest* 22 (Winter 1971): 99.

6. Burton B. Turkus and Sid Feder, *Murder, Inc.* (London: Victor Gollancz, 1953), p. 40.

7. Robert F. Kennedy, *The Enemy Within* (New York: Popular Library, 1960), p. 20.

8. Henry A. Ziegler, ed., *Sam The Plumber* (New York: Signet Books, 1970), p. 32.

9. *Ibid.*

10. Turkus and Feder, *Murder, Inc.,* p. 40.

11. Ziegler, *Plumber,* p. 160.

12. Ralph Salerno and John S. Thompkins, *The Crime Confederation* (New York: Popular Library, 1969), p. 208.

13. *Ibid.*, p. 209.

14. Ziegler, *Plumber*, pp. 196-197.

15. *Ibid.*, p. 155.

16. *Hearings Before the Permanent Subcommittee on Investigations of the Committee on Government Operations* (McClellan Committee), 88th Cong., 1st Sess., 1968, p. 115.

17. Mike Royko, *The Boss: Richard L. Daley of Chicago* (New York: E. P. Dutton and Co., 1971), p. 50.

18. Sidney Hook, *The Quest for Being* (New York: Dell Publishing Co., 1961), pp. 26-27.

19. *Ibid.*, p. 27.

20. Mario Puzo, *The Godfather* (Greenwich, Conn.: Fawcett Publications, 1969).

21. *Ibid.*, p. 14.

22. *Ibid.*, p. 276.

23. See, for instance Gay Talese's treatment of a purported Mafia don in *Honor Thy Father* (New York: World Publishing Co., 1971).

24. Bob Peterson, "The Wealthy Father of the Godfather," *Life*, vol. 69, no. 2, p. 44.

25. Slater and Reynolds, "Inside the Mob," p. 39.

26. *Ibid.*, p. 50.

27. Jimmy Breslin, *The Gang That Couldn't Shoot Straight* (New York: Bantam Books, 1970), p. 35.

28. *Ibid.*, p. 68.

29. *Ibid.*, pp. 163-164.

30. Estes Kefauver, *Crime in America* (Garden City, N.Y.: Doubleday Co., 1951), p. 51.

31. Ziegler, *Plumber*, p. 165.

32. *The Voices of Organized Crime*, New York State Joint Legislative Committee on Crime, 1968, pp. 52-53.

33. Turkus and Feder, *Murder, Inc.*, p. 114, 116, 132.

34. *Ibid.*, p. 114, 12.

35. Peter M. Blau and W. Richard Scott, *Formal Organizations* (San Francisco: Chandler Publishing Co., 1962), p. 252.

36. For an excellent discussion of Blau and Scott's position see Michael A. Weinstein, *Philosophy, Theory and Method in Contemporary Political Thought* (Glenview, Ill.: Scott, Foresman and Co., 1971), pp. 141-145.

37. Ziegler, *Plumber*.

38. Peter Maas, *The Valachi Papers* (New York: Bantam Books, 1968), p. 262.

39. Blau and Scott, *Organizations*. "New problems are internally generated in organizations in the process of solving old ones" (p. 250).

40. *Voices of Crime*, p. 20.

41. Turkus and Feder, *Murder, Inc.*, p. 92.

42. Ramsey Clark, *Crime in America* (New York: Pocket Books, 1971), p. 67.

43. Hank Messick, *Lansky* (New York: G. P. Putman's Sons, 1971), p. 164.

44. John A. Gardiner, *The Politics of Corruption: Organized Crime in an American City* (New York: Russell Sage Foundation, 1970).

45. Clark, *Crime in America*, p. 53.

46. Messick, *Lansky*, p. 221.

47. Maas, *Valachi*, pp. 134-135.

48. *Voices of Crime*, pp. 52-53.

49. Joseph Heller, *Catch—22.* (New York: Dell Publishing Co., 1955).

50. "The Mafia: Back to the Bad Old Days?" *Time*, 12 July 1971, p. 14.

51. *Ibid.*

52. *Hearings* (McClellan), 88th Cong., 1st Sess., 1963, pt. 2, p. 590.

53. The concepts "garlic and guns" and the "melted pot" are my own creations used to clarify the conclusions of other practitioners in the field.

54. See abbreviated definition of organized crime in Chapter 1.

55. Herbert Gans, *The Urban Villagers* (New York: Free Press, 1962).

56. Edward C. Banfield, *The Unheavenly City* (Boston: Little, Brown and Co., 1968), chapters 3 and 4.

57. Banfield, *Unheavenly*, p. 70.

58. Daniel Bell, *The End of Ideology* (Glencoe, Ill.: Free Press, 1960), pp. 115-116.

59. Luigi Barzini, *The Italians* (New York: Bantam Books, 1964), p. 286.

60. Nathan Glazer and Daniel Patrick Moynihan, *Beyond the Melting Pot* (Cambridge, Mass.: MIT Press, 1963), p. 224.

61. Glazer and Moynihan, *Melting Pot*, p. 225.

62. Ziegler, *Plumber*, p. 224.

63. Larry Collins and Dominique La Pierre, "The French Connection— In Real Life," *New York Times Magazine* (6 February 1972): 14-16, 51-53.

64. Barzini, *Italians*, p. 271.

65. Salerno and Thompkins, *Confederation*, p. 370.

66. Turkus and Feder, *Murder, Inc.*

67. Harry J. Anslinger and Will Oursler, *The Murderers* (New York: Farrar, Straus, and Cudahy, 1962), pp. 20-21.

68. Collins and La Pierre, "French Connection," p. 14.

69. *Ibid.*

70. Henry Barrett Chamberlain, "Some Observations Concerning Organized Crime," *Journal of Criminal Law and Criminology* 22 (January 1932): 661.

71. Messick, *Lansky*.

72. Talese, *Honor*, pp. 11-14.

73. Barzini, *Italians*.

74. Maas, *Valachi*, p. 246.

75. Glazer and Moynihan, *Melting Pot*, pp. 273-274.

76. Bell, *Ideology*, p. 117.

77. *Ibid.*, pp. 116-119.

78. Richard Cloward and Lloyd Ohlin, *Delinquency and Opportunity*, (Glencoe, Ill.: Free Press, 1960).

79. Irving Spergel, *Racketville, Slumtown, Haulberg* (Chicago: University of Chicago Press, 1964), p. xii.

80. *Ibid.*, p. xv.

81. *Ibid.*, p. xvi.

82. *Ibid.*, pp. xvi-xvii.

83. Chamberlain, "Some Observations," p. 660.

84. Francis A. J. Ianni, *A Family Business* (New York: Russell Sage Foundation, 1972), p. 194.

85. *Hearings* (McClellan), 88th Cong., 1st Sess., 1963, pp. 413-14.

86. Nicholas Gage, "Informants Give Mafia Reaction to Colombo Shooting," *New York Times*, 30 June 1971, p. 26.

87. Gage, *Not Equal*, p. 127.

88. Ianni, *Family Business*, p. 86.

89. Richard "Dixie" Davis, "Things I Couldn't Tell Till Now," pt. 2, *Colliers*, 104 (29 July 1939): 21.

90. Ianni, *Family Business*, p. 193.

91. *Ibid.*, pp. 87-106.

92. *Ibid.*, p. 96.

93. *Ibid.*, pp. 88, 100.

94. Bell, *Ideology*, pp. 121, 130-133.

95. Ziegler, *Plumber*, p. 122.

96. Puzo, *Godfather*, pp. 440-441.

97. Robert K. Merton, *Social Theory and Social Structure*, rev. ed., (Glencoe, Ill.: Free Press, 1957), chapters 4-5.

98. Edwin H. Sutherland, *White Collar Crime*, supra n.1, chapter 2.

99. Salerno and Thompkins, *Confederation*, p. 136.

100. David Finn, *The Corporate Oligarch* (New York: Simon and Schuster, 1969), p. 89.

101. Talese, *Honor*.

102. Anslinger and Oursler, *Murderers,* pp. 9-10.
103. Ziegler, *Plumber,* p. 208.
104. Joseph Crapsey, *The Nether Side of New York* (New York: Sheldon, 1872), p. 138.
105. Anthony Downs, *Inside Bureaucracy* (Boston: Little, Brown and Co., 1966), p. 20.
106. Salerno and Thompkins, *Confederation,* p. 100.
107. Downs, *Bureaucracy,* p. 20-21.
108. Ziegler, *Plumber,* p. 30.
109. *Ibid.,* p. 213.
110. *Voices of Crime,* p. 27.

Chapter 4

1. Donald R. Cressey, *Theft of a Nation* (New York: Harper and Row, 1969).
2. Francis A. J. Ianni, "The Mafia and the Web of Kinship," *Public Interest* 22 (Winter 1971); also Francis A. J. Ianni, *A Family Business* (New York: Russell Sage Foundation, 1972).
3. See for example, Thomas C. Schelling, "Economic Analysis and Organized Crime," in *Task Force Report: Organized Crime* (Washington: Government Printing Office, 1967).
4. David Easton, *The Political System: An Inquiry into the State of Political Science* (New York: Alfred A. Knopf, 1953).
5. Henry Barrett Chamberlain, "Some Observations Concerning Organized Crime," *Journal of Criminal Law and Criminology* 22 (January 1932): 652.
6. *Task Force Report: Organized Crime,* p. 6.
7. Schelling, "Economic Analysis."
8. *Ibid.,* p. 115.
9. Henry A. Ziegler, ed., *Sam The Plumber* (New York: Signet Books, 1970), p. 240.
10. Chamberlain, "Some Observations," p. 655.
11. Hank Messick, *Lansky* (New York: G. P. Putnam's Sons, 1971), pp. 31-32.
12. Ralph Salerno and John S. Thompkins, *The Crime Confederation* (New York: Popular Library, 1969), p. 127.
13. Vincent "The Cat" Siciliano, *Unless They Kill Me First* (New York: Award Books, 1970), p. 44.
14. Chamberlain, "Some Observations," p. 655.

15. Estes Kefauver, *Crime in America* (Garden City, N.Y.: Doubleday Co., 1951), pp. 111-12.

16. Siciliano, *Unless They Kill,* p. 46.

17. *Ibid.,* p. 47.

18. Norval Morris and Gordon Hawkins, *The Honest Politician's Guide to Crime Control* (Chicago: University of Chicago Press, 1970), p. 222.

19. Salerno and Thompkins, *Confederation,* p. 177.

20. Messick, *Lansky,* p. 14.

21. *Hearings Before the Subcommittee on Criminal Laws and Procedures of the Senate Committee on the Judiciary,* [hereafter referred to as *Hearings . . . Judiciary*] 90th Cong., 1st Sess., 11 July 1967, p. 943.

22. *Ibid.,* p. 946.

23. Ziegler, *Plumber,* p. 263.

24. Max Singer, "The Vitality of Mythical Numbers," *Public Interest* 23 (Spring 1971): 6.

25. Cressey, *Theft,* p. 75.

26. Ianni, *Family Business,* pp. 90-91.

27. Cressey, *Theft,* p. 243.

28. Ramsey Clark, *Crime in America* (New York: Pocket Books, 1970), p. 56.

29. Cressey, *Theft,* p. 2.

30. Ziegler, *Plumber,* p. 181.

31. *Ibid.,* p. 182.

32. *Ibid.,* p. 241.

33. John Gardiner with the assistance of David J. Olson, "Wincanton: the Politics of Corruption," *Task Force Report: Organized Crime,* p. 66.

34. *Summary and Principal Recommendations: Commission to Investigate Allegations of Police Corruption (New York),* 3 August 1972, p. 12.

35. William Foote Whyte, *Street Corner Society* (Chicago: University of Chicago Press, 1943), p. 129.

36. *Ibid.*

37. *Hearings . . . Judiciary,* 90th Cong., 1st Sess.

38. Cressey, *Theft,* p. 127.

39. *Hearings . . . Judiciary,* 90th Cong., 1st Sess., 11 July 1967, p. 952.

40. Ovid de Maris, *Captive City* (New York: Pocket Books, 1970), p. 15. Six attorneys were used when Giancana was granted immunity before a grand jury in 1965.

41. Gardiner, "Wincanton," p. 64.

42. Messick, *Lansky,* p. 221.

43. Peter Maas, *The Valachi Papers* (New York: Bantam Books, 1968), p. 194.

44. *Hearings . . . Judiciary*, 90th Cong., 1st Sess., 11 July 1967, p. 951.

45. Maas, *Valachi*, p. 188.

46. Ziegler, *Plumber*, p. 242.

47. Maas, *Valachi*, pp. 192-94.

48. Ziegler, *Plumber*, pp. 113, 173.

49. *Task Force Report: Organized Crime*, pp. 1-24.

50. Talcott Parsons, "The Monopoly of Force and the 'Power Bank,'" in M. E. Olson, *Power in Society* (New York: Macmillan Co., 1970), pp. 54-55.

51. Richard "Dixie" Davis, "Things I Couldn't Tell Till Now," *Colliers* 104 (22 July 1939): p. 9.

52. Ziegler, *Plumber*, p. 104.

53. Mario Puzo, *The Godfather* (Greenwich, Conn.: Fawcett Publications, 1969), pp. 69-70.

54. Davis "Couldn't Tell," (12 August 1939): 16-17, 29.

55. Ziegler, *Plumber*, p. 160.

56. Gilbert Geis, "Violence and Organized Crime," *Annals of the American Academy of Political and Social Science* 365 (March 1966): 87.

57. Maas, *Valachi*, p. 107.

58. *Ibid.*

59. Norman MacKenzie, ed., *Secret Societies* (New York: Collier Books, 1967), p. 222.

60. Ziegler, *Plumber*, p. 261.

61. *Ibid.*, p. 263.

62. Geis, "Violence and Crime."

63. Ziegler, *Plumber*, p. 248.

64. John Landesco, *Organized Crime in Chicago* (Chicago: University of Chicago Press, 1968), p. 212.

65. *Ibid.*

66. John Kobler, *Capone* (New York: G. P. Putman's Sons, 1971), p. 209.

67. Chamberlain, "Some Observations," p. 660.

68. Frederic Sondern, Jr., *Brotherhood of Evil* (New York: Farrar, Straus and Cudahy, 1959), pp. 242-43.

69. Ianni, *Family Business*, p. 134.

70. Cressey, *Theft*, pp. 174-185.

71. Salerno and Thompkins, *Confederation*, pp. 108-129.

72. Ianni, *Family Business*, pp. 139-48.

73. *Hearings . . . Judiciary*, 90th Cong., 1st Sess., 11 July 1967, p. 945.

74. *Ibid.*

75. Ziegler, *Plumber*, p. 17.

76. Ianni, *Family Business*, p. 143.

77. *Ibid.*, p. 144.

78. Salerno and Thompkins, *Confederation*, p. 127.

79. Cressey, *Theft*, p. 177.

80. Ianni, *Family Business*, p. 144.

81. *Ibid.*, p. 147.

82. *Ibid.*

83. Ziegler, *Plumber*, p. 249.

84. Salerno and Thompkins, *Confederation*, pp. 119, 124.

85. Ziegler, *Plumber*, p. 33.

86. *Ibid.*, p. 154.

87. Cressey, *Theft*, pp. 174-185.

88. Maas, *Valachi*, p. 106.

89. Ianni, *Family Business*, p. 113.

90. Whyte, *Street Corner*, pp. 14-25.

91. Ziegler, *Plumber*.

92. Messick, *Lansky*, p. 9.

93. Cressey, *Theft*, p. 51.

94. Messick, *Lansky*, p. 9.

95. *Ibid.*

96. *Ibid.*

97. *Ibid.*, p. 23.

98. *Ibid.*, p. 25.

99. *Second Interim Report of the Special Committee to Investigate Organized Crime in Interstate Commerce* (Washington, D.C.: United States Government Printing Office, 1951).

100. Nicholas Pileggi, "Maps of Current Battlefield," in Thomas Plate, *Mafia at War* (New York: New York Magazine Press), p. 85.

101. Cressey, *Theft*, p. 51.

102. *Ibid.*, p. 52.

103. Morris and Hawkins, *Honest Politician's Guide*, p. 203.

104. Ziegler, *Plumber*, pp. 86-87.

105. See previously cited material.

106. Talese, *Honor*.

107. *Task Force Report: Organized Crime*, p. 8.

108. John Seidl, *Upon the Hip, A Study of the Criminal Loan-Shark Industry* (Washington, D.C.: United States Dept. of Justice, 1969), p. 62.

109. *Ibid.*, p. 68.

110. *Ibid.*, p. 75.

111. Maas, *Valachi*, pp. 107, 121.

112. Puzo, *Godfather*, pp. 276-300.

113. Maas, *Valachi*, pp. 245-246.

114. Salerno and Thompkins, *Confederation*, p. 137.

115. Talese, *Honor*; Ziegler, *Plumber*.

116. *Hearings Before the Permanent Subcommittee of Investigation of the Committee on Government Operations* (McClellan Committee) 88th Cong., 1st Sess., 1963, part 1, p. 159.

117. Ziegler, *Plumber*, pp. 22-24.

118. *Ibid.*, p. 24.

119. *Ibid.*, p. 60.

120. *Ibid.*

121. Salerno and Thompkins, *Confederation*, p. 133.

122. Ziegler, *Plumber*, pp. 30, 229.

123. Clark, *Crime in America*, p. 55.

124. Ziegler, *Plumber*, p. 229.

125. Reid, Ed, *The Grim Reapers* (New York: Bantam Books, 1970), p. 65.

126. *Hearings Before the Permanent Subcommittee in Investigations of the Committee on Government Operations United States Senate*, 86th Cong., 1st Sess., 1963, p. 117.

127. Salerno and Thompkins, *Confederation*, pp. 91-94.

128. Peter Blau and W. Richard Scott, *Formal Organizations* (San Francisco: Chandler Publishing Co., 1962), p. 222.

Chapter 5

1. From conversations with Sergeant Nick Gulling, Indiana State Police, summer 1972.

2. According to Burton Turkus, Harry Feeney of the *New York World Telegram* came up with the name Murder Incorporated. Burton Turkus and Sid Feder, *Murder, Inc.* (London: Victor Gollancz, 1953), p. 19.

3. Ralph Salerno and John S. Thompkins, *The Crime Confederation* (New York: Popular Library, 1969), p. 354.

4. Data from mimeo obtained from the Chicago Crime Commission, spring 1972, entitled *Gang Murders, Chicago Area, 1919 –*.

5. Ovid DeMaris, *Captive City* (New York: Pocket Books, 1968), pp. 55-65.

6. Richard D. Lyons "Jersey Detergent Maker Tells of Payments to Mafia Figure," *New York Times*, 6 October 1971, pp. 1, 32.

7. See for example, Ellen Warren, "2 More Die in Gary Dope War," *Chicago Daily News*, 2 August 1972, p. 9.

8. Robert D. McFadden, "Scores of Detectives Search for Clue in Gangland Slaying of Gallo," *New York Times*, 9 April 1972, p. 22.

9. Salerno and Thompkins, *Confederation*, p. 334.

10. *Ibid.*, p. 335.

11. *Ibid.*, p. 334.

12. For the difficulties involved in obtaining convictions even when the case appears airtight, see James Mills, *The Prosecutor* (New York: Pocket Books, 1969).

13. Turkus and Feder, *Murder, Inc.*, pp. 43-62.

14. In some localities running an adult bookstore has been considered illegal as well.

15. John L. McClellan, *Crime Without Punishment* (New York: Duell, Sloan and Pearce, 1962), p. 118. A further sampling of organized crime's businesses can be obtained from citizens' crime commissions. For example, the Chicago Crime Commission reproduces a document called *Spotlight on Legitimate Businesses and the Hoods* which lists individual businesses and the "known" criminals who are associated with them.

16. The Internal Revenue Service in its 1971 annual report listed the types of legitimate business organized criminals are engaged in. The major and minor racketeers are involved in the following legitimate businesses:

Real estate and insurance	186
Legalized gambling, including casinos and race tracks	117
Finance	86
Professions, including lawyers, doctors, and accountants	82
Entertainment and recreation	77
Construction	71
Hotels and motels	68
Manufacturing	64
Food sales	62
Auto sales and service	56
Trucking and transportation	52
Liquor sales	50

The IRS definition of organized criminals differs from that of other agencies so accountings of businesses of organized criminals may also differ. They divide criminals into major and minor racketeers with two thousand in the former category. "Racketeers' Business Holdings Tallied Up," *Lafayette Journal and Courier*, 12 February 1972, p. B9.

17. *Deskbook on Organized Crime* (Chamber of Commerce of the United States, 1969), p. 4.

18. *Ibid.*, pp. 6-7.

19. Thomas C. Schelling, "What is the Business of Organized Crime," *American Scholar* (Autumn 1971): 647.

20. John Kobler, *Capone* (New York: G. P. Putnam's Sons, 1971), p. 51.

21. Jimmy Breslin, *The Gang That Couldn't Shoot Straight* (New York: Bantam Books, 1969), p. 59.

22. *Ibid.*

23. *Deskbook on Organized Crime*, pp. 26-27.

24. Pete D'Andreoli, "Organized Crime Enterprises—Legal," in S. A. Yevsky, ed., *Law Enforcement Science and Technology* (London: Thompson Book Co., 1967).

25. The same kind of manipulation of company names is found in stock fraud transactions. See *Organized Crime: Stolen Securities: Hearings Before the Permanent Subcommittee of Investigations of the Committee on Government Operations.* 92nd Cong., 1st Sess., pt. 3, p. 675.

26. See, for instance, the *Report on Organized Crime* (Harrisburg: Pennsylvania Crime Commission, Office of the Attorney General, 1970), p. 28, and the *Task Force Report: Organized Crime* (Washington: Government Printing Office, 1967), p. 3.

27. Donald R. Cressey, *Theft of a Nation* (New York: Harper and Row, 1969), p. 74.

28. *Task Force Report: Organized Crime*, p. 3.

29. See Gordon H. Cole and Sidney Margolius, "When You Gamble—You Risk More Than Your Money," *Public Affairs* (Pamphlet 354, 1964), p. 3.

30. John Gardiner, *The Politics of Corruption* (New York: Russell Sage Foundation), 1970.

31. Cole and Margolius, "When You Gamble," p. 2.

32. William J. Duffy, "Organized Crime—Illegal Activities," *in* Yevsky, *Law Enforcement*, pp. 30-31.

33. *Ibid.*

34. Cressey, *Theft*, pp. 127-133.

35. *Ibid.*, p. 127.

36. *Ibid.*, pp. 127-133.

37. Duffy, "Organized Crime," p. 31.

38. *Report on Organized Crime*, p. 26.

39. Peter Maas, *The Valachi Papers* (New York: Bantam Books, 1968), p. 139.

40. *Ibid.*, p. 140.

41. Gardiner, *Corruption*, pp. 79-80.

42. Johnathan Craig and Richard Posner, *The New York Crime Book* (New York: Pyramid Books, 1972), pp. 56-57.

43. Tim Cohane, "Irresponsible Recruiting is the Chief Reason Behind the Basketball Scandal," *Look*, 13 February 1962, p. 85.

44. *Ibid.*

45. *Ibid.*

46. Lou Brown, "I Worked With Basketball's No. 1 Briber," *Look*, 27 February 1962, p. 71.

47. Jack Cavanaugh, "Basketball, Betting and Borscht," *Sports Illustrated*, 7 June 1972, p. M3.

48. Steve Cady, "A Fixer Describes Drugging Hundreds of Race Horses," *New York Times*, 14 June 1972, p. 55.

49. Lou Brown, "No. 1 Briber," p. 79.

50. *Task Force Report: Narcotics and Drug Abuse* (Washington: U.S. Government Printing Office, 1967), p. 2.

51. *Ibid.*

52. *The Drug Crisis: Report on Drug Abuse in Illinois* (Chicago: Illinois Legislative Investigating Commission, 1971), p. 73.

53. *Ibid.*, p. 91.

54. *Ibid.*, p. 75.

55. *Ibid.*, p. 76.

56. *Task Force Report: Narcotics and Drug Abuse*, pp. 12, 5.

57. See *Marihuana: A Signal of Misunderstanding: The Official Report of the National Commission on Marihuana and Drug Abuse* (New York: Signet Books, 1972).

58. James M. Markham, "A Long War on Drugs," *New York Times*, 4 August 1972, p. 6.

59. Larry Collins and Dominique La Pierre, "The French Connection—In Real Life," *New York Times Magazine*, 6 February 1972, p. 53.

60. *Ibid.*

61. *Task Force Report: Narcotics and Drug Abuse*, p. 7.

62. *Ibid.* See also "Mexican Mobsters In Drug War," *Indianapolis Star*, 17 September 1972, sec. 1, p. 21.

63. *Task Force Report: Narcotics and Drug Abuse*, p. 7.

64. Kathleen Teltsch, "Asian Area is Aim of Drive on Opium," *New York Times*, 13 March 1972, p. 11, and James M. Markham, "A Long War on Drugs," *New York Times*, 4 August 1972, p. 6.

65. For an excellent description and history of the cocaine traffic see Charles Siragusa, *The Trail of the Poppy* (Englewood Cliffs, N.J.: Prentice Hall, 1966), pp. 185-199. See also Harold M. Schmeck, Jr., "Cocaine Is Re-emerging as a Major Problem, While Marijuana Remains Popular," *New York Times*, 15 November 1971, p. 74, and Joseph Novitski, "U.S. Drug Watch Shifts Its Focus," *New York Times*, 12 March 1972, p. 17.

66. James M. Markham, "South Florida is Emerging as Center of Drug Traffic," *New York Times*, 1 May 1972, pp. 1, 53.

67. William Shakespeare, *The Merchant of Venice in The Works of William Shakespeare* (New York: Oxford University Press), p. 392.

68. Eric Partridge, *A Dictionary of the Underworld: British and American* (New York: Bonanza Books, 1949), p. 625, and Charles Siragusa, *The Loan Shark Racket (Juice Racketeering)* (Indiana State Police Organized Crime School, 1972), p. 1.

69. *Task Force Report: Organized Crime*, p. 3.

70. *Ibid.* See also *The Loan Shark Racket* (New York State Commission of Investigation, 1965), pp. 10-12.

71. John M. Seidl, *Upon the Hip, A Study of the Criminal Loan-Shark Industry* (Washington, D.C.: United States Dept. of Justice, 1969), pp. 32-33.

72. *Ibid.*, p. 39.

73. *Ibid.*, p. 40-41.

74. From a series of articles which appeared in the *Pharos Tribune and Press*, Logansport, Indiana, in March of 1972 by Mort Golden as told to Ira Berkou entitled "Loan from Chicago Outfit Drew Victim into Gangland Nightmare," "Justice Squeeze Pushes Him to FBI," and "Informer is Still Running from Mafia."

75. *Ibid.*

76. *Ibid.*

77. Testimony of Ralph Salerno in *Hearings Before the Select Committee on Crime: House of Representatives*, 91st Cong., 1st Sess., p. 155.

78. *Ibid.*

79. Fred J. Cook, "Just Call the Doctor for a Loan," *New York Times Magazine*, 28 January 1968.

80. Joseph Volz and Peter J. Bridge, *The Mafia Talks* (Greenwich, Conn.: Fawcett Books, 1969), p. 106.

81. Siragusa, *The Loan Shark Racket*, p. 2.

82. Salerno and Thompkins, *Confederation*, p. 96.

83. *Ibid.*

84. Mary Owen Cameron, *The Booster and the Snitch* (New York: Free Press of Glencoe, 1964), pp. 146-147.

85. *Ibid.*, p. 57.

86. *Ibid.*, p. 58.

87. Lawrence Van Gelder, "Indictment of 2 Men Here Links Dominican Aides to Car Thefts," *New York Times*, 18 November 1971, p. 36.

88. *Hearings before the Permanent Subcommittee on Investigations of the Committee on Government Operations, United States Senate*, 92nd Cong., 1st Sess., pt. 3, p. 683.

89. "7 Arrested in Theft of Millions in Stocks," *Lafayette Journal and Courier*, 12 November 1971, p. 1.

90. *Hearings before the Permanent Subcommittee on Investigations*, 1st Sess., pt. 3, p. 697.

91. *Ibid.*, p. 687.

92. *Ibid.*, p. 614.

93. *Ibid.*, p. 616.

94. *Ibid.*, p. 684.

95. *Ibid.*, p. 697.

96. *Ibid.*, p. 676.

97. *Ibid.*, pp. 643-645.

98. *Ibid.*, p. 656.

99. Henry Raymont, "Counterfeit Paperback Covers Plaguing Publishers," *New York Times,* 7 April 1972, p. 58.

100. Cameron, *Booster and Snitch,* p. 158.

101. *Ibid.*, p. 159.

102. Lawrence R. Zeitlin, "A Little Larceny Can Do a Lot for Employee Morale," *Psychology Today* (June 1971): 24.

103. *Ibid.*, p. 64.

104. Schelling, "Business of Crime," p. 646.

105. Morton Mintz, "AT&T Officials Took Presents From Mob-Related Suppliers," *Washington Post,* 9 June 1972, p. A2.

106. Henry E. Peterson, "Winning the War Against Organized Crime," *U.S. News and World Report,* 5 June 1972, pp. 66-67.

107. James Q. Wilson, "Corruption Is Not Always Scandalous," *New York Times Magazine,* 28 April 1968, p. 55.

108. *Ibid.*

109. J. S. Nye, "Corruption and Political Development: A Cost-Benefit Analysis," *American Political Science Review* 61 (June 1967): 419.

110. James C. Scott, *Comparative Political Corruption* (Englewood Cliffs, N.J.: Prentice-Hall, 1972), p. 5.

111. Martin and Susan Tolchin, *"To the Victor . . . Political Patronage from the Clubhouse to the White House* (New York: Vintage Books, 1972), p. 9. This scheme is implicit but not clearly delineated in their book.

112. *Ibid.*, p. 5.

113. *Ibid.*, p. 25. For example, "James Boyd who, as Secretary of Transportation approved a $25.2 million grant to the Illinois Central Railroad in December 1968, became the railroad's $95,000-a-year president the following month."

114. John Kobler, *Capone* (New York: G. P. Putman's Sons, 1971), p. 199.

115. Donald R. Cressey, "The Functions and Structure of Criminal Syndicates," *Task Force Report: Organized Crime,* p. 35, and Cressey, *Theft,* pp. 250-252.

116. William F. Whyte, *Street Corner Society* (Chicago: University of Chicago Press, 1943), p. 128.

117. *Ibid.*, pp. 128-129.

118. *Ibid.*, p. 132.

119. "Excerpts from the Knapp Commission's Findings," *New York Times*, 7 August 1972, p. 32. It must be noted that Robert M. McKiernan, president of the Patrolmen's Benevolent Association, and others have leveled severe criticism at the Knapp Commission and its final report. See "Knapp to Carry Cash to Albany," *New York Times*, 8 August 1972, pp. 1, 23. Denials would be expected from in-house agencies, and their criterion that testimony comes from "pimps, prostitutes, perjurers, rogue cops, and other self-confessed criminals to besmirch the department's reputation" is not convincing to this reader. Where else could the evidence come from?

120. Gardiner, *Corruption*, p. 55.

121. *Ibid.*, pp. 55-56.

122. "Panel Urges State Name Prosecutor," *New York Times*, 7 August 1972, p. 32.

123. *Ibid.*

124. *Task Force Report: Organized Crime*, p. 6. Also, uniformed policemen received money on not so nearly the grand and organized scale as their supervisors or special gambling or vice squads. "Uniformed policemen, particularly those assigned to radio patrol cars, participated in gambling pads [payoffs] more modest in size then those received by plainclothes units." "Excerpts from the Knapp Commission Findings," p. 2.

125. Gardiner, *Corruption*, p. 24.

126. *Ibid.*, p. 26.

127. Whyte, *Street Corner*, p. 139.

128. Robert A. Dahl, *Pluralist Democracy in the United States: Conflict and Consent* (Chicago: Rand McNally Co., 1967), pp. 171-72.

Chapter 6

1. *Hearings before the Permanent Subcommittee on Investigations of the Committee on Government Operations, U.S. Senate* (McClellan Committee), 88th Cong., 1st Sess., 1963, pt. 1, p. 80.

2. *Ibid.*, p. 183.

3. *New York Times*, 3 August 1972, p. 37.

4. Murray Kempton, "Too Late for the Panthers?" in Theodore L. Becker and Vernon G. Murray, eds., *Government Lawlessness in America* (New York: Oxford University Press, 1971), pp. 49-52.

5. Victor S. Navasky, *Kennedy Justice* (New York: Atheneum, 1971), p. 26.

6. John A. Gardiner, *The Politics of Corruption: Organized Crime in an American City* (New York: Russell Sage Foundation, 1970), p. 57.

7. Hank Messick, *Lansky* (New York: G. P. Putnam's Sons, 1971), p. 8.

8. Richard O. Curry and Thomas M. Brown, eds., *Conspiracy: The Fear of Subversion in American History* (New York: Holt, Rinehart and Winston, 1971), p. 111.

9. *New York Times*, 23 July 1972, p. E4.

10. James M. Markham, "Funeral of Adonis is Passed Up by Other Members of the Mafia," *New York Times*, 7 December 1971, p. 93.

11. Joseph Bruce Gorman, *Kefauver: A Political Biography* (New York: Oxford University Press, 1971), p. 92.

12. Ralph Salerno and John S. Thompkins, *The Crime Confederation* (New York: Popular Library, 1969), p. 329.

13. Gerard L. Goettel, "Why the Crime Syndicate Can't be Touched," *Harpers* (November 1960): 34.

14. *Ibid.*

15. Navasky, *Kennedy*, pp. 49-50.

16. *Reports on Crime Investigations Senate Reports*, vol. 6, 82nd Cong., 1st Sess., January 3–October 20, 1951 (Washington: United States Government Printing Office, 1951), p. 53.

17. *Ibid.*, p. 118.

18. Ramsey Clark, *Crime in America* (New York: Pocket Books, 1970), pp. 57-58.

19. *Ibid.*, p. 66.

20. Norval Morris and Gordon Hawkins, *The Honest Politician's Guide to Crime Control* (Chicago: University of Chicago Press, 1970), p. 5.

21. *Ibid.*, p. 6.

22. *Ibid.*, p. 203.

23. *Ibid.*, p. 234.

24. Salerno and Thompkins, *Confederation*, p. 327.

25. James Q. Wilson, *Varieties of Police Behavior* (Cambridge, Mass.: Harvard University Press, 1968), p. 7.

26. *Ibid.*

27. "Knapp Plan for Prosecutor Scored," *New York Times*, 9 August 1972, p. 41.

28. *Testimony of John Edgar Hoover, Director, Federal Bureau of Investigation, Before the House Subcommittee on Appropriations on March 17, 1971, Regarding Organized Crime*, p. 5.

29. See a case study of the process in James Mills, *The Prosecutor* (New York: Pocket Books, 1970).

30. For the exception, see Meyer Berger, "Lepke," *Life*, 28 February 1944, pp. 86-98 to learn how Lepke Buchalter was charged and convicted of ordering gangland executions.

31. William E. Farrell, "Colombo Shot, Gunman Slain At Columbus Circle Rally Site," *New York Times*, 29 June 1971, p. 1.

32. "Assassin's Mistake Triggers New York Crackdown on Mobs," *Lafayette Journal and Courier*, 17 August 1972, p. 8.

33. *Ibid.*

34. Reprint of "Gambling Investigations," *FBI Law Enforcement Bulletin* (July 1969), pp. 1-2.

35. *Task Force Report: Organized Crime* (Washington, D.C.: U.S. Government Printing Office, 1967), pp. 2, 3.

36. "Knapp Panel Urges State Name Prosecutor to Lead a 5-Year Corruption War," *New York Times*, 7 August 1972, p. 1.

37. Robert K. Merton, "Social Theory and Social Structure," rev. ed. (New York: Free Press, 1957), pp. 19-87, and Eric L. McKitrick, "The Study of Corruption," *Political Science Quarterly* 72 (December 1957): 502-514.

38. James C. Scott, *Comparative Political Corruption* (Englewood Cliffs, N.J.: Prentice-Hall, 1972), p. 21.

39. McKitrick, "Corruption," p. 5.

40. See Nicholas Gage, *The Mafia is not an Equal Opportunity Employer* (New York: McGraw-Hill Book Co., 1971), pp. 159-168, for an excellent description of a gambling junket to Las Vegas.

41. Charles Winick and Paul M. Kinsie, *The Lively Commerce: Prostitution in the United States* (New York: Signet Books, 1971), pp. 195-97.

42. Gardiner, *Corruption*, p. 2.

43. *Ibid.*, p. 23.

44. Peter Maas, *The Valachi Papers* (New York: Bantam Books, 1968), p. 28.

45. Navasky, *Kennedy*, p. 13.

46. *Ibid.*

47. *Ibid.*

48. William W. Turner, *Hoover's FBI* (New York: Dell Publishing Company, 1970), p. 150.

49. *Ibid.*, p. 151.

50. Gary Talese, *Honor Thy Father* (New York: World Publishing, 1971), p. 403.

51. *Ibid.*, p. 405.

52. Goettel, "Syndicate Can't be Touched," p. 38.

53. *Ibid.*, p. 35.

54. Navasky, *Kennedy*, p. 103.

55. Michael Dorman, *Payoff* (New York: David McKay Co., 1972), p. 7.

56. Sanford Kadish, "The Crisis of Overcriminalization," *The Annals: Combatting Crime* (November 1957): 157-170.

57. Morris and Hawkins, *Honest Politician's Guide*, pp. 2-3.

58. Henry E. Peterson, "Winning the War Against Organized Crime," *U.S. News and World Report*, 5 June 1972, p. 67.

Index

Index

Chicago, 33, 40, 45
Chicago Crime Commission, 74
Church, in Italian society, 51-52
Civil liberties, 174-175
Clark, Ramsey, 7, 59, 60, 102, 132, 178
Client-centered violence, 140-141
Cochiaro, Frank, 85, 92, 110, 112
Cohesion, 110, 137
Colisimo, Jim, 32
Collective representations, xii
Colombo, Joseph, 2, 43, 44, 52, 62, 82, 93
Commission, of criminals, 126-128, 135
Compulsive behavior, 50-51
Confederation, 12, 38, 127-131
  decentralization of, 130
  in Italy, 38
  strength of, 127-131
Conflict subculture, 78-79
Consensual crimes, 187
Consiglieri, 44
Constitutional makeup, of criminals, 47-48
Consumers, 17-18
Continental Press, 56
Cooperation, among groups, 34, 40
Corleone, Don Vito, fictional character, 54-55
Corleone, Michael, fictional character, 85
Corruption, 59, 104-105, 150, 162-168, 185
  as byproduct of criminal activity, 162
  definition of, 162
  dishonest, 163
  elitist, 168
  functions of, 162-168
  grass eaters, 164
  honest, 163
  as interaction, 165
  meat eaters, 164
  in New Jersey, 45
  nut, 104
  pad, 105
  corruption producers, 185
Corsicans, 70, 73
Cosa Nostra, 11, 51
  attention on, 43
  definition of, 37
  as definition of organized crime, 9
  as society, 44
  on tapes, 22

Costello, Frank, 27, 38, 41, 43, 85, 129, 130, 177, 178
Costs, of criminal business, 162
Cottage industries, 134
Counterfeiters, 158-159
Crapsey, Joseph, 90
Cressey, Donald, 94, 102, 103, 114, 115, 122, 146, 147
Crime reporter's theme, 27
Curtis, Carl T., 19, 133

Dahl, Robert, 168
Data available
  primary sources, 20-26, 27, 28
  secondary sources, 26-29
Davis, Dixie, 38, 82-83
Dawson, William, 53
De Cavalcante, Samuel Rizzo ("Sam"), 22, 23, 49, 50, 56-57, 58, 69, 85, 89, 92, 95, 96, 100, 103-104, 107, 108, 111, 117, 131, 155
Defectors, 20-26
Degrees of involvement, 16-17
Delinquent subculture, 78
Depression, economic, 106
Deterrence, 50
Dewey, Thomas E., 1, 40-41, 60, 111
Diamond, Legs, 32
Differential law enforcement, 97-98, 187-189
Di Gregorio, Gaspar, 44
Diogardo, Johnny, 42
Diogardo, Tommy, 42
Discrete reportage of events, 27
Dishonest corruption, 163
Dissention, in societies, 33
Diversification, of criminal business, 35, 98, 132-135
Division of labor, 60
D'Mento, Francis, 106
Dorman, Michael, 193
Downs, Anthony, 91
Dream books, 161
Dues, to bosses, 132
Duffy, William J., 146-147
Durkheim, Emile, xi

Easton, David, 94
Eboli, Thomas, 173
Economics, of criminal organizations. *See* organized crime
Edwards, George, C., 81
Efficiency, of organized criminals, 47, 54-62

Index

Index